Andrew Root
& Kenda Creasy Dean

THE
THEOLOGICAL
TURN IN
YOUTH MINISTRY

IVP Books

An imprint of InterVarsity Press
Downers Grove, Illinois

InterVarsity Press
P.O. Box 1400, Downers Grove, IL 60515-1426
World Wide Web: www.ivpress.com
E-mail: email@ivpress.com

InterVarsity Press® is the book-publishing division of InterVarsity Christian Fellowship/USA®, a movement of students and faculty active on campus at hundreds of universities, colleges and schools of nursing in the United States of America, and a member movement of the International Fellowship of Evangelical Students. For information about local and regional activities, write Public Relations Dept., InterVarsity Christian Fellowship/USA, 6400 Schroeder Rd., P.O. Box 7895, Madison, WI 53707-7895, or visit the IVCF website at <www.intervarsity.org>.

Scripture quotations, unless otherwise noted, are from the New Revised Standard Version of the Bible, *copyright 1989 by the Division of Christian Education of the National Council of the Churches of Christ in the USA. Used by permission. All rights reserved.*

Discussion and reflection exercises are adapted from the following: The Skillful Teacher, *2nd ed., by Stephen D. Brookfield. Copyright ©2006. Reproduced with permission of John Wiley & Sons, Inc.;* Discussion as a Way of Teaching, *2nd ed., by Stephen D. Brookfield and Stephen Preskill. Copyright ©2005. Reproduced with permission of John Wiley & Sons, Inc.;* Becoming a Critically Reflective Teacher, *by Stephen D. Brookfield. Copyright ©1995. Reproduced with permission of John Wiley & Sons, Inc.*

While all stories in this book are true, some names and identifying information in this book have been changed to protect the privacy of the individuals involved.

Design: Cindy Kiple
Images: teenage girl: ©David H. Lewis/iStockphoto
        three teenage boys: Stockbyte/Getty Images

ISBN 978-0-8308-3825-7

Printed in the United States of America ∞

Library of Congress Cataloging-in-Publication Data

Root, Andrew, 1974-
    The theological turn in youth ministry / Andrew Root & Kenda Creasy
Dean.
        p. cm.
    Includes bibliographical references.
    ISBN 978-0-8308-3825-7 (pbk.: alk. paper)
    1. Church work with youth. 2. Theology—Miscellanea. I. Dean,
Kenda Creasy, 1959- II. Title.
    BV4447.R6625 2011
    259'.23—dc22

2011013716

| P | 19 | 18 | 17 | 16 | 15 | 14 | 13 | 12 | 11 | 10 | 9 | 8 | 7 | 6 | 5 | 4 | 3 | 2 | 1 |
| Y | 27 | 26 | 25 | 24 | 23 | 22 | 21 | 20 | 19 | 18 | 17 | 16 | 15 | 14 | 13 | 12 | 11 |

To Roland Martinson and Richard Osmer

Thanks for getting us started!

CONTENTS

PART TWO: THEOLOGY ENACTED
Exploring Youth Ministry Practice

ACKNOWLEDGMENTS

This book is about "turns," the kind of pivotal moments when lives and ministries change direction. If you've rounded such a corner recently, you know how important the people are who encouraged you along the way. So you will understand why, before going even a paragraph further, we must say thank you. We owe thanks to more people than we can possibly name here, but for all of you on that list, we hope you know how grateful we are for your patience with us, your encouragement to us and your brazen belief in us. You convinced us that God was up to something good, in young people and in the church, and that we were called to be part of it.

Two people deserve special thanks, because more than anyone else, they helped *us* make the theological turn in youth ministry. The first is Roland Martinson, whose incomparable energy for changing the church is matched only by his incomparable love for those who serve it. The initial steps of any turn are the hardest; to simply get momentum moving in a new direction is often a brutal task. Rollie (as he is lovingly called by students and colleagues alike) gave momentum to a generation of church leaders whom he inspired to take youth ministry in a new direction. It was Rollie, speaking at a Group youth conference in the late 1980s (back when Kenda was still in seminary), who first sparked her imagination with the idea that theology and youth ministry belong together. When Andy joined the faculty at Luther Seminary, it was Rollie who encouraged him to take his passion for theological reflection into the classroom, and who provided the space and motivation to write—and write *theologically*—about youth ministry. As he did for countless youth pastors throughout his career, Rollie reminded us constantly that working with young people is a theological calling. If anyone deserves thanks for pushing a theological turn in youth ministry forward, it is Rollie Martinson.

The second person who deserves special thanks is our shared teacher, Richard R. Osmer, whose passion for practical theology is matched only by his delight in those who take it seriously. We showed up, a decade apart from one another, on Rick's academic doorstep at Princeton Seminary. Recognizing us for the theological vagabonds that we were, Rick took us under his wing and opened up the world of practical theology to us, showing us that the kind of thinking we desired for youth ministry had a home in this discipline that helps people think deeply about practice. Rick pushed both of us to keep our eyes on the hands-on practice of youth ministry, but to do so with all the theological depth we could muster. If there is anyone who secretly stands behind our writing on this subject, it is Rick Osmer. Both Kenda's book *Practicing Passion* and Andy's book *Revisiting Relational Youth Ministry* were originally written (in different forms) under Rick's supervision. It was Rick who supported and helped us craft these theses, giving them the theological depth we hope they offer.

We would also like to thank our wonderful editor, Dave Zimmerman. Here we share an overwhelming desire to write our appreciation in caps and bold. For one thing, it was Dave's editorial magic that turned a collection of disparate essays into the whole and single volume you are reading. Another reason is that Andy is still beating himself up for forgetting to thank Dave in the preface of *Revisiting Relational Youth Ministry*. If that book has been a blessing to anyone, or added theological depth to the practice of youth ministry, Dave should get credit. Dave had, and continues to have, a significant vision for the theological potential of youth ministry, and he is an enthusiastic cheerleader for those of us who write about it. That, and he has the patience of Job. We couldn't ask for a better editor, or a better colleague. Or a better friend.

Because this book reworks articles that have been published elsewhere, we would like to thank the editors of a number of journals for allowing us to reprint these articles here. Chapter one originally appeared in the now-defunct *Methodist Quarterly Review*, and later in the *Journal of Youth and Theology*. We are grateful to coeditors Ted Campbell, Rex Matthews and Russell Richey of the *Methodist Review* for allowing it to see the light again here. Chapters two, eight, nine and fourteen were originally published in *Immerse Journal* (which used to be *The Journal of Student Ministries*). Thanks go to Mike King, chief editor and visionary for that journal, as well as a great friend and supporter of youth ministry's theological turn, for allowing us to use these articles here. Chapter three appeared in the *Journal of Youth Ministry*, and we thank editors and fellow youth ministry professors Mark Cannister and Tom Bergler for their important work on that journal, and for allowing us to use this essay. Chapter four first appeared in *Theology Today*, and has been liberated for our use by editor and dear friend Gordon Mikoski. Chapters five, six and seven were originally published in the international *Journal of Youth and Theology,* edited by the sharp-minded Nick Shepherd, who has been a good friend and a great midwife of that fine journal.

Chapters ten and fifteen began as lectures for the Princeton Lectures on Youth, Church and Culture, published by Princeton Theological Seminary's Institute for Youth Ministry. It is impossible to overestimate the IYM's importance in creating openings for theological reflection on youth ministry among scholars and practitioners over the past fifteen years. Thanks especially go to IYM director Dayle Gillespie Rounds for inviting us to participate in the Princeton Forums' creative conversations about youth ministry and theology—conversations that put scholars, pastors and youth leaders across the table from one another, swapping notes and visions for ministry. Chapter eleven is included thanks to editor (and former youth minister) Cynthia Rigby, who helms Austin Theological Seminary's *Insights* and who first commissioned that article. Likewise, chapters twelve and thirteen originally appeared in *Connect* (the journal of the ELCA youth ministry network) and *Dialog* respectively. Thanks to Todd Buegler, Michael Sladek and Kristin Largen for their support.

One last thing: we should note that the postscript introduces a new author into the discussion, Blair Bertrand, who assists Andy in beginning to locate youth ministry scholarship in a broader philosophical and theological context. We include this essay as a postscript because it represents a first attempt to "map" the conversation about youth ministry and practical theology. If you are primarily interested in hands-on youth ministry, you may find this essay extraneous; if you are interested in practical theology, and especially in the way God's action and human action intersect in the practice of youth ministry, you may want to read the postscript first in order to get a philosophical "lay of the land."

Finally, and most importantly, we'd like to thank our families for their constant support and love. Thank you for being the people who turn us back to what really matters, in heaven and on earth. You are our greatest blessings.

INTRODUCTION

KENDA CREASY DEAN

For I am about to do something new.
See, I have already begun! Do you not see it?

ISAIAH 43:19 NLT

At the new Anglican seminary in southern Sudan, the first four courses that students take are Hebrew, Greek, agriculture and public health.[1] That news brought me up short. I started thinking about my students' first-semester courses, and the way we douse these future pastors with biblical criticism, church history and speech. These are critical subjects for pastors to know, after all; our students (most of them) come to learn how to lead churches, to become knowledgeable "theologians-in-residence" for congregations. Sometimes a first-year student slips into a course on pastoral care or ethics, but if you were to look at our graduation requirements, you would see that our school's curriculum tilts decisively toward the church's saints, sources and traditions. Students readily comply, assuming that they will figure out how to be "practical" later on. One day, they hope (and we hope), they will get the alchemy right and spin all this knowledge into ministry.

In Sudan, apparently, it's a different story. To imagine God apart from on-the-ground realities of hardship, hunger and hope—to separate biblical Greek and Hebrew from agriculture and public health—is unthinkable. What took my breath away about the Sudanese curriculum was not the classes themselves, but what those classes suggest that ministry is *for*. What

Sudanese pastors-in-training need to learn is not how to lead a church but how to *stop people from dying*. In Sudan, the church is a life-force. Those who lead congregations find living water in Scripture for their thirsty flocks while staving off threats like starvation, HIV/AIDS, malaria. As a result, theological education in Sudan dare not dawdle long in abstraction. It must prepare Christians to preach the gospel and to practice it by helping pastors learn to lasso holy texts for people who are literally dying for a story of resurrection.

RUINED FOR YOUTH MINISTRY

One of the things I love about youth workers is that most would feel right at home with the theological education of Sudan. We understand why Christian leaders there bring the story of Jesus Christ into conversation with the growing and healing arts. As youth workers, these are our arts as well. We too translate the story of Jesus so that young people can hear it for themselves. We too tend the soil of young souls so that the seeds of God's self-giving love will be more likely to take root and grow. We too strive to build healthy communities where children are not ravaged, and we try to create ecologies of grace where young people can flourish. There is no doubt: youth workers are in the translating, growing and healing business, for we are called to *stop young people from dying*. Our vocation is to help young people "choose life" (Deut 30:19) by equipping them with the faith, hope and love needed to recognize God's forgiveness and embrace the life God intends for them. Wherever young people struggle, or lack nourishment, or are no longer flourishing, we—the church—are called to practice resurrection.

Given how desperate our flocks are for someone to stop them from dying, youth workers are famously impatient with theological abstractions. Instinctively we know that ministry precedes theology, that (as Andy points out in chapter two) the God we meet in the pages of Scripture is not a theologian, but a *minister*. Everything we know about who God is and what God does emerges from God's extravagant, reckless love for and ministrations to humanity. The church's response to particular young people (and they are always particular; there is no such thing as "generic" youth) is conditioned by God's particular response to us in Jesus Christ. The name *Jesus* means "YHWH will save." Ministry with young people, therefore, must ultimately reflect God's saving ministry with us.

One of the foundational assumptions in practical theology is that all decent theology begins and ends in practice. Unfortunately, those of us who are youth ministers have not always assumed that our vocation also implies a call to be practical theologians. As a species, youth workers have quick triggers; we notice a need and we respond speedily with the best of intentions but often with minimal reflection, theological or otherwise (and then we wonder how we stepped on so many toes). If anything, we may be guilty of believing that youth work is too important to be left to people with theology degrees. When I told the teenagers I worked with in college that I was thinking about going to seminary, they were aghast. One girl shook her head sadly, remembering a string of failed pastoral attempts to reach young people. "Seminary," she said ominously, "*ruins* you for youth ministry."

MAKING THE THEOLOGICAL TURN

We hope, obviously, that this book won't ruin you for youth ministry. We're going to gamble and say that it might even help, regardless of whether you work primarily with teenagers, emerging adults, families, children or whole congregations.

The essays included here represent two people's efforts to think about youth ministry as theologians. All of the essays have been published before, and while we updated where we could, some are unapologetically time-bound, as their footnotes and popular-culture references will reveal. When updating a particular piece felt cheesy and fake to us, we chose to leave the words alone and let them speak to the times for which they were written. Moreover, we chose not to try to unite them around a common theme, or develop a single argument. Our main goal with these articles was simply to bring them out of the attic, dust them off and reconsider what they say for a new era in youth ministry.

The era we have in mind is just now peeking over the horizon, as youth leaders today continue to enter into what Andy calls "the theological turn in youth ministry." It's an era in which theological reflection is becoming the norm in youth ministry instead of the exception. What we mean is that while the practice of youth ministry has been with us for quite a while now (70 to 120 years or so, depending on how you count), it has not always been concerned with theological reflection. This is not to say that theology wasn't happening, or that youth workers didn't care about theology. But it is to say that youth workers' actions and self-conceptions were rarely informed by significant theological reflection. In fact, when I started writing about youth ministry nearly twenty years ago, theological reflection with and for young people was rare and awkward. Youth workers groped for ways to describe the spiritual significance of our work after decades of justifying our ministries for their sociological, educational or therapeutic usefulness.

In the last several years, though, this has started to change. In our own work, Andy and I have, admittedly, been rather blatant in pushing for these new theological directions.[2] But our writing reflects a "turn" that youth leaders were already making as they began to acknowledge the theological depth and possibilities of churches' ministries with young people. Thanks especially to a new generation of sophisticated lay theologians serving "on the ground" as church youth workers, the practice of reflecting theologically on youth ministry is becoming both normative and necessary. In blogs, classrooms and continuing-education events (not to mention churches), youth workers are pushing for theological depth in their practice, for lenses to help them understand that what they do is essentially about navigating the sacred connection between God and humans. This palpable "turn" in youth ministry reveals our longing for something solid and deep on which to stand with young people, a way to move beyond the consumer habits and entertainment focus that too often consume youth ministry.

Since you're reading this book, chances are that you also share this longing. If you have started to think about your work less as a church job than as a holy vocation . . . or if you approach youth ministry less as a place to groom future church members than as a missionary activity that translates Christian faith for new contexts and new generations of disciples . . . or even if you find yourself less interested in filling teenagers with moral information than in walking alongside them in Christ's name . . . then you too are already making this "theological turn."

The shift has happened none too soon. Anthropologists know that the health of a community can be assessed by the well-being of its children. Given the continued hemorrhaging of young people from American churches, Christian communities have cause for concern.

Yet the "sign potential" of young people is promising too. If youth tend to be the barometers of their communities' health, then replenishing young people's theological water supply could have the effect of bringing water to a thirsty church. In every corner of the globe, youth ministry acts as the church's "research and development" department, an unofficial laboratory where youth and adults alike try to figure out new ways of being the church for our surrounding cultures. When young people bear witness to the gospel in their own lives, Christ's living water flows through them into parched churches and communities that are literally dying for new life.

WHAT DO WE MEAN BY PRACTICAL THEOLOGY?

A shorthand way to define practical theology is that it is reflection on Christian life. In other words, practical theology studies those moments, contexts, situations and practices in which God's action intersects with our actions, and transforms paltry human effort into something holy and lifegiving. This book is particularly focused on the context of youth ministry and on helping youth leaders notice where these points of divine-human connection occur, making us—and making young people—vessels of divine grace in the world.

For that reason, we have organized these essays into two parts. Part one, "Theological Starting Points: What Does Youth Ministry Have to Do with Theology?" offers a series of reflections about what we mean when we assert that youth ministry and theology have something to say to each other. We take it a step further, claiming that youth ministers, and even youth themselves, are practical theologians, and therefore theology lies at the very heart of ministry with young people. In part two, "Theology Enacted: Exploring Youth Ministry Practice," we mobilize theology for the practice of youth ministry itself, looking at issues of particular importance to adolescents such as discernment, sexuality, doubt, hope, even the "where" of God. We then offer examples of how we might respond to these issues in ways that reflect our understanding of who God is and what God is up to in the world and with us.

These two sections are followed by a brief postscript, "Reflecting on Method: Youth Ministry as Practical Theology." As I mentioned before, if you are the kind of reader who is dying to get down to the actual practice of ministry, then skip the postscript and go find some teenagers in need of the gospel. Or, if you're the kind of reader who likes to have a "map" of the conversation ahead of time, you might want to read the postscript first. In it, Blair Bertrand helps Andy "out" some unspoken philosophical assumptions behind various practical theological approaches to youth ministry. The result is a bird's-eye view of the ways scholars in youth ministry tend to think about the field of practical theology, and especially the ways we understand the intersection of divine action and human action.

WHAT *DON'T* WE MEAN?

Of course, there are a few things that we assume youth ministry as practical theology is *not,* as well. Perhaps now is the time to mention them, just to make sure we are all starting on the same page.

1. *Youth ministry as practical theology is not new.* You have been doing practical theology at some level from the first moment you started intentionally living as a Christian. In part one you'll notice that the activities involved in practical theological reflection are what thoughtful people of faith (including youth ministers!) have done for centuries to make decisions about ministry and mission: (a) understand a situation calling for a faithful response, (b) reflect on this situation with all relevant tools of discernment, including those offered by the gospel itself, and (c) construct a faithful response to this particular situation. For us as youth workers, this includes becoming more thoughtful about our practices and more aware of the way our work reflects (or fails to reflect) the gospel of Jesus Christ. Practical theology simply gives us direction and language to describe this process.

And this language matters. Youth ministry has only recently emerged as a viable option for pastoral ministry, and it still struggles for a proper name ("youth" only describes some of the people we work with) as well as vocational legitimacy (you know the rhetoric: it is a "stepping stone" into "real" ministry, a holding tank for pastoral neophytes until they get "a church of their own," and so on). One of the reasons for these misconceptions is youth workers' tendency to work at the margins of the church, physically and symbolically. Many people drawn to youth ministry are not invested in the credentialing aspects of church leadership. We are often somewhat allergic to (or disdainful of) "insider" Christian language and tend to feel at home in the church's boundary waters, where the gospel becomes entangled in real life and where translating "churchy" language into a useful vernacular for people on the edges of the faith community is a daily necessity.

The reason for our self-imposed marginality is simple: most teenagers are on the church's margins too—not fully opposed to Christian faith, but not invested in it either.[3] The result is that we do what all missionaries must learn to do: we wing it with whatever resources we have. Confronted with the particularities of a given young person, we translate faith on the fly, trying to make connections. Many (and often most) of the young people who cross our paths aren't Christians. They will never go to youth group. They don't know that the message we bear belongs to Christ, or that they belong to God as surely as stars belong to the nighttime sky. Yet *we* know, and as a result, we are determined to encounter these young people—no matter who they have momentarily become—as cherished children of God.

The problem with "winging it" is that we operate without checks and balances—a precarious position for people in ministry. Google "clergy" and you will quickly be reminded that ministers are as capable of damaging young people as helping them. Practical theology offers youth ministers an intentional process that allows for considered, creative pastoral responses to the particular situations facing adolescents.

It also helps counter the sin of making ministry about *us*. Without such intentionality, we become victims of our own best intentions. Either we become mired in reflection at the expense of action, or (more likely) we jump too soon, responding out of our own needs instead of out of what either the young person or Jesus Christ requires. As I look back at my own "crash and burn" moments in youth ministry (the list is long and humiliating), it is obvious that most of them could have been avoided if I had been a more self-aware practical theologian at the time. When I hear youth workers complain about a heavy-handed retreat talk, a diabolical senior pastor, sex talks gone bad or pointless mixer activities, I know that an intentional process of practical theological reflection is in order.

2. Youth ministry as practical theology is neither "relational evangelism" nor Christian education—though it involves both. When youth ministry first attracted academic attention, evangelicals were in the habit of assuming that youth ministry was a form of evangelism, following the model of parachurch organizations where the primary theological method involved leveraging relationships with teenagers in order to "earn the right to be heard." Once a relationship of trust could be established between a Christian adult or teenager and his or her young friend, this friend (so the thinking went) would be likely to convert and join ranks with Christians. Meanwhile, mainline Protestant and Catholic youth workers viewed their ministry primarily as a form of Christian education or catechesis. In this view, the chief goal of youth ministry was to nurture disciples, a practice that by definition took place in congregations. The goal of conversion seldom occurred to these youth workers; after all, the young people they met with grew up in churches, which implied (so the thinking went) that they were already Christians.

Over the years, these two approaches became suspicious of one another and perfected the art of ecclesial potshot. Parachurch organizations, popular among teenagers for their appealing leadership, were considered theologically suspect and were accused of siphoning off teenagers from local churches (both charges were occasionally true). Meanwhile, mainline Protestant and Catholic congregations that struggled to get youth involved were accused of not being "Christ-centered" and for lacking methodological know-how with teenagers (both charges were occasionally true).

As youth ministry became increasingly professionalized in the late twentieth century, these two approaches started to learn from each other. Literature on youth ministry became more available, and evangelicals, mainline Protestants and Catholics regularly commingled at youth ministry training events that quickly became nonnegotiable for new "professional" youth workers. A new generation of mainline Protestant and Catholic youth ministers—many of whom had positive experiences in parachurch ministries when they were adolescents themselves—imported a form of "relational ministry" to congregations, and young evangelicals, including those in parachurch organizations, adopted discipleship formation as a critical feature of their ministries. Today, most youth ministers (from all theological persuasions) would agree that relationships, evangelism *and* discipleship formation are important for contemporary Christian youth work.

At the same time, it is still common for congregations (and seminaries) to consider youth ministry as either a tool for evangelism or as a subarea of Christian education. Both of these views misrepresent what actually goes on in ministry with young people. What makes youth ministry distinctive is not its form, but its flock. Ministry with young people is, after all, *ministry*—not so different from ministry with anybody else. Yet because young people demand that the church address them in their particularity (in other words, from the perspective of their specific cultural and developmental experiences as adolescents), youth ministry serves as a laboratory where we can learn to contextualize ministry. When we walk alongside young people as Christ's representatives, we become incarnational witnesses, people who must use our own lives to "put wheels on the gospel" for the flock at hand. If there is any practice that every shepherd of young souls must learn, it is the ability to think missionally—the ability to translate Christ's love incarnationally, through our own lives, while sharing the lives of those we are called to love and serve in Christ's name. Youth ministry means responding to the flock God has given us in ways that are particular to them.

3. Youth ministry as practical theology is not boring. As soon as you say the word *theological* (and we've said it a *lot*), eyes start to glaze over. Here is what we *don't* want you to do when you start putting theology at the heart of youth ministry: (a) Organize your youth group around a systematic theology syllabus, (b) drone on in your next youth meeting about sin and atonement, or (c) make Karl Barth's *Church Dogmatics* your confirmation curriculum.

Now that I've said that, let me backpedal a little. While I don't know youth pastors who have organized their youth calendar around a theology syllabus, I know plenty who read in the great works of Christian theology issues that weigh heavily on the hearts of teenagers. They therefore find ways to let these voices speak to teenagers—usually without fanfare or much in the way of "making it shiny" (we know youth workers who use Bonhoeffer's *Life Together,* C. S. Lewis's *Screwtape Letters* and John of the Cross's *Dark Night of the Soul* "straight up" with theologically curious young people, with great success).

In addition, we absolutely *should* discuss sin and atonement with young people—as well as other "heavy" theological issues in Christian theology (try theodicy if you want to wake up the crowd)—as long as we can do so with humility, in ways that communicate our confidence in *their* abilities as practical theologians. When I was a campus minister, I logged the longest string of failed Bible studies in the history of college ministry. I planned killer Bible studies every semester, and two people would show up. Convinced that I needed better marketing, I stole the title of a Bible study used on another campus and mailed out postcards announcing our new unit, "Hard Core B.S." (of course it stood for "Bible study"). I scrambled for the most off-putting subject I could find *(doctrine!)* and hunted for one people still argue about *(election!)*. This was a Methodist campus ministry, after all.

That's when Paul, one of the most perceptive students in our campus ministry group, caught me after church. "Will it *really* be hard core?" he asked. "I'll come if it's really hard core." I promised (what did I have to lose?), and he came. So did ten of his friends—and then twenty, then thirty, then forty. We drilled down into doctrine, into tricky passages of Scripture, into theologians who had something to say on the subject. We had to find a bigger room, and it was still standing-room only, every Wednesday afternoon. From that point on, "Hard Core B.S."—which always came back to two questions *(Where is God in the story? Where are you in the story?)*— became a staple of our ministry, attracting students who had outgrown our usual weekly activities and who, as a result, were frequently overlooked.

Here is what I learned: Young people are not bored by theology. They are bored by theology that doesn't *matter.* Theology is the most relevant of all disciplines; it is reflection on what God is doing with *us,* in human time through the Holy Spirit, as revealed through the life, death and resurrection of Jesus Christ—which is why theological reflection can never be separated from life itself. Theology begins and ends in life's concrete situations, and presenting it as anything else will surely misfire.

Moreover, young people long to be taken seriously. Witness the *Invisible Children* and *Do Hard Things* phenomena—both launched by teenagers fed up with pablum offered by schools and churches. These experiences strike a chord with teenagers who long for someone who believes in them enough to challenge them. Unfortunately, most youth are routinely undersold by their churches.

Finally, for the record, I actually do know a pastor who uses Karl Barth's *Church Dogmatics* as youth curriculum—and it works because he wasn't fishing around for a great program model. He uses *Church Dogmatics* for ministry with teenagers because he uses it for ministry with everybody, because his own affection for Barth's theology is nothing short of contagious. You cannot know Christian Andrews without seeing Barth's vital connection to his life, which somehow makes you think that Barth might be useful to yours. Christian and his wife, Michelle, launched a network of reading groups for teenagers and emerging adults in their small congregation as they read through portions of Barth's *Church Dogmatics* together. Engaging young people in this process of theological reflection has helped forge a common faith language that increases opportunities for theological conversation throughout the entire congregation, and improves young people's chances of seeing their own lives in theological terms.

4. *Youth ministry as practical theology is not optional.* Without theology, we have no language to describe our experience of God, no way to prevent ministry from devolving into social science or social service, no way to point ministry beyond ourselves toward Christ. Of course, we do not need to use academic, technical or polarizing language to ground our practice of youth ministry in theological reflection. Theology simply gives us a vehicle to talk about what matters most. And unless youth ministry deals with the ultimate issues—Why am I and why is God? What is worth living for and what is worth dying for?—it has no place in the church. As C. S. Lewis remarked, "Christianity, if false, is of no importance, and if true, of infinite importance. The only thing it cannot be is moderately important."[4]

To approach youth ministry theologically is to help others give it equal footing alongside other forms of ministry. It's to open the eyes of others to see young people's status as human beings, created and loved by God, who have the right to be taken seriously by the church. In solo pastor situations, this means attending to young people as full-fledged participants in the congregation. In multistaff churches, this also means removing the disparity between youth pastors and everyone else.

When I was speaking at a youth ministry training event recently, someone raised a question about prioritizing youth ministry in our present economic crisis, when churches seem to be cutting youth ministry positions to make budget. Tongue in cheek, I remarked, "Who says it has to be the youth minister who gets cut? Why not cut the senior pastor—let volunteers do that job, and keep the youth minister?" The audience laughed, and we continued the discussion, recognizing youth ministry's "down" position in an economy of scarcity. But when I got home, a letter was waiting for me. It was from a woman who had been at the conference. She recalled the joke about cutting the senior pastor's position in order to keep the youth minister, and said: "I just wanted you to know that our congregation here in Minnesota did exactly that. It was clear to us that, to be true to the mission of the church, we had to remain faithful to our commitment to young people. So when it came time to adjust our pastoral staff, we let the senior pastor go, and we kept the youth minister. Today volunteers are doing the preaching and pastoral care, and the youth ministry is a strong presence in our community."

Wow.

AS WE BEGIN

I want to be clear about something. I am honored to share these pages with Andy Root, and even more honored to have spent a significant amount of time with him during his doctoral program, a season that made us friends as well as colleagues. But as you can see from the contents, this is mostly Andy's book. And because these pages are filled with brief, pastoral reflections rather than sustained academic arguments, you are about to see the pastoral side of one of the most sophisticated American practical theologians ever to write about youth ministry. You'll recognize Andy Root's gifts as a pastor and teacher (he remains the only teaching assistant I've ever had who received a standing ovation after a lecture), but you will also encounter his self-deprecating wit, his passion for reality TV, his angsty hypochondria, his affinity for obtuse diagrams, his debt to Ray Anderson, his bias toward crisis, and his soulful devotion to his wife and children. And though, if you were to press the details in this book, you might find that we differ on a few of them, Andy has taught me at least as much about practical theology and youth ministry as I have taught him. In short, I *trust* Andy Root: I trust his scholarship because I trust his heart.

As we head into these pages together, I hope you will trust your heart too. I hope you will recognize your own ministry in these chapters. I hope you will be reminded of the theological importance of the work you are already doing, even as you adopt some new practices of theological reflection to guide you in the future. Above all, I hope you will be energized by remembering the urgency of your vocation. This is the work that you do: you stop young people from dying. You nourish them with the Bread of Life, sow seeds of hope that take root and create communities where adolescents can thrive as God intends them to. Christ has called you, and you have been faithful—with or without a theology degree, with or without a job description, with or without an education from Sudan (or anywhere else). The church is stronger because of you.

So now: let's get to work.

PART ONE

THEOLOGICAL STARTING POINTS

What Does Youth Ministry Have to Do with Theology?

THE NEW RHETORIC
OF YOUTH MINISTRY

KENDA CREASY DEAN

While cleaning out my office recently I finally had to face facts: my shelves were bloated with youth ministry books I would never use: tried-but-discarded strategy books, tie-dye cool gospel vernaculars like *God Is for Real, Man,* outdated youth culture commentaries, game guides and "idea" books that included everything from noncompetitive parachute games to the now-suspect chubby bunny contest.

Equally noticeable were the books that were absent. Almost nothing on ministry with young people outside of suburban, white, middle-class North America. Almost nothing on the globalization of contemporary culture, or on how technology and changing social expectations increasingly challenge the notion of adolescence itself. Despite the throngs of scholars lamenting "problems of American youth," few mention religion or the church as a possible road to cure.[1] Disturbingly, neither do theologians.

THE LITERATURE OF LAMENT:
YOUTH MINISTRY'S RHETORIC OF DESPAIR

The rhetoric of youth ministry in the late twentieth century, especially among mainline Protestants, was born of slippage: declining church memberships, decreasing moral influence and—save for the religious Right's brief political apex in the 1980s—evaporating social power. As mainline churches gradually admitted their new marginal status in American society, the rhetoric surrounding their ministry with young people could aptly be described as "a rhetoric of despair." Denominations bemoaned the loss of young people from their ranks, and ministry analysts launched a new literature of lament that blamed the church's adolescent hemorrhage on everything from inadequate leadership training, poor educational models and dwindling denominational support to demographic shifts, economic cycles and, of course, the onslaught of secular culture.[2]

Notably absent from these rebukes was any mention of *theology*. For the most part, churches remained naive to their own complicity in the loss of young people from the pews. Liberal Christians blamed conservatives for promising young people easy answers (sometimes true) and conservative Christians blamed liberals for comforting them with cheap grace (also sometimes true). The fact was that most young people had never *been* in the pews to begin with, and their fading voices signaled an increasingly toxic culture and a distressingly impotent church. In 1965, the World Council of Churches called for an end to the segregation of young people into isolated "youth programs," urging congregations to integrate youth into the total mission of the church.[3] Financially strapped denominations responded by amputating costly youth departments—yet, as youth staffs and budgets shriveled, no mechanism emerged to help local churches absorb young people into their larger ministries. The Carnegie Council on Adolescent Development declared the 1980s "an era of massive cuts in youth ministry" in terms of denominational personnel and resource deployment.[4] By the end of the century, young people's absence, not their presence, had become normative for American Christianity.

SIGNS OF HOPE

Surprisingly, despite the litany of crises that ushered in the twenty-first century, the rhetoric of despair that had come to typify the conversation about youth ministry has begun to soften. By the first decade of the twenty-first century, three developments had slowly gathered momentum, setting the stage for a rhetorical change of heart and allowing a "rhetoric of hope" to emerge in the church's conversation about young people, and about youth ministry in particular.

The first development was the late-twentieth-century's renaissance in practical theology. Overwhelmed by the information age's glut of data, modern fractiousness and moral uncertainty, secular scholars and theologians alike welcomed the practical wisdom of local communities as an alternative route to truth, which had the effect of rekindling academic interest in concrete communities of faith. Meanwhile, a new generation of students entered Christian colleges and seminaries—students whose coming of age coincided with the demise of many denominational youth ministry programs, which meant they increasingly traced their faith formation to parachurch youth and mission organizations rather than to traditional catechesis in congregations. As schools found themselves preparing candidates for ministry who had little experience in (or affection for) congregations, youth ministry provided a curricular bridge between students and local churches. For many of these young leaders—whose experiences in life-changing youth groups shaped their expectations for Christian community—youth ministry offered a template for how to "do church" with all age groups, and informed their approach to ecclesiology, mission and ministry as well. As a 1994 report to the Lilly Endowment conceded: "What has become clear . . . is that youth ministry is ultimately about something much more than youth ministry. . . . These [Christian youth] movements are redrawing the ecclesial map of the United States."[5]

The second development that signaled changing attitudes toward youth ministry was the Lilly Endowment's decision in the late 1980s to seed youth ministry initiatives in colleges and seminaries. Flush with profits from the "irrational exuberance" of the American stock market, Lilly gave innovative youth ministry the financial encouragement once provided by denominations—with a crucial difference. Lilly tendered this financial support primarily through Christian higher education, not denominations or parachurch groups—a decision that created a new "center of gravity" for innovative youth ministry, not in grass-roots ministries or in church bureaucracies, but in theological institutions whose primary focus was Christian vocation, and especially the education of pastors.[6] Besides spawning curricular changes, the decision to fund youth ministry at the level of theological education gave it new stature as a theological subject, and sent an unmistakable signal to pastors-in-training that their ministries should include young people.

The infusion of Lilly dollars placed youth ministry squarely on the agenda of mainstream Christian colleges and seminaries in the U.S. Before Lilly's entry into the discussion, youth ministry (widely considered a place to "do time" until a chance for "real"—read: adult—ministry came along) floated on the periphery of the church's consciousness. Youth ministry classes in higher education, where they were offered at all, were often outsourced to talented pastors instead of taught by regular faculty. Now, however, theological schools actively cultivated youth ministry initiatives in order to qualify for grant support, and churches responded by adding pastoral positions in youth ministry. While evangelicals had been professionalizing youth ministry throughout the late twentieth century, in the 1990s mainline Protestants began to follow suit. A small but influential number of mainline schools (including Emory, Princeton and Duke) launched youth ministry initiatives and added lines for pedigreed professors who brought theological substance to youth-related coursework. By the mid-1990s, the number of professors of youth ministry reached a critical mass, spawning professional guilds and a serious debate about whether youth ministry should constitute a "discipline" of its own.

Meanwhile, a third development contributed to the rhetoric of hope in youth ministry: a rising interest in spirituality among young people themselves, especially outside the U.S. As young people around the globe turned to religion to interpret cultural shifts and resist globalization's homogenizing juggernaut, scholars and policymakers took note. Sociologists who had predicted the triumph of secularization recanted;[7] social and developmental psychologists, once skittish about religious subjects, began to acknowledge religion's positive impact on healthy communities and adolescents.[8] Tragedies like the Columbine High School shootings and the terrorist attacks of September 11, 2001, soldered the connection between young people and faith in the public eye, and in this cultural milieu, youth ministry grew bolder, demanding legitimacy as a ministry of the church.

REDEFINING CHURCH: THEMES IN THE RHETORIC OF HOPE

In short, just as adolescence itself has expanded to include nine-year-olds entering puberty as well as twenty-nine-year-olds struggling to make adult commitments, the rhetoric of hope has expanded youth ministry's scope. In some ways, this rhetoric underscores long-accepted themes in Christian youth work—the need for relational methods and radical contextualization, for instance. But the new conversation about youth ministry sounds these themes with a new and almost brazen sense of purpose. Because this rhetoric views young people as capable of theological critique, the new conversation sets out to do more than redefine youth ministry. It aims to redefine the *church*, with passionate communities of youth playing a central role, on the premise that young people are reliable barometers of the human condition, and their actions may therefore be considered Exhibit A of humanity's desire for God. At the same time, this rhetoric is intensely local and highly personal, echoing the apostolic community's emphasis on personal, even mystical, encounters with Jesus Christ. As in the early church, this rhetoric tends to emphasize informal enclaves of care and spiritual practice that provide fidelity, transcendence and intimacy to young people starved for all three.

For those of us who take more than a casual interest in ministry with young people, this rhetoric offers promise but also invites caution. Youth ministry both challenges existing ecclesiologies and risks making them puerile; indeed, new church movements are frequently accused of being "adolescent." Many visible leaders of today's "alternative" congregations—church movements where pastors intentionally refashion styles of worship, patterns of polity and forms of nurture to attract Baby Boomers and/or their progeny—admit strong roots in youth ministry. A quick scan through their proliferating publications shows that, by and large, these leaders simply adapted the visions, methods and rhetoric of youth ministry to address the adults these youth inevitably became. (As one "alt-church" pastor put it, "I basically do youth ministry for people who can drive and vote and drink."[9]) At the same time, the rhetoric of hope reveals a broader sense of calling on the part of young people and in youth ministry itself, as youth and their ministers seek to refashion what it means to be "church" in a frankly post-Christian culture. The rhetoric of hope's investment in practical theology, global postmodern culture and communities of faith practice, for instance, suggests an expanding purpose, context and curriculum for ministry with young people. In short, youth ministry is no longer only about youth.

A broader purpose: From Christian education to practical theology. What is at stake in the rhetoric of hope's interest in practical theology is rescuing youth ministry from decades of foster care in the social sciences in order to return it to its theological home.[10] For more than a century, the church has conceived youth ministry as a "department" (or sometimes as the unruly stepchild) of Christian education. The label never quite fit; youth ministry acts more like a microcosm of the church than as an arm of education—which means that it actually provides a premiere laboratory for engaging laypeople (in this case, teenagers) in practical theological reflection. The perspective of youth ministers themselves also shifted; as they sought more professional credibility, they demanded more substantive training, and therefore began to think of themselves and their vocations theologically.

This did not eliminate a relationship between Christian education and youth ministry; it simply put the relationship in a different perspective, recognizing that education is *one* practice of youth ministry that helps young people discover themselves called by Christ to carry out the church's mission in the world.[11] Youth ministry is, after all, *ministry,* and the practicing Christian community is its "curriculum"—a curriculum that is meaningless unless participation accompanies cognition. The language of formation and discipleship stresses the embodiment of faith, as young people encounter and incarnate Christ through the mediating practices of the church. For this reason, the rhetoric of hope stresses spiritual formation over "Christian education," discipleship over membership, small enclaves of community over youth fellowships. On the one hand, these distinctions are largely semantic. Spiritual practices, after all, are enacted beliefs; doctrine inheres in the imitation of Christ in all its forms.[12] On the other hand, religious education's alliance with American pragmatism throughout the twentieth century perverted ancient understandings of *catechesis.* The "handing on of the faith" was never intended to be a dogmatic exercise but rather provided a route for spiritual transformation through practices that demonstrate trust in the risen Christ. Living out such trust sometimes did, and sometimes did not, perpetuate "adult" faith norms.

A broader context: From youth culture to global postmodernity. Like all ministry, youth ministry is highly contextual; what is distinctive about youth ministers' rhetoric of hope is that they view their ministry's "context" as the broader culture of global postmodernity, making adolescents' reactions to culture emblematic of the human condition as a whole. Fifty years ago, it was possible to speak of an emerging "youth culture." The invention of portable technologies like the transistor, the mandatory age-stratification of American high schools following World War II, the growing disposable income of adolescents that allowed advertisers to develop a "teen market"—all of these factors invited young people to create and consume their own subculture away from the watchful eyes of parents. Consequently, the "adolescent society," as James Coleman called it in 1961,[13] represented a new civilization, as foreign to the American church as any far-flung place on the globe, and as much in need of Jesus.

No more. Youth ministry is still missionary work, and adolescents still need Jesus. But the "adolescent society" no longer exists, not because it has vanished but because it has devoured everything around it. Today, *all* popular culture is youth culture, and vice versa, and *all* age groups participate in it—forcing young people to turn to increasingly marginal and dangerous alternatives in order to distinguish themselves from adults. Youth ministry no longer focuses on the cultural idiosyncracies of the young as a homogenous group simply because youth culture is no longer idiosyncratic, and because adolescents are not (and have never been) homogenous. The rhetoric of hope assumes that young people live betwixt and between multiple cultures. "Youth culture" theory is supplanted by "generational" theory, the unsurprising (but highly marketable) observation that people are shaped by the events and popular cultures of their youth.

Yet the new rhetoric of youth ministry also assumes that young people's immersion in broad cultural and ecclesial trends gives them unique resources (cultural literacy and a heightened sense of context come to mind) for navigating culture that could benefit the entire church. Far more important to the contemporary adolescent experience than "youth culture" are the tectonic plates shifting under the weight of globalization and postmodernity, cultural changes that affect adults and youth alike. According to the new rhetoric of youth ministry, cultural upheaval provides opportunities for rediscovering the gospel, even as it threatens to disarm the church. Like cracks in a sidewalk that allow dandelions to push through, the cultural fissures created by global postmodernity give certain themes crushed by post-Enlightenment rationality space to reemerge, find light and blossom.

This point of view is a main feature of the rhetoric of hope, namely, that despite the manipulative nature of popular consumer culture, the church can and should *use* the rips and tears in our cultural fabric as portals to discover more adequate narratives in Jesus Christ. The rhetoric of hope frequently turns to popular culture to amplify revelation, pointing out gospel themes inadvertently revealed in the culture that the modern church overlooked or undervalued. The contemporary insistence on personal experience, mystery and utter connection might illuminate, for instance, the personal, relational nature of faith, the experiential side of Christian community, the suffering of Christ and the need for God's transcendence, not to mention Christ's call for solidarity with those who are not like us. In the rhetoric of hope, even postmodern relativism itself is a sign of spiritual unrest, as our restless souls, as Augustine observed, seek their rest in God. These themes are not revealed to adolescents because of any latent Christology lurking underneath the surface of popular culture. Rather, faith enables those also conversant in culture—

teenagers, for instance—to baptize culture for Christ.[14]

A broader curriculum: From programs to communities of spiritual practice. Perhaps the most noticeable change in youth ministry in the early twenty-first century is the diminished role of denominations, youth programs and events in favor of relationships and spiritual practices—those ongoing activities of the Christian community that shape us in relationship to God and to one another—as the primary vehicles through which adolescents recognize God encountering them. The popularity of mission trips (inevitably low-tech, limited, human operations) offers a case in point. Youth mission trips typically trade razzmatazz for drama, relying on communities of radical care and belonging that are constructed through shared practices of prayer, service, hospitality and celebration. In the Christian community, practices that imitate the self-giving love of God shape relationships that echo Christ's love. To be sure, the interest in faith practices and the relationships that emerge from them do not eliminate the need for youth programs; good youth programs are communities of faith practices. But contemporary adolescents—justly suspicious of adult abandonment—distrust the institutional ring and relational sterility suggested by "program" ministries and gravitate to them only insofar as they engage practices that foster personal relationships with God and one another.

Christian practices therefore assume critical importance. They are the curriculum of youth ministry. In the first place, prayer, preaching, tolerance, tithing, living simply, living chastely, conferencing with other Christians, searching Scripture, serving others and so on tether young people to a faith tradition without shackling them to a particular institutional expression of it, giving faith flexibility and portability. In addition, practices shift youth ministry's attention away from activities and events to communities, which are the fruit of Christian practices. Practices also stress the lived nature of faith, for practices *embody* Christ's suffering love, thereby preventing Christianity from deteriorating into abstract intellectualism or vapid, generic "feel good-isms." And, by enfleshing God's love in word, deed and act, practices offer concrete points of connection that provide a sense of divine accompaniment in daily life. In short, faith practices allow young people a way to encounter God without needing a priest, a program—or, for that matter, an adult—to guide them.[15]

Two examples of how youth ministry turned to the historic practices of the church to foster authentic community are youth ministry's recent passion for worship and identification with mission. Borrowed in part from alternative church movements in Europe and in part from creative young pastors who sought to replicate youth ministry's tight-knit communities and experiential methods with entire congregations, worship in particular became recognized as a context with unparalleled potential to form community. Drawing on practices like praise and lament, preaching and teaching, hospitality and healing, teenagers gathered to experience the presence of God. The term *experience* was important; in both mission and worship, young people sought an *experience* of God in which God inhered even if youth did not "feel" God emotionally. The availability of technology in worship, for instance, allowed for innovative forms of piety (that had been long practiced in youth camps, conferences and fellowship groups) to be played out in a larger chancel as youth ministry began a clear drift toward the sanctuary. By the late 1990s, the prominence of worship as a feature of youth ministry served as a sign of youth workers' desire to locate ministry with young people at the center of the Christian community, just as mission expressed young people's insistence on an active Christianity that tangibly follows Jesus into the world.

IMAGINING CHURCH

The effect of the rhetoric of hope in youth ministry has yet to be calculated. On the one hand, it promises a new sense of vocation for youth ministry, and a theological sense of direction as youth ministry becomes more than a platform for placating teenagers. Indeed, youth ministry's great potential may lie in its ability to reimagine the church on behalf of the wider Christian community, a church in which God has called young people to play an irrepressible and irreplaceable part.

On the other hand, the rhetoric of hope in youth ministry has risks, not the least of which is hubris and the possibility that it promises more than it can deliver. Will adolescents be able to reimagine the church in ways that are any less jaded than the adults before them? Or will youth ministry's expanded vocation on behalf of the church lead to a loss of focus—an abandonment of the church's mission with young people themselves, returning youth ministry to the "stepping stone" status it has so earnestly tried to shake? Above all, what is the source of the rhetoric of hope in youth ministry? Is it grounded in the optimism and idealism of young people, or in the hope of Jesus Christ, who somehow manages to save the world daily without our help?

The verdict, of course, will be for another generation to decide. What we can ascertain is that the rhetoric of hope enlarges youth ministry's territory for the twenty-first-century church. Youth ministry's broader sense of purpose, broader view of context and broader understanding of curriculum leave no doubt about its vocation on behalf of the larger church. And if the predicament of adolescents is intimately linked to the predicament of the *church*, then the transformation of one implies the transformation of both.

• DISCUSSION AND REFLECTION EXERCISE
Tales from the Trenches

This exercise seeks to get you thinking about theology from within your practice and action of ministry in the church.[16] The idea is not to simply remember and retell stories, but to discuss how your experience of youth ministry was influenced by a local congregation. Think about the congregation where you first encountered youth ministry. How did the activity of the larger church affect your understanding of what youth ministry is all about? How did the church's implicit or explicit theology impact the youth ministry (and you in particular)? How did youth ministry lead the church in dealing with cultural transitions?

Each person should come with a tale to tell—one story from his or her experience described above—and be ready to share this narrative in three to five minutes. After each tale allow for discussion.

(Note: It often works best if the leader of the conversation begins by telling a tale. This allows the leader to model the kind of reflection and time use desired—not to mention personal vulnerability.)

GOD IS A MINISTER

Youth Ministry as Fundamentally Theological

ANDREW ROOT

The other day I was sitting with two fellow seminary professors, both talented biblical scholars, discussing the present and future of our seminary. I explained to them that those of us in the Children, Youth, and Family Department were planning on deepening our commitment to our Ph.D. program in the next few years. They both responded positively and encouraged the possible new endeavor. When it became clear that the conversation was about to shift topics, however, one of them turned to me and, with a half smile that said he knew his next comment would draw my ire, inquired, "My only question is, who is going to teach the Ph.D. seminar on group mixers?"

Despite youth ministry's long history, its practice has often been viewed by senior pastors and academics as lightweight. It has been assumed that the youth worker is a hyperactive person in their early twenties who prefers unserious kid stuff to the responsible practice of shared suffering and proclamation of the Word in pastoral ministry. So, while the theology, history and Bible people discuss rigorous theories, youth ministry people teach students how to do things like plan trips, play games and lead Bible studies—all important in practice, but low on the food chain of academic scholarship.

Is all this true? And if not, what is it that we are really up to in youth ministry?

I believe, in fact, that the practice of youth ministry has been seen as lightweight both intellectually and ministerially because we have failed to see *ourselves* as theologians doing a fundamentally theological task. But what does that mean? What difference could it make to see ourselves as theologians? And how does theology work within the practice of youth ministry?

SINGING A NEW SONG: YOUTH MINISTER AS THEOLOGIAN

A frequent sight on the early episodes of *American Idol* (which I have to admit I'm addicted to) was profanity-laced tirades of some of the very worst singers when they left the audition room. Through their rage and tears they often asserted that they're great singers, and the judges were wrong. We as viewers know, of course, that the individuals are actually very bad singers, which makes their angry tantrums sadistically funny and so entertaining to watch (at least to me). Sure, the judges may be harsh, but they're not wrong when it comes to these contestants' singing ability.

Much like the *American Idol* candidates who can't sing, some of us have a conflated view of ourselves that has developed out of the imagined, or actual, perception of youth ministry as shallow. *We* aren't the problem, we assert; it's the uptight pastors or ivory-tower academics who judge wrongly. Our ministries are actually singing beautifully, or would be if our so-called ministry judges just understood us. But it may be that the genesis of the perceived thinness of our craft actually does rest more with us and our explicit or hidden insecurities about who we are and what we do.

Desiring to be respected but feeling a lack of acclaim, we've often fallen into two problematic traps. The first trap that our insecurity has led us into is the overwhelming need to justify ourselves. We have made arguments for why we are important and necessary to personnel committees and church boards. We have also spent a great deal of energy and ink explaining why youth ministry is important both as a ministerial office and as an academic discipline.

The second trap of insecurity is isolation. We have decided to spend all of our time reading, writing and participating in conversations solely about youth work. We have been slow to enter into crossdisciplinary or crossministerial conversations that would open up our understanding of our vocation to those in other fields. In staff or faculty meetings, rarely have we understood the doctrine of reconciliation or the writings of a leading theologian as well as (or better than) the senior pastor or senior professor. We have networked ourselves with fellow youth workers but have been less willing to network with other pastors.

If youth ministry is to have a future that avoids these deadly traps of self-justification and isolation, it must move boldly into deep theological construction. What I mean is that we must begin to see ourselves not primarily as youth ministry directors but as theologians who do constructive theology in the context of ministry with the adolescent population.

Truth be told, the theological legitimacy of the senior pastor is often based more on ordination credentials or years of past education or a pulpit to preach from than on constructive theological thinking in the practice of ministry. But this only makes things more difficult, giving senior pastors and others a reason to keep us youth workers theologically ignorant so that we might not see that all pastoral ministry needs a turn to the theological. I know this is cynical, but too often it plays out like this. And when it does, we youth workers find ourselves always scratching for some respect.

But seeing ourselves as theologians has the potential to move us beyond concern for de facto respect by drawing us into more meaningful and significant conversations with our colleagues in ministry, if they are willing. As we enter into mutually significant conversation beyond our isolation, they will recognize that we are not seeking to justify ourselves but rather are trying to construct deep theological articulations of how God is at work within the world. Claiming our place at the table of meaningful ministry will thus only be achieved by *a richer theological imagination.*[1] But to make such a move we must begin by understanding how theological reflection happens in the context of ministry (not just youth ministry) and what difference it might make.

THEOLOGY AS MINISTRY/MINISTRY AS THEOLOGY

In the first class session of my core children, youth and family course called "Theological Frameworks for CYF," I often set up my students by giving them a pop quiz. They're to circle all of the following phrases that they believe are true:

> Good theology leads to good ministry.
> Good ministry leads to good theology.
> Bad theology leads to bad ministry.
> Bad ministry leads to bad theology.
> Good theology can lead to bad ministry.
> Bad theology can lead to good ministry.

There is more than one right answer depending on how a person perceives the statements, but I assert that "good ministry leads to good theology" is the (most) correct answer. My point is this: that ministry always precedes theology and becomes the fodder for constructive theological thought because of our claim that God is living and active in the world—which means that God is a Minister.

By looking at God's Ministry of creation, covenant, incarnation (including crucifixion and resurrection) and Pentecost, it is obvious that God is not a theologian but a (the!) Minister. *God has committed to be the Minister of creation, and theology is reflection on and articulation of God's Ministry.* If we confess that God is active, that God is moving creation to its completion, then ministry is participation in God's own act of Ministry, and theology is nothing more than reflecting on God's action. And if it is true that God is alive and moving in the world as Minister, then all constructive theological work must be done in conversation and connection with this same world to which God is in God's tri-unity. To be in contact with this world is to be in ministry, and therefore is to do theology.

Our own ministries in the world, then, are only truly ministries if they are connected to God's continued Ministry, and theology is only constructive (and helpful) if it is done in the context of God's continued Ministry in the world. Because youth ministry is ministry that seeks to connect *not* primarily to adolescents but to God's own Ministry as God ministers to adolescents, theological construction is demanded. To be faithful ministers we must begin to articulate how God is active in their (and our own) lives (by the way, it's this that makes us very different from the local after-school program). This means that the very humanity of each adolescent becomes significant to us, not because it is our job to love them but because God has so loved them, and to join God's Ministry we too must love them. Therefore, we love through the power of God in God's Ministry and not by our own ability.

This all leads me to assert that to do theology you must be in ministry. By this I mean you must be seeking to discover how God is active in the lives of concrete people in the world, and join that. Our actions in ministry with people whom God loves and stands with and for then become the material of original and deep theological thought. But our ministerial actions themselves also loudly assert theological truths. Stepping back from our actions in ministry allows us to both consider them theologically and begin to recognize the unconsidered theology present in them. For example: a youth director stands in front of a group of six eighth graders and says, "Hey, where is everyone?" What seems purely utilitarian is actually a claim laced with theology: "You six eighth graders do not constitute a faith community. You are not 'everyone,' or really 'anyone.' Bigger is better. We have failed to capitalize on our influence." In our failure to reflect theologically on our actions, to have a vision of God's own Ministry, we stumble in the dark, and sometimes we stumble onto paths that lead away from God's Ministry. This is all to make the point that in a real way, ministry is a theological task, for if it is ministry of the gospel it seeks to be faithful to God's own Ministry.[2]

WHAT DIFFERENCE WILL THIS MAKE?

But what difference will it make to see ourselves as theologians? Could this have any significant impact? I offer four ways it makes an important difference.

First, seeing youth ministry as a theological task *moves youth ministry beyond utilitarianism and demands that we do real reflection on the practice of ministry and the young people to and with whom we minister.* By understanding yourself as a theologian, you are freed to function as more than the congregation's program director. Rather, you are called to discern the multiple layers and nuances of God's activity and the actions of people, and then to seek creative ways to facilitate their understanding of and participation in God's action in the world.

For example, during a weekend retreat you may discover that five of the seven adolescents in your cabin come from families with parents who are divorced, separated or were never married. You must stop and reflect on this experience, evaluating it both theologically (What is God's desire for families and children? How do estranged and separated bonds between parents shape children's experience of their world and the way they see themselves? And how is God active in transforming their brokenness?) and psychosocially (How does such a family form psychologically affect a child? How does it affect the relational resources available for their development?[3] And what resources can I or the church provide to them?). If you are only a programmer you may be justified in ignoring an adolescent's deep suffering; your job is to provide meaningful events, and suffering throws wrenches into well-oiled programmatic machines. But if ministry is not about the utilitarianism of programming but about seeking to join God's Ministry in the world, then you cannot turn from the suffering adolescent, for with her stands the crucified Christ.

Second, I believe seeing ourselves as theologians helps us *move past much of the fragmentation of ministries within the church.* The Protestant Reformation stood, at least in part, upon the belief that all Christian believers were priests—the priesthood of all believers, in other words. In that Reformation context this worked out radically in the areas of prayer, Bible reading and confession; the Reformers asserted that all believers were priests, so all believers could pray, read the Bible and confess their sins without a priest standing between them and God. Almost all churches and traditions would affirm this strongly today. But what is interesting is that this conception of the priesthood of all believers hasn't continued on to its logical conclusion, which is that *all* believers are participants in God's Ministry and are therefore *all* involved in a theological task. In other words, anyone participating in any way in the ministry of God is swept up into a theological task.

What's often assumed instead is that the theologian on the church staff is the senior pastor; everyone else is just trying to keep things running smoothly. But from a constructive theological perspective, all those involved in ministry within the church are involved in theological reflection, and any individual who deliberately reflects on God's action in light of concrete people is involved in theological construction. I believe this perspective releases youth ministry from being merely an appendage, connected but not integrated into the church's ministry, and instead roots it within congregational life. Every staff member, every congregation member, is a theologian, and it is your job (as paid pastor) to help them see how and why this is so.

Third, embedding youth ministry in theology demands that we *see the adolescent from a contextual perspective, as one who is affected by multiple forces.* It is not enough to only be concerned with programming for the adolescent on Wednesday night or Sunday morning; as youth workers we are called to relate to youth within their families and cultures. Moreover, by giving direct attention to how an adolescent exists in multiple systems, we come to recognize that the young person's family is also affected by the forces of a pluralistic world. God is active in multiple contexts, not only in the church's youth ministry but also within the family and larger world. By understanding ourselves as theologians, our ministry is directed beyond the four walls of the church and into the familial, community and socio-political contexts in which students and their families live.

Finally, I believe that by seeing youth ministry as a theological task, *theory and practice are held together.* It is too often assumed that youth ministry is for doers and not for thinkers. Yet good doing demands good thinking. Understanding yourself as a theologian demands that you become astute at moving from experience to reflection and then to action by learning to discern and articulate the connections between God's action and human persons.

REFLECTING ON OUR EXPERIENCE OF GOD'S ACTION

To live as theologians in youth ministry we must learn to dance, in a sense— to continually operate from three distinct, but connected, steps.

Experience. Imagine taking the seat behind two tenth-grade girls on your bus trip home from camp. Seeking to start a conversation you ask, "Are you both looking forward to getting home?" The one seated on the aisle turns to you and says, "I know she is," pointing to her friend who is leaning against the window. She continues, "She hasn't seen her boyfriend in a week and she can't wait to get some!" You spend the next forty-five minutes hearing stories and asking questions about high-school dating and sexuality. You've just had an experience!

Reflection. Now that you have had the experience, you begin to reflect on it. You may look at some social scientific research (maybe a book like *Unhooked*[4]) to help you see why adolescents do the things they do. Could it be a psychological issue with their fathers? Could it be the effects of consumer culture? The Internet can connect you with other helpful sources as well; blogs and RSS feeds of articles can easily put information and ideas in your inbox. To do the kind of theological reflection that's desired, you have to do the work to really see the young person. This kind of reflection may not be theology proper (it may not immediately be bringing forth ideas of God's action) but it nevertheless helps you join in God's Ministry of loving solidarity with and for adolescents. As a constructive theologian, you're seeking here to understand, through reflection on experience, the concrete humanity of those with whom you are in ministry.

But reflection on our experience demands more if it is to be theological. It is here that the normative texts of the Christian tradition become essential. For instance, asking what Scripture says about our human sexuality and what other theologians in the tradition understood about this issue in their own time and place helps us have a broader and deeper vision of how our experience should be understood in light of God's Ministry. Scripture is not God, but it is, after all, a normative set of assertions about the shape of God's Ministry. We need Scripture and the Christian tradition (the thoughts of the theologians who went before us) to have a vision to see God's action in and through our experience.

Then, very practically, it will be helpful to have a theologian or two with whom you are in constant conversation through reading his or her writings. Drawing from the Christian tradition can feel overwhelming; no one can draw on the full breadth of it. We therefore have to pick dialogue partners to accompany us on this journey of seeking God's action. I have a circle of close dialogue partners, some living, others not, to which I always take my theological questions (Karl Barth, Dietrich Bonhoeffer, Eberhard Jüngel, Douglas John Hall, Kathryn Tanner and Ray Anderson). In confronting the issue above, I would think through how it connects with what Barth has said about the imago Dei (image of God) in *Church Dogmatics* 3.2 or Bonhoeffer in *Creation and Fall* or Hall in *Imaging God,* and how the cross must lead me into a compassionate response (Hall) that calls me into deep solidarity (Anderson).

I don't agree with everything my theological dialogue partners have said (they don't all agree with each other, either), and I try to read as many other theologians as possible. But these five theologians are significant to me, not for getting everything right but for how they have helped me see the beauty and wonder of God's Ministry in the world, which, in turn, helps me make theological sense of my experiences in ministry (we'll discuss this all further in chapter five). When you take your experience on the bus and place it in conversation with social scientific research and theological discussions (which we'll discuss more in the next chapter), you've reflected on your experience!

Action. If reflection is born from experience it will blossom into action. So now, having reflected on your experience on the bus, you may decide to revamp the next month of Wednesday nights, making the topic sexuality, or you might decide that all-girl and all-guy retreats are in order. It's important to see that experience leads to reflection and then to action, but you also need to understand that the process doesn't end with action. In actuality, once you have made your way through these three steps, the third (action) has a way of instantly sweeping you back to the first (experience). It is not a sweeping that means you must start all over but rather one that opens your eyes to see that all actions become new experiences and take you again (and again) into the three steps. After the all-girl and all-guy retreats, for example, you'll have new experiences to reflect on which will no doubt lead to new reflections and then new actions. This three-step process helps us do constructive theology that is grounded in the practice of ministry and that seeks to be faithful to God's continued Ministry in the world.

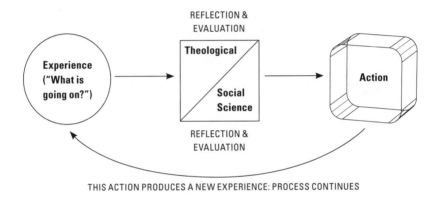

Figure 2.1. The process of practical theology

NEGLECTING THE STEPS

The theological academy has been accused (often rightly) of failing this three-step process. The perception is that we have locked ourselves in stuffy libraries far away from the experience of contemporary people in our context, and that many of us academics care little about action, about what the church actually does; we're more concerned with writing commentaries and articles for our guilds than producing work that will impact the church. The academy would do well to remember that our ultimate attention is to be given to the living God, as opposed to editorial boards and guild meetings.

Traditionally, youth ministry has also failed to hold to this three-step process, but in the exact opposite way as the academy. Our mistake in youth ministry is *not* that we have been closed to experience; youth workers are

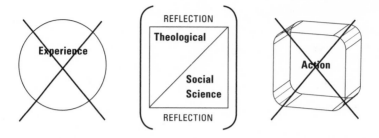

Figure 2.2. The academy's neglect

great at having experiences. And it is not that we have failed to move into action; our calendars are generally filled with planned actions, and we're often willing to do new and different things. The problem is that we have often failed to attend to deep, rigorous, reasoned reflection; we've been too anxious (rebellious) to slow down and think before doing.

I believe that this is the root of our insecurity and of the perception of youth ministry as lightweight and shallow. For this stigma to melt away we will most likely have to correct ourselves by spending more time and thought in reflection. And for youth ministry to see itself as theological in nature, we must learn to consistently and deeply move within the three steps of experience, reflection and action.

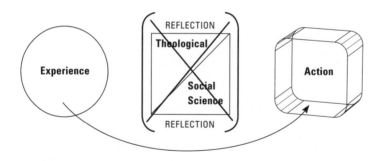

Figure 2.3. Youth ministry's neglect

CONCLUSION

It is my hope that in seeing ourselves as theologians, taking on a new theological rhetoric (to follow chapter one), we might be drawn more deeply into the continued Ministry of God in the world, which is to be with and for adolescents. I am confident that, by doing this, we can free ourselves from our stances of justification and isolation and become significant voices within the church for what God is doing in God's Ministry in the world, and for how human beings can faithfully join it.

• DISCUSSION AND REFLECTION EXERCISE
Role Model Profile

This exercise invites you to reflect on past youth workers, pastors or volunteer leaders you've known, examining how they sought to think theologically or how theology impacted their ministry and their person.[5]

- As you look back, which youth workers, pastors or others best represent what a theologian in ministry should be (in your opinion)?

- What characteristics have you observed in these people that, in your mind, make them such good theological thinkers in ministry?

- As you think about how these people work, which of their actions most encapsulates and typifies that which you find so admirable about their theological reflection?

- As you think about what these people do well, which of their abilities would you most like to be able to borrow and integrate into your own ministry?

Our answers to these questions can give us a picture of the parts of ourselves and our practice that we yearn to develop. Review your responses and make a list of those areas.

YOUTH MINISTRY AS AN INTEGRATIVE THEOLOGICAL TASK

Toward a Representative Method

ANDREW ROOT

Heather is fifteen and has attended Grace-Trinity Church since she was in third grade. She seemed like a normal, average kid who almost disappeared into the background, until six months ago. In a small group discussion, Heather shattered the perceived ordinariness of her life by revealing, almost matter-of-factly (as if no one would care anyhow), that she had missed quite a few days of school recently (which she figured few people had noticed). Most mornings she felt so depressed she could barely get out of bed. Her mother, she said in an aside, was unavailable to her because she had a drinking problem, and her stepdad had enough to worry about; she disclosed that he had recently lost his job at the local factory, forcing her family to go on food stamps while he searched unsuccessfully for another job.

Sara, the youth director at Grace-Trinity, stared back at Heather, stunned. She was moved both by the depth of suffering Heather was experiencing and by the fact that she chose to share it. In the weeks preceding this confession, Sara had found it impossible to get Heather to share anything at all. The multiple layers of the issues affecting Heather became instantly obvious, but Sara feared that confronting any of them would move her far from her expertise (whatever that expertise might be).

Sara finally returned her gaze to the open Bible in her hand. As the late chapters of Mark's Gospel stared back at her, she wondered what difference it made. How would another poorly planned Bible study have any impact as Heather faced poverty, abuse, addiction, isolation and depression?

Could theology assist Sara in ministry in this situation?

As I stated in the last chapter, youth ministry is fundamentally a theological task, a task that seeks to participate in God's own Ministry by moving from experience to reflection to action. Or, to broaden and deepen this, we could say that youth ministry attends to divine action: it aims to do its work in a manner that is faithful to (and that strives to articulate) God's action in the world. Our job, then, is not to simply apply Bible verses to research on adolescent behavior; when we do this we overlook our theological calling. Rather, youth ministry is in the unique business of constructing theology itself by examining how divine action connects to human beings in the first third of the human lifespan.

But here sits Sara, overwhelmed with the issues impacting Heather, issues that are clearly more than theological. They're psychological and economic too. How can theology help? And how can theology enter into conversation with other areas of knowledge to help us reflect deeply on our experience, so that our action might touch the broken humanity of those like Heather?

WHAT IS THEOLOGY?

Proclaiming God's revelation: The kerygmatic emphasis of theology.
The words *theos* and *logos* have been scribbled on the blackboard of almost every introductory class to the study of theology. Students are told that *theos* means "God" and *logos* means "logic" or "study," and that theology is therefore the study of God, like sociology is the study of society, psychology the study of the psyche and biology the study of the organic body. When explained this way, theology, like its other "–ology" comrades, is a science, the science of God.

Yet it is at this point that we confront a gigantic problem. For while the other sciences look to unveil what is hidden within a phenomenon (why the economy works like it does, why childhood trauma reappears in later life, why certain drugs can shrink a tumor), theological study looks beyond what can be known in the natural world. Indeed, theology can unveil nothing of its subject of study, for its subject—the eternal God of Israel—transcends time and space and any human tool that could be created or imagined to unveil God.[1] In this way, theology is fundamentally different from the other sciences. The process of unveiling is God's own work; it is God who chooses to make Godself known to a world that God is completely other than.[2]

This process of God's unveiling is called *revelation,* and revelation is what we're talking about when we assert (as I did in the last chapter) that God is a Minister. God's revealing of Godself (revelation) is God's Ministry; it is God's coming near to us to overcome that which keeps us from God (our death and sin). Douglas John Hall states, "Christian faith does not base itself on general observations about the world, human beings, nature, divinity, and so forth. . . . It begins with revelation. That is, its point of departure is a disclosure, an 'unveiling' of something not otherwise accessible to human knowing."[3] Theology, then, is not the process of unveiling God to the world but rather the process of articulating how God has unveiled Godself in the world—in other words, it's kerygma, the proclamation of God's Ministry.

As Sara sits with her small group of young people she must acknowledge that she does not control God's unveiling. No matter how prepared, talented or equipped she may be, it is not her job, or even in her power, to make God known to these young people, as though with the right questions or moving story *she* could pull God from her pocket to offer God to her small group, like a pack of gum. Rather, as a theologian it is Sara's job to seek to articulate (as best she can) how God is making Godself known in the life of this community.

Making a case for God's revelation in context: The apologetic emphasis in theology. While God is other than the world and is the one who does the unveiling, this unveiling (revelation) nevertheless happens within time and space. In other words, revelation may come from outside of human history and be out of our control, but it nonetheless breaks into and penetrates human existence. Moreover, there is no such thing as generic revelation, for revelation is not a concept but the event of revealing a person (God's very self). Revelation as personal being therefore always encounters persons, whether through covenant, burning bush or (in its fullest form) child born unto a virgin. It's "the movement of a loving presence towards world and self,"[4] Hall says.

Thus, while theology proclaims that God is unveiled, the theologian must argue for how God is unveiling Godself in this time, in this context.[5]

While God in God's being is other than the world (making revelation necessary), God nevertheless makes it clear by being Emmanuel (God with us) through creation, covenant, incarnation and re-creation that we can know God only in the world. Therefore, as Hall explains, "Faith is the grace-given courage to engage that world. Theology is a disciplined reflection and commentary upon faith's engagement. Theology therefore is contextual, and that by definition."[6]

This means theology must work in dual directions.[7] It must proclaim the gospel, the *kerygma*, of God's unveiling in the world through its Scriptures (the normative articulations of God's unveiling) and its tradition (its trusted commentary on the articulations of God's unveiling). But because theology confesses God's continued action, it must also work in an apologetic spirit, observing and then searching to articulate what God is up to now, in specific times and places, and how human persons and communities can be faithful. Hall puts it this way: "Theology lives between the stories—God's story of the world, and humanity's ever-changing account of itself and all things. Theology is what happens when the two stories meet."[8] Thus we—as theologians in ministry—must each work to understand our context and the (young) people within it.

THEOLOGY AND INTERDISCIPLINARITY

It is in this dual movement of attention to revelation and attention to context that theology can (must) engage in conversations with those in other disciplines of the social and hard sciences. But theology makes the claim that revelation gives individuals a distinct vision of reality that cannot be perceived outside of God's unveiling love. In other words, encountering God's revelation lightens our darkness, causing us to see reality differently. It is dangerous, then, to simply jump from one discipline to another as we pursue answers to questions (placing theology on a shelf in the meantime, which too often youth workers do), with no reasoned method that keeps theology in the conversation. Yet to maintain a true dialogue, we also cannot force another discipline, such as sociology, to be molded around theological or ministerial needs; this would prevent our work from being truly interdisciplinary or our research from being sociologically valid. Instead, theology, with its different kind of subject (the eternal God, as opposed to phenomena in time and space), must enter into these conversations in such a manner that the distinct scientific pursuits of each (the articulation of

God's unveiling or the unveiling of certain phenomena) are upheld. We therefore need a method for relating theology and other fields.

Interdisciplinary methodologies (the twentieth-century classics). We'll look at two well-known methods (the correlational and Chalcedonian) before I present my own. The correlational and Chalcedonian perspectives have been very popular within theology. We find their positive and negative implications not only in our interdisciplinary methods, but also in our very perspective of ministry.

Correlational method. The correlational method is divided into two distinct actions: asking questions and providing answers. It allows the social sciences, hard sciences or arts to provide questions from their distinct locale and logic; theology, then, joins these asked questions with answers drawn from its own tradition and commitments. For the correlationalists, the unveiling of God happens in the apologetic moment where deep questions are asked and ultimate answers are given.

In Sara's situation, then, a correlationalist theologian would give attention to the implicit or explicit questions being asked by Heather and her peers. The poverty, dysfunctional family and depression Heather faces raise deep questions of ultimacy. To understand these questions in their fullness, Sara would have to dig deeply, using multiple disciplines. She might call a local psychologist, for example, or read a sociological article on the breakdown of the working class. Once she understands what questions are being asked, Sara would then bring theological answers to them. As adolescents' deep questions are faced and correlated with answers from theology, God is unveiled and students like Heather are given ultimate answers to their many questions.

The method of correlation was constructed by the great German American theologian Paul Tillich during the swirling change of a post–World War II society, which is when he wrote his *Systematic Theology.* Tillich believed that (post)modernity had wrestled away from the church its ability to hold together the many diverse segments of human existence and religious experience. Science had dethroned theology and the state had dethroned the church. This allowed for a dualism that he believed separated theology completely from public life. For Tillich, theology could no longer focus only on the church but needed instead to turn toward culture (and thus away from a dualistic perspective) so that people could see society and theology as unified in a correlating whole.

Tillich's method was both profound in its application and simple in its construction. He sought to enter into meaningful conversations with depth psychology and existential philosophy to show the innate and nascent religious propensities within culture itself. In that vein, the job of the correlating theologian is to peer deeply into the cultural life of society, looking for the religious theological questions that are seeking answers.[9] Upon discovering these questions, theology, in an apologetic spirit, delivers explanations. For Tillich, the theologian is both detective and relief pitcher, hunting for unanswered questions and then entering the game to give closure with theological answers of ultimacy.[10] As James McClendon notes, "Thus theology's task was . . . the discovery of implicit religion lurking in society's crevices."[11]

While there is much to be admired in the apologetic focus of Tillich's correlational method (e.g., its openness and desire to face the deep questions of existence), it nevertheless leaves itself open to a number of problems. First, though it contends that revelation (God's unveiling) is other than cultural realities, it is bound to them, for correlationists believe that revelation is only present after the questions have been discerned. Revelation plays no part (or little part) in enlightening your understanding of the questions themselves.

The second concern is that innate within the correlational perspective is the fundamental belief that all questions can be easily and harmoniously correlated with answers. The attempt to find a happy harmony between question and answer, culture and gospel, however, denies theology the uniqueness of its own questions and ignores the fact that some perspectives may be, in their very essence, antithetical to God's unveiling in the world, such as questions rooted in corruption or evil. For instance, Dietrich Bonhoeffer saw no possibility of finding correlation with the ideologies of national socialism. The church, he believed, could only deny and refuse these perspectives. Moreoever, a commitment to God's unveiling in the world (such as stating that the gospel illustrates nonviolence, or declaring that the last shall be first) will be offensive to other disciplines or to culture. To think that those who are offended will always be willing to listen to and accept correlationists' answers is naive; correlation is unlikely in those instances. As Douglas John Hall comments, "There appears to be little awareness here of a gospel which, while it may indeed be the 'right answer,' is offensive precisely for that reason."[12] So, in Sara's quest to address Heather's situation, for example, Sara may become so concerned about understanding the questions that the need to proclaim the gospel is compromised. The gospel, however, doesn't need or seek harmony with the questions. And indeed, this was not Tillich's desire—but in the end the otherness of God's unveiling becomes lost or dependent on what is happening within culture.

Chalcedonian method. Those using this method assert that the way to relate theology and other disciplinary perspectives can be drawn from the Council of Chalcedon's definition and understanding of Jesus' divine and human natures. The Chalcedonian model enters constructive theological work through Karl Barth's use of the divine and human natures of Christ, in particular.[13]

What makes this position distinct from the correlational method is that it holds strongly to the belief that theology should never abandon its own subject matter, and should only appropriate the findings of other perspectives in a second-order manner. Therefore, intrinsic within this perspective is a kerygmatic thrust. Where Tillich's method is essentially apologetic (putting questions and answers together to make a case), the Chalcedonian method is constructed around proclamation (the confession of the faith) and the transformation that occurs in the moment of profession when the Word of God is encountered.

Deborah van Deusen Hunsinger uses the Chalcedonian pattern in her book *Theology and Pastoral Counseling* to associate theology and psychology so that the pastoral counselor can use both in his or her work.[14] Thus, she first asserts in a kerygmatic style that there is no way from psychology to theology, but there is a way from theology to psychology. The pastoral counselor must therefore learn to be bilingual, she goes on to explain, able to speak psychologically but with an understanding that this psychological language has its true etymology in theology. She also shows that this relationship between theology and psychology must be governed by three terms that are at the core of the Chalcedonian pattern: indissoluble differentiation, meaning the two fields must be related without being confused and without changing one into the other; inseparable unity, meaning that the fields must be related as a whole, without separating or dividing them into parts; and indestructible order, meaning that the theological has asymmetrical control over the other, for it has a wider vision.[15]

If Sara is a theologian that uses the Chalcedonian method, then, she will work to speak in a bilingual fashion to her small group. She may use a psychological perspective to help her understand Heather's situation, and she may even enter into a conversation with Heather and a local psychologist. But in doing this, Sara is not looking for answers to deep questions of existence per se. Rather, she's searching for ways that psychology and its theories are secular parables of the more encompassing reality of God's action through God's Word.[16] So while Sara may use a number of different perspectives for a time, her work will ultimately be concerned with providing her small group with moments of proclamation where they can both individually and corporately be transformed.

The problem with the Chalcedonian model of interdisciplinarity is that it may succumb to the very problem of the doctrine itself. Douglas John Hall has made a convincing case that Chalcedon was not only constructed under Constantinian political pressure but was also ultimately constructed around the logic of a Hellenistic-Athenian perspective of substance rather than a Hebraic-Jerusalem understanding of relationship.[17] Therefore, instead of being based on the relational life of God in the person of Jesus Christ for other concrete persons (i.e., relationships, which draw us into the suffering of our neighbor), the method focuses on the substantive structure of each field and its ability to relate (or witness) to God's Word. As a result, God's unveiling gets placed outside the construct of human relationality (outside of being representatives or place-sharers for and with young people, as we'll see below) and attending to the substance of the moment of proclamation becomes primary—making the kerygma potentially more important than the humanity of concrete persons in the world and thereby eclipsing our need to concern ourselves with human action.

Both of the above perspectives are insightful but deficient; they've both given direction to the practice of ministry but have ultimately been more concerned with how to relate the substances of multiple academic perspectives. So let me try to offer my own perspective. We'll turn to Luther's *theologia crucis* for a method that is open to the suffering humanity of the other as both apologetic and kerygmatic, and that therefore offers a meaningful way to do theology as the practice of ministry (as we began in chapter two).

A representative method. At the center of the great turn that would lead to the Reformation, Martin Luther made the assertion that human beings can have no knowledge of God that doesn't begin with God's own unveiling on the cross of Christ.[18] Luther believed that theology within the Christendom of his time had failed to follow Paul's desire to "to know nothing . . .

except Jesus Christ, and him crucified" (1 Cor 2:2) and had fallen into what Luther called a *theologia gloria*, which he defined as "calling evil good and good evil." Or, to say it less dramatically but just as forcefully, the Christendom of Luther's day had made theology something other than reflecting on and then articulating the cross of Christ and the weak and hidden truth of God's revelation in the peasant Jesus "who had nowhere to lay his head" (Mt 8:20). Rather, in the *theologia gloria* the cross was used as a logo of triumph and power, divorced from the humanity of Jesus.

Luther sought to correct this error by returning theological attention to "Christ and Him Crucified," creating what he called the *theologia crucis* ("the theology of the cross"). Unlike the *theologia gloria,* the *theologia crucis* "calls a thing what it is." Because it is a theology that seeks God's unveiling in the grittiness of the broken humanity of Jesus, there is no fear in speaking about sin or evil, or in facing the crushed or mangled humanity of another. The *theologia crucis* can call a thing what it is because it bravely enters into the darkest corners of human hells, claiming God's presence there through the cross of Christ. The place of God's unveiling (and, as such, our salvation) is in the place of suffering—ours and Christ's.

The *theologia crucis* claims that Jesus Christ is our representative (our place-sharer, as I have developed in other places). A representative is one who stands fully in the place of the other, not overcoming the other but (in both differentiation and identification) standing beside and for the other, sharing the other's reality even to the point of shared culpability. By being incarnate, crucified and resurrected, Jesus Christ shares our place *(Stellvertretung).* But he also, by being incarnate, crucified and resurrected, is shown to be the fullness of God.[19] Therefore, Jesus stands simultaneously as the true representative of God and the true representative of humanity; it is in this dual representative nature that salvation is achieved. Hall says it this way: "Jesus is with us so unreservedly that he may represent us before God; and Jesus is with God so unreservedly that he may represent God to us."[20]

How might this representative perspective on *theologia crucis* help us understand how to go about doing interdisciplinary work in youth ministry? By starting with the humanity of "Christ, and him crucified," a representative perspective immediately draws us into the deep suffering of the human condition that our neighbor experiences. Through the cross, God in Christ stands with and for all humanity as our representative; as followers of Christ, we share in his life by becoming representatives ourselves. So, unlike starting somewhere other than Christology (correlational) or starting in christological doctrinal theory (Chalcedonian), a representative perspective begins with the living God who is known in the crucified humanity of Jesus (it starts with God's Ministry).

This means two things for our purposes. First, it means that the cross and resurrection are an invitation to live in the deep relational life of God, who gives Godself for the love of humanity. The *theologia crucis* claims that our neighbor is no longer lost but forever found in the suffering humanity of Jesus; stranger is made friend and enemy is made beloved. But, second, to love the other in relational solidarity, the representative nature of the *theologia crucis* demands that we face the concreteness of reality (calling a thing what it is). The followers of the cross must be brave enough to make their way deep into the gullies of human suffering. The cross is not solely a spiritual reality but a concrete historical event that occurs in time and space. Representation in the image of *theologia crucis* therefore demands that we pay attention to concrete historical reality and its effect on human persons. But the *theologia crucis* also demands that this entering into suffering not be done over against the other but with and for the other in such a manner that we recognize the other as our brother or sister through the humanity of God in Christ. Thus, through the representative humanity of Christ on the cross we are led to relate the social sciences and theology to one another. But what would this look like?

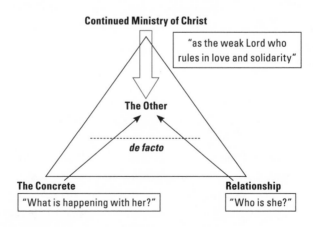

Figure 3.1. Interdisciplinarity from the representative perspective

Figure 3.1 shows three points that make up a triangle in an interdisciplinary position from the representative perspective. At the top is the continued ministry of Christ as the weak Lord who rules in love and solidarity. God's rule of love and solidarity through Jesus the representative means that the neighbor, the other, becomes the center of our attention, for God is found unveiled in the world as the representative for this other. At the two corners rest "the concrete" and "relationship," two points we drew from the *theologia crucis*. "The concrete" refers to the work that must be done to understand the fullness of the other's reality and discover how and why their world is impacting them like it is. By "relationship," I mean that the other has become dear to us—which is what causes us to do "the concrete" and seek to understand who they are within the multiple systems and situations that impact their person.

This then means we use the social sciences (or any other form of knowledge) to answer two questions that are bound to the humanity of the other that is taken up and represented by the cross of Christ. The first question is, "What is happening with this other?" This question is governed by the cross of Christ and by my call to be a representative for the other. It is more than scientific—it's pastoral—but if I'm going to love and care for the other, I must seek the assistance of multiple disciplines in answering the question. This question is also more than existential—it's social too, in that it attempts to understand how large cultural and societal structures are impacting the adolescent. For example, it desires to know how a lack of health insurance, the community the adolescent lives in and the education they are receiving play a role in their situation. Therefore, while representation gives significant attention to the individual, it knows that to care for the humanity of the individual—to really be able to understand what's happening with the other—it must engage (through the social sciences) the multiple contexts the adolescent lives in.

The second question that must be asked, also born from relationship, is, "Who is this other?" We ask this question too as representative and not as scientist, in order to know how to minister and care for the adolescent's very humanity. The use of other disciplines in this process is governed by the humanity of the other. In other words, the other disciplines are used only as they are needed alongside the other's humanity and only in a utilitarian, de facto manner to assist the representative in caring for the other. And we use them within the bound reality of Jesus Christ who stands with us, participating and healing through his own representative humanity.

The use of any discipline must serve to bring us close to the other. All disciplines are free to be used in assistance of my ministry as long as they exist only in a christologically bound reality of representation and never distract me from concrete action as the representative for my neighbor. I may have a good handle on Freudian psychology, for example, but if the issue at hand is economic, or if a Freudian perspective is found (in this context) to be detrimental, I must abandon it. It is the ministry of Christ for the humanity of the other that sets the terms for interdisciplinary work. And seeking answers to the questions, "What is happening with the other?" and "Who is the other?" is the action of representation which connects back to the representative ministry of Christ in the cross.

As Sara sits across from Heather, then, she is *not* struck by the multiple theories and disciplines that come into vision. Rather, what strikes Sara is Heather: her suffering humanity and her bravery to speak of her suffering in front of her peers. Sara had thought she loved Heather; she wasn't one of her favorites, but she had believed that she loved them all. But now, hearing Heather speak of her suffering, Sara is drawn to her broken humanity, drawn to be Heather's representative—and so she must ask again, *Who is she?* To answer this Sara might turn to family-systems theory in an effort to discover how alcoholism affects the youngest child, or she may look at object-relations psychology. But the use of these disciplines, and any others Sara uses, will be governed by her desire to be a representative to Heather, to love her by being with her. Therefore, the interdisciplinary conversation partners will be determined by Heather's humanity and will therefore be used de facto—in other words, they will be used only to help Sara love and care for Heather.

In addition to the *who* question Sara must also ask, *What is happening?* This question too is connected to Heather's humanity—her humanity in her place, in the concrete location of time and space. So Sara might use educational theory to understand why Heather is failing in school, or she may use sociology to understand why factories and mills are closing in small towns. But again, these questions are explored with and for Heather. The multiple disciplines are not used for apologetic or kerygmatic purposes solely but rather for ministry in the shared suffering of the other which seeks to call a thing what it is!

Seeing interdisciplinarity from this representative perspective keeps the person of Christ (Christology) and the work of Christ (soteriology) connected. The two other theories above seem to unknowingly divide Christology and soteriology. The Chalcedonian perspective uses Christology as an organizing principle for multiple disciplines but seems to care little about how the use of these disciplines participates in Christ's work of soteriology. Participation in Christ's soteriological work is left solely to the moment of proclamation. The correlationalists, on the other hand, desire greatly to find the apologetic pulse of culture so that they might make a soteriological dent, but they do so to the detriment of Christology. Significant conversation about the person of Christ takes a backseat. The representative perspective provides us with a way to hold Christology and soteriology together, connecting Jesus' *identity* as representative and his *work* of representing.[21]

Like the Chalcedonian method, the representative perspective begins with God's action of unveiling in the person of Jesus Christ. However, it uniquely claims, following Luther, that God's action of unveiling is seen in its fullest in the hiddenness of the beaten peasant of Nazareth. In other words, the Word unveiled is seen in the weak One of the cross and nowhere else (at least intentionally). Also in congruence with the Chalcedonians, a representative perspective claims that God's action (in the cross of Christ) is an incomparable reality and therefore cannot be correlated with any other occurrence in culture or society. But the representative method asserts that God's action in the cross of Christ penetrates the depths of the brokenness of humanity and creation: estrangement, dehumanization and death. Thus the deep questions of human existence, to which the correlationists point, are taken up and borne in the weakness of the crucified. In this way, both the kerygmatic and apologetic emphases are connected in the representative perspective by the suffering humanity of God in Christ.

Representative interdisciplinarity is born from and practiced within concrete relational ministry. But how do we teach others to be representatives for adolescents? How do we draw from this perspective in intentional interdisciplinary work in the congregation? Douglas John Hall has offered five points that frame representative action in a way that can direct us in the ministry of Christ. For each point, I've added a question or two specifically for youth workers.

- A representative is qualified. Jesus was qualified to be our true representative by incarnation, crucifixion and resurrection. Have we helped our volunteers and young people do deep theoretical reflection on human action (social sciences) and divine action (theology)? Or have we settled for a programmatic focus?

- A representative must regularly face in two directions. Jesus, as the church confesses, was simultaneously the Son of Man and the Son of God, human like us and also completely other. Youth workers and volunteers are told to identify with adolescents, but have we also taught them the importance of differentiation?

- A representative must suffer. God in Jesus suffered the fullness of the human condition. Have we understood that (youth) ministry demands suffering? Are we aware that youth ministry is more than fun and games, that it is a call to bear the suffering of the adolescent as one follows the suffering Christ?

- Representation flows from a vocation. Jesus could not be distracted from his vocation of the cross that bore the suffering love of the Father for the world. Can youth workers articulate how suffering love in youth ministry is about doing but also about thinking? Have we seen our vocation as local theologians, reflecting and articulating God's continued unveiling in the world?

- Those who are being represented know themselves as being involved in the representational event or act. Jesus calls his disciples to love the world as he does; discipleship (as Bonhoeffer has asserted) is the invitation to follow Christ to the cross. Have youth workers helped adolescents see and participate in representation? Do youth workers see their part in helping adolescents themselves become representatives of Christ for the world?

CONCLUSION

Youth ministry is no doubt an integrative endeavor, requiring an interdisciplinary approach. For youth ministry to live into the theological turn it will be essential for us to have some conception of how to relate to different disciplines. After all, as the case of Sara and Heather shows, this interdisciplinarity is often inevitable. But what their situation also shows is that relating these disciplines should always be governed not by the rigor of the university but by the Ministry of God, by a pastoral vision. Sara is sent on a journey of theological reflection because she experiences Heather's broken humanity. And in experiencing it she is called to act for the Ministry of God by seeing and understanding the depth of Heather's person and situation. Sara leans on other disciplines in her theological action of care for Heather, but the use of these other disciplines is only to connect her heart to her hand so that she might be with and for Heather as God is with and for us all as his very Ministry in the world.

• DISCUSSION AND REFLECTION EXERCISE
A Protocol for Critical Reading

Critical reading often is assumed to have three elements:[22]

1. The epistemological: What schools of knowledge is the author coming from or looking to bring together?

2. The experiential: How do these schools of knowledge relate to you? Do you find them helpful in articulating your reality or the reality you perceive?

3. The communicative: What do you find helpful in this author's argument? What do you find unhelpful or underdeveloped?

Each participant should answer these questions for the three elements of critical reading and then present the answers to each other, allowing ample time for discussion.

PROCLAIMING SALVATION

The Ministry of Youth for the Twenty-First-Century Church

KENDA CREASY DEAN

Y ou could almost hear the sigh of relief when the ball dropped in Times Square announcing January 1, 2010: America's *decadus horribilis* had come to a close. Already the twenty-first century was known for terrorist attacks, economic disaster and—especially chilling—alienated teenagers who fingered society by opening fire on their schoolmates. After one of the most shocking shootings, Columbine High School in the spring of 1999, *Time* columnist Lance Morrow reminded us that the writing had been on the wall for some time. He pointed to "one of the founding documents of American adolescence," J. D. Salinger's *Catcher in the Rye*. In a prescient passage, Holden Caulfield—expelled from prep school—is wearing a red hunting cap. A pimply kid named Ackley mocks him, calling it a "deer shooting hat." "Like hell it is," Holden retorts, closing one eye as if taking aim. "This is a people shooting hat. I shoot people in it." Morrow added quickly: "Holden is kidding, of course."[1]

Youth ministry came of age during Holden Caulfield's adolescence, a time when teenagers were still kidding when they took aim at one another. The fellowship groups, parachurch clubs, summer camps, mass rallies and teen programs—modules of peer culture that came to characterize mainstream (mostly Anglo-European) "youth ministry" by the mid-twentieth century—all promised moral fortitude and a measure of protection from the demands of adulthood. The widely touted objective of youth ministry was to claim youth for "the church of tomorrow" by socializing them into the ecclesial mores of the church of today.

By the 1960s, however, the "church of tomorrow" was being sent to Vietnam with orders to kill. Summer camp and Bible Bowls paled beside emerging claims on the adolescent soul—the civil rights movement, "flower power," even rock and roll—that sought immediate involvement from youth who, in essence, had been put on hold by American institutional life. Reacting to the hyper-institutionalism of postwar America (and responding to the World Council of Churches' admonition that youth be integrated into the total mission of the church), mainline churches in the 1960s and 1970s dismantled denominational support systems for youth ministry and released adolescents from their destiny as "the church of tomorrow." At the same time, youth began to vanish from the ecclesial radar screen like disappearing ink.

We're now in a new millennium—but intense interest in spirituality still fails to translate into adolescent church involvement in most Protestant congregations. Confirmation, the rite of initiation into lifelong church participation, more often than not serves as a graduation ceremony for bored adolescents and weary parents; more than half of those confirmed as adolescents leave the church by age seventeen. Girls tend to exit congregational life around age fourteen or fifteen, boys somewhat sooner. Meanwhile, youth ministers practice disappearing acts of their own. By the turn of the century, the average tenure for a full-time youth minister was 3.9 years (a dramatic increase from the widely cited "eighteen-month to three-year" expiration date of youth ministers a decade before), no doubt thanks to the field's increasing specialization.[2] Still, four out of five youth leaders are volunteers, and more than one-third of full-time youth pastors stay in their placements one year or less. As one researcher noted, "Even when remaining in the profession, youth ministers may rank just behind migrant workers in length of time staying in one place."[3]

ADOLESCENTS AS A SIGN: PROCLAIMING SALVATION IN SPITE OF THEMSELVES

By now American Christianity's well-intentioned impotence with young people has been analyzed to death, scattering blame on everything from budget cuts to training deficits to demographic cycles. Beneath these issues, however, lies the question of *theological credibility:* does the God presented by American churches pacify adolescents with pizza and youth groups, or does this God satisfy their deepest longings and deliver them from their most profound dreads? If nothing else, the events of the last decade force us to repack our theological gear for youth ministry, beginning with a doctrine of salvation in which human development and divine action intersect.

Acknowledging God's role in existential rescue represents a shift in youth ministry's self-understanding. For most of the past hundred years, youth ministry relied on psychology, sociology and education—not theology—to justify its existence. Even evangelicals, who tended to use the language of salvation more readily than their mainline and Catholic counterparts, were pragmatists when it came to youth ministry, frequently equating young people's salvation to quantifiable conversion "experiences." Especially among mainline Protestants, who borrowed pedagogies from social sciences where adolescence was often viewed as an occasion for therapy, these rationales drove churches' ministries with young people for the better part of a century. The need to connect what adolescents must do developmentally (achieve an enduring sense of identity) with what Jesus does theologically (accomplishes YHWH's salvation) was chronically overlooked by the church, although not necessarily by adolescents themselves, who "acted out" the human need for salvation, often implicitly or inappropriately. Christians understand identity to be given, not "found"—ours by redemption, not human development. Adolescents, despite being mired in a distinctly modern search for self, *demonstrated* this profound connection between theology and identity formation. In other words, the adolescent search for self implicitly represented, in the individualistic West at least, humanity's effort to recover the imago Dei given in creation but lost to sin.

INTUITING THEOLOGY: I KNOW IT'S IN HERE SOMEWHERE

Christians have always maintained that the search for self is simultaneously a search for God. Human beings are "hardwired" to seek salvation, even if they cannot articulate "salvation-from-what." Human development need not go according to plan to reveal the divine imprint, but each life stage nonetheless predisposes us toward certain theological moorings. Adolescents in the throes of identity formation, for instance, must daily choose between being and non-being, between the relationships that are self-creating and the isolation that leads to self-disintegration. For teenagers, "salvation"—from disintegration, if not from sin—is a daily and persistent request.

All of this makes salvation a central if implicit motif during adolescence. A brief channel-surf through primetime makes the point (think *True Blood* or any J. J. Abrams project). Moreover, salvation in adolescence always seems to come in the form of a "relationship," that sacred and zealously guarded "in-between-ness" with others that allows youth to develop friendships and intimacies that confirm their existence. The problem is that these identity-forming relationships are pocked by sin, making human identity an incomplete, distorted, even false view of the self given to us by God. Like teenage acne, sin clogs the pores of the soul that simultaneously longs to reveal (even to ourselves) our true identity as God's beloved and forgiven children.

Yet, improbably—while sin obliterates most of the clues pointing to our holy imprint—the imago Dei in human beings remains perceptible, if impossibly distorted. During adolescence, the desire for love and fidelity points always to the passionate love of God (despite myriad forces that attempt to subvert it). The God who desires us also created our desire for others; consequently, the passion that is acute during adolescence (but present in all of us) points us to the One whose friendship restores us, redeems us and re-creates us into the person God made us to be in the first place. Whether we recognize Jesus Christ's re-creating friendship or not, in Christ, all things are made new—including teenagers.

The connection between the psychosocial dynamics of adolescence and the ontological significance of salvation ought to have positioned the twenty-first-century church as a hotbed of possibility for adolescent faith—but so far, this has seldom been the case. Apart from the youth group, most churches have given up on being a hotbed of any kind where teenagers are concerned. In the absence of theological guidance from the community of faith, then, adolescents are left to intuit salvation's trajectory through peer relationships. So they turn to—well, to most anybody, trying various "hit and miss" avenues to intimacy in hopes of finding someone who can love them into being.

"Intuitive" theology inevitably yields questionable ethics (intuition, after all, has the advantage of openness and the disadvantage of boundlessness), but it is far from new. For example, in Acts 16, a local slave girl with a loud proclivity for fortune-telling day in and day out proclaims her intuition that Paul and Silas are bearers of salvation. For days on end she cries: "These men are slaves of the Most High God, who proclaim to us a way of salvation!" (v. 17). Annoyed, Paul finally orders the "spirit" out of her. Luke writes, "When her owners saw that their hope of making money was gone, they seized Paul and Silas and dragged them into the marketplace before the authorities," whereupon Paul and Silas were summarily stripped, flogged and thrown into jail (vv. 19-24)—all because Paul put a stop to adults' exploitation of a teenage girl.

The more familiar part of the story follows: ever optimistic, Paul and Silas sing and pray in prison throughout the night until an earthquake releases their chains. The startled jailer—certain that prisoners have escaped on his watch—sets out to commit suicide, but Paul shouts, "Do not harm yourself, for we are all here!" Apparently amazed as much as frightened, the jailer falls down and asks, "Sirs, what must I do to be saved?" "Believe in the Lord Jesus," is the reply, "and you will be saved—you and your household" (vv. 25-31).

A detail worth noting: it is the girl, not Paul or Silas, who proclaims that salvation is afoot. The presence of Jesus' salvation unhinges her sanctioned exploitation, frees her identity from her earning potential and sets in motion a series of chain-shattering events. Because they liberate a slave girl from the profitable "spirit" possessing her, Paul and Silas are imprisoned. When an earthquake sets them free, we learn that it is the jailer who is bound—by duty, not by chains, but he prepares to fall on his sword nonetheless as penance for irresponsibility. Paul spares him the trouble by redefining liberation. The prisoners have not escaped—yet they are free! The Holy Spirit then delivers apostles and jailer simultaneously. The jailer, however, asks a curious question for someone whose life has been spared: "What must I do to be saved?" Clearly, in this passage salvation—deliverance— implies something more than physical life and death. Deliverance always ushers in new life (we say we "deliver" babies for a reason). The jailer becomes beholden to Jesus Christ instead of to the magistrates. He can no longer view himself, or anyone in his household, apart from the salvific work of God.

Adolescents, of course, seldom articulate the human desire for salvation as pointedly as the jailer: "What must I do to be saved?" The adolescent in this story is the slave girl, a youth who intuits the possibility of salvation before she can say what it means, and whose proclamation is inappropriate, unwelcome—and unavoidable. She "smells" salvation in the air, and gropes for a way to lay claim to it. The adult, on the other hand, practically misses

God's deliverance right under his nose. Like so many of us, the jailer confuses his identity with his professional competence, and is so ready to fall on his sword that he almost misses the crucial point: No need! He has been delivered! Youth and adult balance one another in this story: the jailer needs the slave girl's bold proclamation of possibility, while the slave girl needs the jailer's ability to ask for salvation by name—specifically, Jesus' name.

THE SIGNIFICANCE OF SALVATION IN
THE FORMATION OF SELF

Historically, Western societies have viewed adolescence as an anomaly, with "diagnoses" ranging from a lack of conversion to a form of mental imbalance. Today, the line between medication and ministry is no less fuzzy. School shootings inevitably focus public attention on mental illness. After Eric Harris and Dylan Klebold's infamous shooting rampage at Columbine High School in April 1999—a story rife with both horror and testimonies to faith—Channel One and the National Association for Mental Illness posted a webpage listing symptoms of teen manic depression, including "increased talking—the adolescent talks too much," "distractibility," "unrealistic highs in self-esteem—for example, a teenager who feels specially connected to God."[4] Long before twenty-three-year-old Seung-Hui Cho killed thirty-two people at Virginia Tech in April 2007, his mother had turned to a church, hoping that involving her son in religious formation would modify Cho's troubling behavior. The pastor deemed Cho in need of "spiritual power" (whether the Chos also sought psychiatric help for their son is unclear).[5]

Though the media may dismiss it, teenagers themselves often intuit salvific significance—not mental illness—in a divine-human connection, a connection that they sense counters death with life. Following the Columbine massacre, many young people saw a "special connection to God" as something teenagers their own age had been willing to die for. Salvation is never an eschatological category for adolescents; it is a near and present hope. The onset of formal operational thought allows them, for the first time, the luxury of existential reflection. Teenagers realize with new force that they could live or they could die, and they do not want to live or die "for nothing." So they act out a deeper question: "What must I do to be saved?" Ministry geared to such questions sets out to shape the soul, not merely modify behavior; it traffics in Christian practice and doctrine, not miniature golf. Soul-shaping ministry knits together the developmental and cultural questions that lie at the hub of adolescent experience and places them in the service of Christian tradition. Youth ministry that transcends the "church of tomorrow" helps youth put away their identities as slaves and jailers in favor of their freely given identities in Christ.

Salvation and identity formation: Trying not to disappear. Every adolescent engaged in the life-work of identity formation senses the ease with which he or she could vanish, especially given the magnetism of other, stronger identities and pseudo-identities that easily absorb the developing self into their powerful orbits. Without skills of resistance, youth frequently resort to outlandish and obnoxious behavior to escape absorption by powerful others. The slave girl described in Acts—who made Paul "very much annoyed" (16:18)—points her finger at Paul and Silas's message of salvation until Paul literally must stop and take notice. In Salinger's account, Holden Caulfield bolts from the magnetic pull of prep school, friends, family and his one remaining mentor, but his jarring search for autonomy leaves him with (literally) barely enough strength to cross the street:

> I had this feeling that I'd never get to the other side of the street. I thought I'd just go down, down, down, and nobody'd ever see me again. . . . Every time I'd get to the end of a block I'd say [to my dead brother], "Allie, don't let me disappear. Allie, please don't let me disappear. Allie, don't let me disappear."[6]

During adolescence, writes James Loder, "all previous solutions to the major issues of the first ten years of life undergo an upheaval that thrusts the developing person into the abyss of nothingness underlying the ego, and calls that person into transformation."[7] As formal operational thought dawns during early adolescence, so too do new capacities for faith, for possibility, for dread. For the first time, youth recognize that they are dying a thousand deaths they cannot stop—a condition that Christian tradition chalks up to sin, and developmental theorists attribute to identity diffusion. The upshot, either way, is the startling realization that "the me I know" is going to vanish.

Loder believes that the lurking possibility of the "void" that youth sense yawning beneath them—the possibility of disappearance—gives adolescence its theological potential. Encountering the void spurs young people to move out into the unknown futures to which they are biologically, socially and culturally called. In order to avoid vanishing into the abyss, as Loder calls the existential loss of self, youth begin building bridges—relationships that move them closer to others, closer even to God—as they seek a hand that can save them, that will keep them from falling into the darkness.[8]

In recent years, however, some youth who have felt themselves disappearing into this void have turned up the volume on Holden Caulfield's mantra by punctuating it with gunfire. Desperate for clues about motivation, reporters from school shootings invariably pump classmates for character studies. The striking observation, again and again, is how little observation took place. "You just didn't notice them," classmate after classmate reports. Adolescent assassins like Eric Harris, Dylan Kliebold and Seung-Hui Cho, in incomprehensible and grandiose ways, took it upon themselves to be noticed. They demanded that someone, everyone listen. For one terrible day, they decided not to disappear.

Erik Erikson, whose theory of identity formation eventually framed the twentieth-century search for self, believed that identity—the consistent, durable sense of self that gives youth confidence that they will not disappear—enables adolescents *to live for something worth dying for.* For Erikson, achieving identity required being strengthened by the enduring virtue he called "fidelity," the strength of a "disciplined devotion." For Christians, disciplined devotion is the ongoing work of grace, not a static developmental strength we achieve on our own; fidelity—literally, *faithfulness*—is made possible by God's sanctifying grace, and its ultimate test is *marturia:* "witness," or literally, martyrdom. Yet Erikson's psychosocial definition of fidelity hints at the same connection: Fidelity, said Erikson, is "the vital strength which [a youth] needs to have an opportunity to develop, to employ, to evoke—and *to die for.*"[9]

To be sure, martyrdom makes mainline Protestants nervous. We confuse it with the desperate quest not to disappear—a quest that too often leads to violence, not sacrificial love. We lack Catholicism's confidence in beatification, and we do not share conservative evangelicalism's enthusiasm for cosmic drama. In fact, we tend to refer people with martyr complexes to psychologists, and our preaching has been known to devolve into a studied avoidance of death and its pesky theological companion, sin. Atonement theories in particular have received more than their share of theological corruption over the centuries, leading some theologians to want to banish them altogether for seeming to promote divinely sanctioned abuse or the celebration of suffering. But as Roberta Bondi rightly observes:

The early church does not teach that the most basic quality of God's love is a suffering self-sacrifice. What first engages God with us is not a duty or need or self-sacrifice or obligation or the need to be right or good but delight in us as the beloved. . . . Delight makes the lover extravagantly eager to make sacrifices for the beloved. The cross, which is the occasion for God's own terrible pain, is very real, but it is God's delight in and desire for us that calls God to do it.[10]

Of course, adolescents' interest in martyrdom, especially when twisted into a quest for recognition, is justly worrisome. Psychologists remind us that the adolescent predilection for excess, when coupled with an un-formed self, tends to makes youth vulnerable to "totalism," an uncritical fusion of a permeable, "soft" identity with a newly claimed ideology. In totalism, the ideology, in effect, claims the youth instead of the other way around. Although most significant faith claims involve a period of total-ism, youth ministers have a special obligation to allow adolescents the freedom to refuse our ideologies, lest we inadvertently manipulate them into "identity foreclosure" rather than disciple them into genuine commit-ments to Jesus Christ.

At the same time, neither adolescent development nor theology permits youth ministry to avoid passion—a love "to die for"—or its consequences. Identity is forged in the tension between the possibility of gaining a self and the possibility of losing the self, which occurs in the absence of being known intimately and loved unconditionally. In Christian tradition, the conse-quence of God's passion is salvation, as Christ offers divine love so true that he willingly suffers on behalf of the beloved; likewise, sanctification (and especially martyrdom) is always the consequence of a self so identified with Christ that it willingly gives itself for another. True love, as any teenage moviegoer will tell you, is always worth dying for. Youth intuit that salva-tion lies in finding someone who loves them enough to die for them, and the whole of adolescence is directed toward this end.

The totalistic vision of adolescents, then, makes the ultimate sacrifice of martyrdom appealing, if not for its gory glory then for its passion—for its affirmation of a worthy life, a love worthy of life and death, not just a Sun-day night. Far from a form of mental instability, adolescence challenges the church to the kind of passionate self-sacrifice to which all Christians are called, born out of disciplined devotion that is not made possible by up-bringing, education, psychological precocity (or instability) or even sheer determination. It is only possible by God's grace. The Columbine myth included not just two disturbed teen killers but also a lost girl who dabbled in drugs and witchcraft, turned to Jesus, joined a mission to gang members, grew her hair out for children with cancer, and allegedly declared her faith at gunpoint before being fatally shot.[11] The word "witness" literally translates to "martyr" in Greek—and it is part and parcel of the radical faith to which teenagers searching for something "to die for" respond.

Salvation and identity formation: On their own. Add to adolescence the shifting sand of global postmodernity, and the theme of salvation stands out in bas-relief. Adolescents today grow up with less adult contact than any generation in human history, forcing teenagers into what journalist Patricia Hersch aptly describes as "a tribe apart."[12] Although youth pull away from adults at more or less the same rate they have for generations, the adult abandonment of youth in the late twentieth century reached new and unprecedented proportions. Parents, for instance, spend 40 percent less time with their children than a generation ago.[13]

Not only has cultural fragmentation atomized communities and isolated institutions from which identities once were gleaned, but *adults*—traditional contributors to identity—are just plain hard to come by these days. Fifty years ago, adults controlled access to society's primary decision-making, education and earning power, and they functioned as gatekeepers for information necessary to participate fully in American middle-class institutions. In short, it served young people's best interest to eventually identify themselves as grown-ups. Today, however, standing alone in the shadow of the self-esteem movement, adolescents conclude that identity is up to them. Take this example, written for a school assignment by a teenage boy:

I Am an Adolescent
I am smart and strong.
I wonder if there is life beyond ours.
I hear a mime scream.
I see a war with no bloodshed.
I want to live forever.
I am smart and strong.
I pretend that I am someone else.
I feel like drinking from the Milky Way.
I touch God's halo and hold the Devil's hand.
I worry about the day when family dies.

I cry for I know that all good things must come to an end.
I am smart and strong.
I understand people die.
I say fighting is childish.
I dream of a world with no pain.
I try to be all that I know I can.
I hope to be a better person as an adult.
I am smart and strong.[14]

The problem is more subtle than working parents and stressed-out social schedules. Conflict requires relationship. The much-maligned adolescent "rebellion" of the 1960s allowed youth to remain connected with significant adults while at the same time distancing themselves from them. Except in its most destructive varieties, rebellion actually serves identity formation by helping one generation establish autonomy from the generation that has gone before—while at the same time acknowledging the older generation's presence and influence. Today, the adult-youth relationship critical to identity formation is threatened by adult invisibility as much as absence. Postmodern culture views adolescence less as a life *stage* than a life*style,* a choice available to adults as well as youth. Advertisers blur the lines between generations by pitching adult toys and child makeup. Adults strive to prolong their adolescence while teenagers face daily decisions that potentially short-circuit theirs.

Coupled with the unmitigated relativism of postmodern culture and its relentless insistence on choosing between options, adolescents often give up on investing in a coherent, governing life-view (what Erikson called an "ideology"). Facile, piecemeal role-taking along with the hapless compartmentalization of life into distinct, even contradictory, categories encourages a "self" cobbled together through bricolage, not integration. Instead of directing youth toward a center that holds, postmodern culture encourages adolescents to reinvent themselves for each of their proliferating social roles.[15]

WHY YOUTH MINISTRY NEEDS THE CROSS

If youth ministry is to address fragmented, overwhelmed teenagers as human beings, and not as objects to be won and counted for the church, then we must orient twenty-first-century youth ministry unapologetically toward the cross. God's fidelity in Jesus Christ, demonstrated by the cross, is a sign of love. As developmental theorist and ethicist James Fowler argues, the cross of Christ is crucial to adolescents precisely because it shows the extent to which God goes in order to be with them.[16]

In the twentieth century, the cross often served as a backdrop for youth ministry rather than as its raison d'être; it was a rallying point for Christian nurture and prophetic witness, but one that became increasingly devoid of meaning as the theological memory of many Christians began to go the way of the poodle skirt. Instead of stressing the lengths God goes to in order to be with young people in the life, death and resurrection of Jesus Christ, youth ministry has vacillated between two teleological objectives: protection and empowerment—poles that seem increasingly unable to bear the weight of ministry for a generation of youth longing to find not new ways to do church or influence policy, but a person, a God, an ideal worth dying for—which, of course, is what makes it worth living for as well.

To be sure, the poles of religious nurture and social praxis preserve important aspects of Christian tradition and must never be discarded. Churches that approach youth ministry from a "communitarian" perspective seek to protect youth so their faith can mature and be shaped in the context of Christian communities. Communitarian ethics are sometimes associated with conservative Protestantism, but in youth ministry communitarian praxis actually unites certain strands of evangelical Protestants, mainstream Catholics and so-called liberal Protestants with strong sacramental histories. Generally, communitarians view adolescence as a late form of childhood, not adulthood, making it incumbent upon institutions like the church to provide youth with the care, boundaries and resilience they need via the practices of Christian community—a community that defines itself as an alternative to the life and practices of the broader culture.[17]

On the other hand, those who generally champion youth empowerment over protection—we might call them "liberating individualists"—encourage adolescents' interaction with the broader culture, believing that adolescents possess prophetic voices necessary for transforming culture. Since liberal Christianity tends to view adolescence as an early form of adulthood, emphasizing teenagers' relatively advanced biological and cognitive development, liberating individualists are optimistic about youth's capacities. If the communitarian concern is that youth are growing up too fast, the liberating individualist concern is that they are not growing up at *all,* and are therefore denied a public voice critical to the transformation of the adolescent as well as society.[18]

Despite their different emphases, liberating individualist and communitarian Christians actually do share substantial common ground where youth are concerned (making youth ministry a promising point of rapprochement between these two theological perspectives). Liberating individualists concede the central importance of identity during adolescence, just as communitarians recognize the value of social praxis. Both of these approaches have much to commend them—but neither helps adolescents live into a doctrine of salvation capable of offering resilience against "disappearing" in the twenty-first century. The liberating individualist may misread the prophetic voice of adolescence, treating teens as voices in the wilderness when, in fact, they are canaries in the mines who sing out humanity's need for salvation amid toxic cultural conditions, songs that sound benign to an undiscerning ear. Like the slave girl in Philippi, adolescents call on the church to stand behind the gospel's most radical claims to redeem and deliver God's people—not to "fix" them. Communitarians, on the other hand, may tempt adolescent conformity rather than transformation, and socialize youth into community practices that may or may not point to the cross. In so doing, communitarians risk replacing holiness with wholesomeness, and youth risk falling for an ecclesiology that is benignly "nice" rather than dangerously loving.

The psychological and cultural realities facing adolescents in the twenty-first century require a theological perspective in youth ministry that takes seriously the questions of salvation that dominate the adolescent experience: What is worth living for, and what is worth dying for? In the face of imminent destruction, who will save us? If the quest for salvation is fundamental to being human and not just to being sixteen, then youth ministry's contribution to the twenty-first-century church may be its unapologetic witness to the salvific relationship available in Jesus Christ. Christians believe that we humans are *homo religiosus,* creatures whose very existence depends on our relationship with something, or someone, whom we believe will save us. The impetus toward this relationship is so strong, in fact, that when we fail to recognize our relationship with the triune God capable of salvation, we invest our faith in lesser gods instead. "To be a self is to have a god," wrote H. Richard Niebuhr—although Niebuhr conceded that humans are fickle in their divine loyalties, living sometimes for the God of Jesus Christ and sometimes for the god of country, job or school.[19] Without faith, Niebuhr noted, humans might exist, "but not as selves."[20] In short, becoming fully human—having a self or identity—is impossible apart from the God who saves us, apart from the relationship that transforms who we are in light of who God is. As we bring our sin-twisted lives into the presence of Jesus Christ, we behold and reflect the imago Dei. In conforming to Christ's identity, we become new—people whose "selves" reflect not who we are, but who God is in us.

PRACTICAL THEOLOGY: FRESH STREAMS FOR YOUTH MINISTRY

For a century, youth ministry has been conceived of as a junior partner in the Christian education enterprise rather than as a pastoral calling—and certainly not as a colony of practical theologians whose engagement in and reflection on ministry is for the sake of the church, not youth alone. Clearly, Christian education is a critical component of mindful Christianity, but it is not the only component, nor is it the primary one. Indeed, no practice of Christian ministry exempts youth or youth ministry if God calls all of us into lives of passionate obedience. Youth are practical theologians by virtue of calling, not proficiency; their inexperience at using theological categories to understand the longings of themselves and others, coupled with the unparalleled spiritual openness of the adolescent life stage, requires adults to engage in careful and intentional pastoring of these intuitive theologians.

The doctrine of salvation remains the church's most practical doctrine. The practices of Christian life find their origins in the life, death and resurrection of Jesus Christ and are the saving work of God enacted, in human form, as Christ enters the world again and again through those who love him. Engaging youth in these practices of faith provides a way to colonize both the church and the world with practical theologians—young people who have a theological consciousness that "who they are" is both sinful and redeemed. It also strengthens adolescents' identification with the practicing faith community (the communitarian concern). Meanwhile, since practices of faith inevitably lead to practices of ministry, engaging youth directly in these practices strengthens and empowers teenagers for ministry in their own right (the liberating individualist concern). In the historic practices of Christian community, youth dialectically encounter the imago Dei in Jesus Christ, since, on the one hand, practices of the church help us become conformed to Christ. And on the other hand, it is in practicing our faith that we become transformed by Christ—re-created even as we claim, critique and re-create these practices for the faithful ministry of God's people.

In the absence of serious theological reflection on youth ministry, we have missed important opportunities to connect the doctrine of salvation with the developmental and cultural exigencies of being adolescent, and to experience doctrine's overall potential for shaping the soul. Developmentally predisposed to form relationships, in search of the One whose fidelity will not fail, whose desire will not fade, whose love will save them from disappearing, youth still require faithful adults to cast out the spirits of lesser gods that possess them. These faithful adults are those who can say, on behalf of awkward adolescents who are still enslaved by sin: "What must I do to be saved?"

OF MARTYRDOM AND MINISTRY

Standing at the brink between being and non-being, teenagers' loud denunciation of phoniness and clumsy stabs at truth call the church to proclaim salvation, even when we would rather not. We don't know why the slave girl's herald so annoyed Paul, but in the end, the truth she proclaimed could not be ignored. The proclamation that Christ's salvation is near demands an audience, and if the church will not proclaim it, adolescents—simply by being adolescents—will proclaim it in our stead. Like Holden Caulfield or the slave girl in Philippi, their voices can be grating, their announcement untimely, their presence jarring. But in their struggle not to disappear youth cling to the hope that yes, somewhere, someone can save them—and they enact this conviction brazenly. Those of us in ministry are called to put words on their intuition, to name what they hope: that they have not disappeared, or come apart, or gone unnoticed, because the God who loves them is in our midst, and salvation is at hand.

But our ministry with youth in the twenty-first-century church must do more than this. The church must also help teenagers recognize that salvation has come to them, and that as a result God calls them to leave behind their schoolboy or slave girl egos and take on new identities as disciples, empowered for ministry through the practices of Christian faith. God calls youth to become "practical theologians" in their own right, not for the sake of the youth in the church basement, but for the sake of the church. Teenagers reorder their lives daily according to what they think will save them (this week). Often they do not even know the gods to whom they pay homage. Yet youth cannot be faithful to that which is only implied. Fidelity—*fidei,* or "faith"—is the stuff of martyrdom, not of youth groups or even "the church of tomorrow." Indeed, authentic witness may jeopardize tomorrow as we expect it to be, for the sake of living faithfully today.

• DISCUSSION AND REFLECTION EXERCISE
Circular Response Technique

Have each person select a theme from this chapter that they would like to discuss.[21] Have the first person speak for two minutes on her chosen theme. The person to her left goes next, paraphrasing the first speaker's comments, and explaining how his own comments spring from them. After two minutes, the next person to the left continues the process, and so it goes.

No one may be interrupted while speaking. No one may speak out of turn. Each person is allowed only two minutes to speak, and must begin by paraphrasing the comments of the previous person. Each person, in all comments, must strive to show how his or her remarks spring from, and are grounded in, the comments of the previous person.

After each person has been able to speak, the floor is open for reactions and further discussion.

WALKING INTO THE CRISIS OF REALITY

How Theology Is Constructed

ANDREW ROOT

Ryan[1] had just finished his first semester of seminary classes. I was still in college, just a freshman. In our personal conversations he was brewing with insight, combusting with new information and thoughts. As we traveled together to the ninth-grade confirmation retreat, where we would be counselors, he spoke of the need to take kids deep, to get them to understand and dwell on the tradition of their faith. "Youth ministry is about theology. It's taking kids inside the Word," he asserted with great passion. I nodded; this sounded important. He mentioned that youth ministry had spent way too much time on activities, fun and programs; it was time to do theology with young people. I nodded again; deep within me I wanted this as well, though I had no idea what it would mean, since I had very little experience myself thinking theologically. I could barely spell the word and had no idea what he meant when he referenced exegesis, soteriology and covenantal theology. I just kept nodding to hide my ignorance. As the car pulled into the camp that would be the site for our retreat, he said, "I'm going to give it to them. I think young people are thirsting for it; I'm going to give them theology at this retreat." "Sounds great," I said as I slammed the door and entered the electric chaos of a ninth-grade retreat.

The next afternoon it was Ryan's turn to lead the teaching time of the retreat. He grabbed his Bible, pulled a stool to the front, sat down, breathed in deeply and began to teach. Ryan talked straight for fifty-five minutes, weaving in and out of conversations on redemption, Israelite sacrificial practice, theories of atonement and authorship of epistles. He even parsed a few Greek verbs. It was clearly not the programmatic, activity-centered youth ministry he had critiqued in the car. But as I sat there, trying myself to follow his explosion of facts, theories and musings, it was also clear that *none* of it mattered to the ninth graders and that *all* of them were somewhere else, passing notes or simply daydreaming of times and locations beyond the theological oppression of this seemingly never-ending moment.

The session ended, and the ninth graders sprinted to their cabins in hopes that they could outrun the convoluted minutiae that seemed to ooze out of our meeting room and its theological focus. As the leaders gathered, Ryan stood among us painted with both confusion and confidence. He admitted that the young people seemed less than engaged, but he stood his ground, asserting that it was what they needed. "What is essential is that we provide them with theology," he continued to repeat. It was clear both that Ryan was unmovable and that he needed this perspective to keep him from facing the utter disappointment of the experience. Some of us tried to reassure him. "It was good. I'm sure they got something out of it," we said, knowing our words were false but hoping our encouragement would keep him from crumbling. "We just have to keep pushing," Ryan continued. "Right now they may not like theology, but it's important, so we just have to keep giving them theology, even if they don't like it."

As Ryan concluded, Joyce, a wise sixty-year-old grandma who had been a longtime volunteer in the youth ministry, piped up. So far in the conversation she had been quiet, but in that moment she said these prophetic words: "Maybe it's not that they don't care about theology, but maybe what we provided them tonight wasn't theology." That's all she said. We all turned to stare at her for a few seconds, wanting to ask for more but not sure what to say; it was clear her response was significant. And her words have remained with me.

In these pages we have been arguing that youth ministry has taken a theological turn, one to which we hope this book adds momentum. In this new turn, youth ministry has remained committed to cultural, psychological and pragmatic reflection, but it's the theological, the practical theology, as Kenda asserted at the end of the last chapter, that has begun to slide to the center of youth ministry thought. Both academics and practitioners seem to be awakening to the importance of theology for youth ministry.

In the four chapters above we've sought to free theology from confinement in libraries of academic institutions and instead return it to the place of concrete communities of faith. We've been pushing you to see the work you do in youth ministry as fundamentally a theological task.[2] The word *ministry*, after all, is a theological word; it no doubt has something to do with human action (the things that ministers—whether ordained, paid or lay—do), but it also has a great amount to do with what God does, as the One who ministers to the world for the sake of its salvation in the fullness of God's future.[3] If theology's "task is to apprehend, understand, and speak of 'God,'" youth ministry should follow this, seeking to apprehend, understand and speak of God in the lives of young people.[4]

But as my story above highlights, this thinking theologically is not easy, or at least, it has been easily confused for something else, something that in the end becomes meaningless to young people and frustrating for those in ministry, making theology seem always beyond reach. So if youth ministry is in the process of taking a theological turn, both in its thought and action, what does this mean? And if this theological turn is necessary and good, how should a youth worker go about thinking theologically in a way that avoids meaninglessness and frustration?

Ryan may have been right those many years ago about the need for young people to be drawn into thinking deeply about their faith, but in the end his form of theological reflection seemed disconnected from young people's reality and too uninteresting to capture their imagination. But if theology is ultimately about a God who enters our existence for the sake of life through death, then it's hard to label theological construction itself as meaningless and frustratingly boring. Thinking theologically is not necessarily about erudition and puking facts and big words on young people. As Joyce's words point us to, thinking theologically may, if we can conceptualize it correctly, not only become significant for our orientation as youth workers (seeing ourselves as local practical theologians), but may also in the end impact young people, drawing them into deep thought about self, world and, most importantly, God.

Therefore, what seems to be needed as youth ministry takes this theological turn is an understanding (a picture) of how theology itself is constructed, and how it is that you go about thinking theologically with and for young people. And, since theological construction is itself a practice of ministry, we're not only being theologians when we learn to articulate it; we're also doing ministry.

CRISIS OF REALITY

To do theological reflection, especially theological reflection that is connected to ministry, we must first ask, "What does theology start with?" or "What does theology look to address?" It's in answering these questions—the first step of theological construction—that we perhaps make the biggest mistake. Too often we have assumed that theology begins with either dogma (especially if you're in a conservative context) or societal milieu (if you're in a liberal one). By confusing our very starting point, we thereby take a step that actually moves us away from the content of theological reflection.

Ultimately, theology starts with a crisis, the very crisis of reality itself. The crisis is the fact that you live, that you have a life to live. The crisis is the very fact that there is something instead of nothing. The crisis is the very mystery of our existence and the yearning for there to be some kind of meaning to it. But this crisis pushes us even further down this road. Theology is reflection and articulation of God's action, and God's very action in the world is a crisis. When God speaks, making Godself known, we find ourselves in the crisis of encounter. Theology seeks to speak of the crisis of an infinite God who encounters finite human beings, and does so in backwards ways (like the foolishness of the cross).[5]

Theology, then, begins with the crisis of God's action, which reveals that we are near death, that our reality (our very person) is opposed to or stands in opposition to the infinite God. To encounter God and God's Word is to encounter our limit (no one sees God and lives). The very fact that God has broken in to make Godself known is a crisis; it calls all that is into question. As Luther has said, "God first kills before God makes alive"[6]—but not because God is vicious; quite the opposite is true. God first kills because God's action of love stands over against all that is. In other words, his love—and therefore all love—kills because it calls us beyond all that stands in opposition to it. God's love, then, is a crisis that calls the regularity of reality into question. Out of love God's very being calls all that is back to God, thrusting all that is into question in relation to God's love. God's action is a crisis because out of love it seeks to address the crisis of human existence. Therefore, the crisis is God's love and our unbelief; the crisis is God's desire to be with us and our movement toward isolation, death and annihilation. And theology is reflection on God's action, which reveals our crisis.[7]

Theological reflection therefore begins with giving attention to God in relation to the crisis of existence itself. Ryan's so-called theological exposition was irrelevant to the young people listening because it said nothing of the crisis of existence. Theology, in his mind, was not to address the crisis of existence—the crisis of death and limit in light of the love and grace of God. Theology was instead about facts and theories. It was meaningless to young people because nothing was at stake; it was frustratingly boring because it had nothing to do with the beauty and pain of our fundamental existence. Douglas John Hall points out, "For the most part the paradigm of prayer we are given in the Psalms and in other parts of the Bible suggests a spontaneous and utterly honest wrestling of the human spirit with the Spirit of God."[8]

Attention to crisis reveals that there is something universal that theology attends to. If theology begins with dogma or the societal milieu, it ultimately only has something to say to the believer, and only the believer that is beyond doubt. But when theology begins with our shared crisis, it speaks to the core of the human condition, to the crisis all of us (believer or not) face. From our perspective as the human knowers we can see the crisis of reality in two broad forms.[9]

Time and eternity. The first form of the crisis of reality is the problem of time and eternity. We are living but we are moving toward death, and there is no stopping it; life is to be lived in joy, happiness and fulfillment, but even at its greatest, it is ending. We now are, but soon we will not be. Theology begins with the assertion that there is a qualitative distinction between time and eternity.[10] God and God's love are eternal, but we are like the grass on the field, passing away (1 Pet 1:24). We are caught within time and cannot escape it. This is a crisis because, though we can imagine eternity (at least as a category) and imagine living beyond the constraint of time, we cannot actualize it. We are stuck with the fact that (most) all things atrophy or move into something different: the innocence of childhood gives way to the pessimism of adulthood, our favorite shirt wears thin, our hairline recedes, our little children grow and move on. We are caught in the stream of time, and its currents are too strong for us to scramble for the riverbank.

Not only are we passing away, though; we're also infinitely small. It is a crisis to watch *NOVA* (the PBS science show) and discover that there are black holes in the universe that are even now eating entire galaxies. Our minds cannot even fathom the expanse of the universe. In the midst of time and space we are but dust, and yet God has acted. In love God has sought to place God's own being, which is eternal, with our beings that are so quickly fading to nothingness.

When we take young people on outdoor trips (backpacking in the mountains, canoeing, camping, etc.) we usually ignore this crisis, making the trip instead about beauty, about experiencing God's created beauty away from the rush of modern life. This is important, but we're missing the theological potential these trips offer. Being next to mountains, leaning against trees, thrusts us into the very crisis of time and eternity. We do theological reflection with young people when we say, "See these mountains? They've been here for millions of years and they may be here a million more. They've been here long before you and will be here still long after you're gone. Who is this God, then? And who are we that this is our state—that we *are* and exist but are also so quickly passing away?"

It is amazing how often adolescents have these thoughts and conversations with their friends, lying on a basement floor at sleepovers or sitting on the grass looking at the sky on a lazy summer night. Young people know the crisis, but too often we are too busy trying to give them theology (or something else) that we don't see that theology begins with the crisis of reality itself—with the fact that, though we can imagine a world without suffering and death, we can't escape the one we're in, where we are and will soon not be.

Our existence as social beings. The second form of the crisis of reality is the problem of existence as social beings. We are caught in time and infinitely small in comparison to the universe, but we nevertheless *are*—we exist—even if only for a fleeting amount of time. This problem of existing as a social being is encompassed within the question we face throughout our short, small lives: What is a lifetime and why do we live it? In a word, this is the problem of self-awareness, awareness that we have a life to live. As Kenda articulated so well in the last chapter, we are awakened to self-awareness in late childhood and early adolescence. It's in adolescence, then, that we begin to discover that there is a question mark wrapped around our very being. And it's in adolescence that we are still too much of a cultural neophyte to ignore how tightly the question mark is squeezing our diaphragm, making it hard to breath.

The crisis is that some are rich while others are poor, and that they're in this state, so it seems, by blind luck. The crisis is that we are aware of many who live broken, caught, oppressed, overwhelmed by impossibility. What is a lifetime and why do we live it when we so quickly are no more and when so many, even now in their short lives, are overwhelmed by poverty, isolation and pain? Even if we can avoid these things we must live wanting more, wanting to be known, loved and understood more fully than it seems possible for others to do. The crisis is that, though God is justice, we lack justice; that life seems so unfair; that we are always, it seems, left yearning. What is the future in the collision of brokenness—melting ice caps, shattered families, a decreasing job market, betrayal—and God's love? Douglas John Hall discusses this crisis in relation to his own journey of becoming a theologian.

> I could not become a theologian in earnest until I had allowed myself to be plunged into the growing darkness of my own time. . . . As Tillich would have said, I could not really be trusted with "the theological answer" until I had learned for myself "the human question"— in all of its specificity, its here-and-nowness. . . . Luther, too, understood this: "I did not learn my theology all at once," he declared, "but I had to search deeper for it—where my temptations took me!" We need to lose our "answers" if we are going to find an answer that actually engages the real question—which is not just the questions we *ask,* but the question that we *are,* individually and collectively.[11]

So much of what we do in youth ministry is uninteresting, meaningless or (dare I say) boring because it doesn't start in the perplexity of the crisis. And we can't bear seeing the crisis as our starting point in ministry because it's a starting point that thrusts us into theology. We therefore tend to turn our attention to programs, thinking activity can provide the excitement that our uninteresting theology cannot. But constructing theology (especially theology in relation to ministry) means starting knee-deep in the crisis. Sunday school, VBS and ninth-grade confirmation retreats are boring and meaningless not because we haven't given students more theology but because we have often tried to do theology beyond the crisis. Theology is utterly meaningless, though, when it's too busy with other things to direct itself toward the very crisis of reality itself. A theologically engaged youth group or retreat is one that begins by inviting young people to face the crisis and begin to articulate their deep questions and experiences of being stuck, small or broken. In other words, a theologically rich ministry begins with inviting young people to articulate what haunts them.

Crisis of Reality
God's Action and Nature

1. Problem of time and eternity
   (Why is there something instead of nothing?)

2. Existence as a social being
   (What is a lifetime and why do I/we live it?)

Figure 5.1. The crisis of reality

Ryan, who sought to give young people theology, did not understand that theology is something constructed with others, not something we give. And it's constructed with adolescents, as Kenda asserted in the last chapter, because it's born next to the crisis that God is God and we are not; we are passing away and stuck in questions without answers. Theological construction that means anything to young people is theology that dwells in questions with no easy answers—not theology that simply provides answers, as Ryan believed. Indeed, to be a theologian as a youth worker is to walk into the crisis of reality, seeking God in the questions raised.

ADDRESSING THE CRISIS

Tradition. While theology begins with the crisis of reality, it doesn't stop there. Theology is not satisfied with simply articulating the crisis; it also seeks to address it. And the first move in addressing the crisis is turning to Tradition (with a capital *T*). By "Tradition" I mean the very core (the dogma) of Christianity (the triune God, the full humanity and divinity of Christ, the pouring out of the Spirit, the centrality of Scripture, the being and acting of the church, etc.). This very Tradition is what makes Christianity Christianity. When it's used as the starting point for theology, however, it's wooden and dead, because it calls us to ignore the crisis, to stop thinking and simply assimilate. What brings Tradition to life is the very thing that moved it from contemplation to dogma: its ability to address the crisis. In other words, the Tradition is the way faith seeks understanding in engagement with the crisis of reality.

The essentials of the Tradition are essentials because they have been seen to be true, but they have only been seen to be true because they have said something true in relation to the crisis of reality itself, not because they are rational or provable. Simply put, they have said something "real." In late modernity, when societies and people are no longer held together by some kind of shared tradition (Anthony Giddens), it is all the more important for us to recognize that our Tradition *is* authoritative because it's trustworthy, and it's trustworthy because it has been shown to be a faithful way to address the crisis of reality.[12]

As youth ministers who are theologians, we must see the Tradition as the beautiful treasure (dogma, the essential core of what makes the Tradition the Tradition, i.e., that Jesus Christ has borne the crisis) it is—a treasure that speaks of life in the midst of death and hope in a world of despair, that articulates the essence of the beliefs of those who trust in the life and the death of the One who has overcome death with life. Unfortunately, Ryan believed that doing theology meant simply passing on the Tradition—getting kids to swallow it and know it rationally. The Tradition was therefore meaningless to the adolescents because it was no longer living, no longer meeting them in the midst of their questions on the road of their human journey.

This approach to Tradition is what has made catechesis such a difficult—and many times failing—effort in youth ministry. And I think it's the reason why so many Christian young people—even highly committed ones—know so little about their faith (as Christian Smith has documented in *Soul Searching*). Catechesis has been a failure because we've been confused about its role; like Ryan, we've used it to assimilate adolescents into the Tradition, and have tried to get them to know it like they know their multiplication tables and to give it the same degree of importance as their sport, their friendship group and their grades. This, however, makes for boring and often meaningless Sunday school and confirmation classes for youth. Instead, we need to see theological reflection as placing the Tradition in conversation with the crisis of reality itself (there is something like Gadamer's fusion of horizons here). When Tradition is engaged through the crisis, little case needs to be made for its significance. Though it may still be judged as wrong or unhelpful, it cannot be judged as benign, irrelevant and uninteresting. To be a theologian in the context of ministry is to dwell deeply in the Tradition, to even kerygmatically confess and proclaim it, but to do so turned toward the crisis of reality itself.

Tradition and Scripture. There are three elements under Tradition that the youth-worker-as-theologian uses to address the crisis. The first is Scripture. Scripture and Tradition exist in a kind of dialectical relationship. The Tradition is considered normative because of Scripture. Scripture asserts that Jesus Christ is Lord; our very dogma is bound within Scripture itself. But we *always* read Scripture through Tradition, that is, we read it through the lens of thousands of readers who have come before us and who have molded our dogma and our communities through their own reading. No one can read Scripture free or outside of the Tradition—indeed, it's a hermeneutical impossibility—because Scripture is the story of a people and the book of a people, and these people (Israel and the church) exist within the stream of a shared history, a shared Tradition. So, for example, when we read in the Gospels about Jesus teaching his disciples to pray, we are reminded of how and when we have prayed the same prayer he taught them in our communities (before Communion, for instance). If we stop and reflect we'll realize that people of this Tradition have been saying the Lord's Prayer for over two thousand years.

But what makes Scripture normative? What has made it the essential material for constructing our Tradition is that it addresses the crisis of reality itself. It speaks of a God who enters reality, making Godself known as the One who enters this crisis to address it, to overcome death for the sake of new life with God's very self.[13] We complain often about young people being biblically illiterate, but I think we have too rarely shown them how Scripture itself addresses our crisis. If we would do so we could help them see that Scripture is living.

There's a misconception in youth ministry that what makes something theological is how many bullet-pointed Bible verses the worksheet, talk or book contains. In truth, seeing Scripture theologically means seeing it as the story of God engaging creation in the midst of its crisis, and recognizing that we never read this sacred text alone but are always reading it within the community of Tradition. Ignoring these facts is just rigid biblicalism.

Tradition and traditions. The second element under Tradition is tradition (with a lowercase *t*). While there is a shared Tradition (dogma) that encompasses all of Christianity, there are also multiple traditions that make up a beautiful mosaic within the larger Tradition. This is more than denominationalism, which, with its bureaucracy, can lead to unneeded conflict and the stunting of the ministry of the church; indeed, too often these distinct traditions have seen themselves as in a battle for a piece of the religious market (in this sense they are unhelpful).

But another way to view these multiple perspectives (like Catholic, Lutheran, Pentecostal, Reformed and Wesleyan traditions) is to see them as particular ways of addressing the crisis of reality. In other words, these traditions are discrete ways that communities of thought and life have sought to articulate who this God is that has acted in the world—most fully through Jesus Christ—and what this God is up to. When these distinct traditions become insular and have as their main goal the perpetuation and existence of their perspective, they have ossified into something unhelpful. But when they exist as the perpetuators of distinct thoughts and practices in relation to an interpretation of the crisis of reality itself, they are great treasures to the church.

I once had someone ask me if I knew of a book written on Presbyterian youth ministry. This person was thinking of writing a book on Lutheran youth ministry and was already aware of books on Catholic youth ministry. I asked if the book would have a theological focus or only a denominational one, to which he responded that he didn't see a difference. I have to admit that the more he talked, the more boring (and meaningless) I found his proposal. It made the tradition the end, rather than a vehicle to articulate, dwell in and address the crisis of reality. I suggested that he write a book on youth ministry *drawing from* the Lutheran tradition instead. The traditions are rich theological perspectives whose value lies not in being a world unto themselves but in being different ways of addressing the crisis of our social existence or finitude and God's action.

Tradition and dialogue partners. The third and the final element under Tradition is dialogue partners (we've already touched on this some in chapter two). As we seek to be theologians in youth ministry, it is essential that we start with the crisis and from there turn to the Tradition via Scripture and the theological depth of a tradition (or multiple ones), but it is also important for us to find for ourselves some dialogue partners—a theologian or two whom we can invite to journey with us. These dialogue partners may never be referenced directly when we're discussing the cross or baptism with young people, but being in conversation with one or two theologians by deeply reading their writings will make a great difference in our thought.

When Ryan was sitting before the ninth-grade confirmation class at the retreat, he had no big idea he was working from, no articulation of reality and God's action within it that could engage young people's imagination. He crisscrossed through multiple perspectives, leaving us with no real clue how they held together. A couple of dialogue partners could have given him a perspective on the Tradition (through his dialogue partner's reading of Scripture and own tradition) that then could have given him a sharper articulation of the crisis. Too often in youth ministry we spend our time reading how-to books or books on cultural analysis (which are all important), but it would benefit us greatly as theologians if we picked a dialogue partner or two and committed to reading and understanding their work.

Tradition, then, in its engagement of the crisis of reality, is an essential part of theological construction that fulfills the kerygmatic (proclamation) pole of theology (discussed in chapter three). When Tradition fails to address the crisis, it spirals into *traditionalism,* a dangerous viewpoint that sees theology as only about Tradition and ignores or avoids the crisis of reality itself. Figure 5.2 provides a map of how the church engages its Tradition, through its three elements, to address the crisis in a kerygmatic manner (to proclaim the gospel).

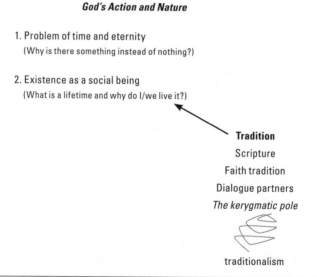

Crisis of Reality
God's Action and Nature

1. Problem of time and eternity
   (Why is there something instead of nothing?)

2. Existence as a social being
   (What is a lifetime and why do I/we live it?)

Tradition
Scripture
Faith tradition
Dialogue partners
The kerygmatic pole

traditionalism

Figure 5.2. Tradition and the crisis of reality

Context. The understanding that theology itself is contextual has gained great momentum in the last few decades. Some argue that theology is always responding to issues within a context, but theology is also done in a place, which means its perspectives are always laced with contextual situations. This contextual reality should not be confused with the crisis of reality, however. Theology addresses the crisis, not primarily the context—or, better put, *it addresses the context through the crisis*. The crisis of reality is more than simply our contextual situatedness; all people (no matter the context) must face the limits of our existence.[14] But cultures have ways of providing practices and perspectives that give meaning to our crisis or even make us think we've transcended it. For instance, in the American context you can avoid the crisis by being a rich celebrity. So people go on reality TV shows, embarrassing themselves, not because they're stupid (not all of them, at least) but because this contextual creation promises the salvation of being a celebrity, someone hidden from the cold wind of the crisis.

In essence, theology is always contextual because it must engage its context's response to the crisis of reality itself (and it does so even if it doesn't intend to). Some may argue that the Tradition is a more trustworthy response to the crisis, and should therefore be given priority over context, because the Tradition (at its best) seeks to explicitly give language and vision to the crisis (even if it's scary—this is why over-positivity cannot be part of Christian theology, why a thing must be called what it is). But this does not eliminate the fact that the context itself seeks to address the crisis, and the fact that the Tradition, while more than the context, can only be known and lived out by those who live within the context and its response to the crisis. Moreover, the context's own operations that confront the crisis can, at their best, also challenge the Tradition with new perspectives that must be considered by it (see the arrow going from context to Tradition in figure 5.3).

On the other hand, every context also has much that seeks to pacify people, deceive people and keep people from reflecting too deeply on the crisis of reality. Indeed, our bureaucratic, economic, educational and even religious contextual structures often try to hold our attention and form our practices in ways that keep us from facing the crisis of reality. In these cases, the church, drawing on Tradition, must address the context and prophetically call it to at least see the crisis (while not necessarily calling it to assimilate to the church's perspective), and remind it that no matter how organized and productive its structures may be, it still has to face the crisis (see the arrow going from Tradition to context in figure 5.3).

The Tradition and context, then, are always in dialogue:[15] It is impossible for those doing theology to escape their context, and the Tradition must remind the context that the crisis exists and that it has responded to it, while the context calls the Tradition to deal with new and distinct perspectives and ideas that address the crisis of reality.

Because of all this, it's essential for us as theologians in ministry to engage context—not simply for relevance but because of the context's own engagement with the crisis of reality. Ryan saw little use in doing this to draw young people into theological contemplation. It seemed like a lightweight approach to him—like giving in to youth ministry's entertainment, activity-driven focus. What he failed to recognize is that theology is not simply about minds assimilating information; it's a way of living, a way of living that must be in dialogue with the context in which we live and its engagement with the crisis. In light of this, as we construct theology for ministry we must be conversant with the two broad ways that the context has sought to address the crisis of reality.

Art. The first way is art. Most often, art is an attempt to express something (even something nihilistic) about the crisis of time and eternity, about the constraints of our social existence, about the need for something transcendent. And it's usually loved or hated based on how it's interpreted: as being real, saying something real or making the participant feel something real.

In our time, especially in relation to younger people, art (at least as high culture) has been replaced by pop art or popular culture. Some may argue that pop culture is devoid of artistic expression, but that argument castrates art's function of addressing the crisis. (Besides, that is an old high culture argument.) Pop culture, with its popular form, may actually have much to say about the crisis of reality—so we should listen and engage it.[16] Obviously, there are forms of it that seek only to distract people from the crisis; the church should oppose these, even the ones that are seemingly moral and benign but that actually seek to pacify us and keep us, through moral religion, from facing the crisis of reality (like Christian T-shirts, some Christian music, some children's entertainment). Overall, though, from a theological perspective, the context is seeking to address the crisis through (pop) art, and the church should honor these efforts, even if the church ultimately finds them misguided or unhelpful.

Many young people listen to the music they listen to and watch the films they watch because of what they say about the crisis, and because of the ways the music and films give them meaning and practices for engaging reality. Thus, to do theological construction in ministry is to see (pop) art as making assertions about reality, which leads us into the dialogue between the context and Tradition as we seek to address the crisis. If Ryan had done this, theology could not have been judged as meaningless or frustratingly boring by young people. Difficult and perplexing, maybe, but not meaningless and boring if it was reflecting on the crisis of reality in conversation with the articulations of the Tradition and the students' deeply held artistic expressions of this reality.

The sciences. The second way the context has sought to address the crisis of reality is through science (whether social or hard). A misguided and ultimately idolatrous belief during high modernity was that science was king, that science would solve all human problems, that science would be our salvation. As we saw in the twentieth century, science can usher in the technology of hell as much as and maybe more than that of utopia. So while science can no longer be considered king—the unveiler of what is real and the solver of the crisis—it does nevertheless address the crisis and seeks to give us perspective on it. Physics, biology, sociology and psychology, for example, all confront the crisis of why there is something instead of nothing, of what a lifetime is and why we live it.

Of course, science can still become an idol when we think it possesses all the answers (as can Tradition if it has closed itself off from dialogue about the crisis), but when it's seen in its proper place, as seeking to explore the very crisis of reality through its instruments and perspectives, it is a valuable tool. Indeed, to tend to context in theological construction is to be in dialogue with science. The science, however, must be judged by its ability to say something to the crisis. If it can't, then it needs to be impounded and placed in the same lot as a theology that is more concerned with academic credibility than reality.

It is not unusual, at least for high schoolers, to feel like they're in conflict with science. For example, conservative young people often feel perplexed as they seek to make sense of evolution, while young people who are more liberal struggle with how to hold on to any authority within their Tradition in light of psychological studies. Unfortunately, though we as youth ministers may encourage conversation about these topics, we've often failed at providing young people in both groups times and venues where they can

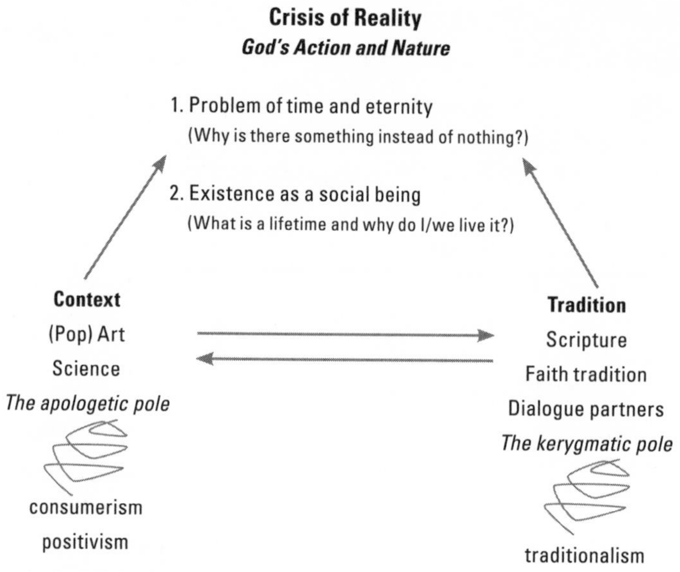

Crisis of Reality
God's Action and Nature

1. Problem of time and eternity
(Why is there something instead of nothing?)

2. Existence as a social being
(What is a lifetime and why do I/we live it?)

Context   **Tradition**

(Pop) Art   Scripture

Science   Faith tradition

The apologetic pole   Dialogue partners

                                                                The kerygmatic pole

consumerism

positivism   traditionalism

Figure 5.3. Apologetics and the crisis of reality

ask questions and talk with others about issues of science and faith and the crisis of reality.

What we need to do is place the crisis of reality as the starting point of theological construction. Then science (or art) cannot assume totality in its perspective, and the Tradition cannot ignore the context's (science's and art's) assertions about reality. And we can turn young people to reflect more deeply on the crisis not necessarily in an effort to find what is right (for "right" is a category of a rational epistemology that cannot bear the fullness of the crisis) but to discover what speaks with depth, hope and wonder about the crisis—in other words, what is true. Christianity, at its core, is not about rightness but about being encountered by truth. It is the call for faith to seek understanding next to a God who acts in the world of death, thinness and yearning.

In conversing with context this way—seeking to truly consider and understand the context's perspectives and situations—we honor the apologetic essence of theological construction (as Tradition honors the kerygmatic essence; see figure 5.3). But, just as there is a danger of the Tradition spinning into traditionalism when the crisis is not addressed, so too the context possesses its own dangers. If (pop) art and science believe that they can, in their operations, articulate the full totality of existence, and that they possess all truth, then they can spin into consumerism and positivism, respectively. Positivism clouds us from seeing the crisis because it believes that science knows all. And consumerism blinds us from the crisis by making its texts (movies, music) about numbing our minds instead of about opening us up to see reality differently.

THEOLOGY AND PRAXIS

What all of the above asserts is that to make the crisis the focus of theological attention as we dialogue with the Tradition and the context is to see theology not as an academic exercise but as the very heart of ministry itself (see, in figure 5.4, the arrows moving to the heart of the picture, which is the praxis of ministry). In this light, the praxis of ministry comprises more than just defending a tradition or being culturally relevant. If the crisis is that God has acted and is acting, then *ministry is confrontation with the crisis of reality and with God who is already there;* participating in ministry is therefore participation with God where God can be found, in the crisis of reality in people's lives.

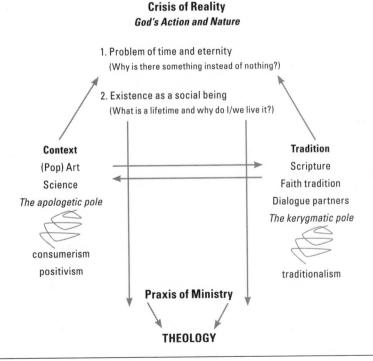

Figure 5.4. Practical theology and the crisis of reality

It's through this praxis of ministry in relation to the crisis, as the Tradition and context dialogue with it, that we have theology. In short, *theology is the articulation of the crisis and God's act and being within it,* so doing theology means turning to the crisis in ministry as we dialogue with the Tradition and the context (see the arrows in figure 5.4 that point from the praxis of ministry to theology).

Questions about existence, death and social location in relation to the possibility of God are asked from the core of our humanity and therefore call for theology that is done in ministry, in conversation and within the embrace of relational care.[17] Ryan's talk that afternoon was not theology, as Joyce profoundly stated, but not because he didn't try or have the ideas right. It was not theology because it didn't mean anything; it didn't address the crisis that young people face, and it missed that theology is essentially a conversation (between Tradition and context) that leads us into ministry. Theology can only be constructed within the lives of people yearning for God in a world of death, life, love and brokenness. It was Luther, after all, who said, "It is by living—no rather, by dying and being damned—that a theologian is made, not merely by understanding reading and speculating."[18]

• DISCUSSION AND REFLECTION EXERCISE
Haunting Reflections Journal

The purpose of this journal is twofold.[19] First, it can give you insight into your own existential reflections. In other words, you will become more aware of how you are confronting the crisis of reality in yourself and in the world. Second, it will help you discuss with others the theological significance of your own experiences with the crisis. Because theology is always done in community, you will be asked to share elements from the journal with others.

You should write about anything that haunts you and causes you to think deeply about the crisis of reality. However, it may help to frame it this way:

- Write one entry on a song (any song) that causes you to think deeply about your existence or the world.

- Describe in one entry a scene from a movie that haunted you, causing you to reflect on the question, What is a lifetime and why do we live it?

- Write one entry on a quote from a theologian (a quote that is not in this book) that has haunted you and caused you to think deeply about God and God's action in the world.

- Describe in one entry how a biblical text has haunted you and pushed you to see God, self, world and reality itself differently.

(Note: The leader should tell participants how many entries are required and the length they should be. For instance, participants could be asked to write three entries of four hundred words each over the week this chapter is read.)

YOUTH MINISTRY AS DISCERNING CHRISTOPRAXIS

A Hermeneutical Model

ANDREW ROOT

A few days after the semester was over I received a letter in my campus mailbox. It was addressed to the youth ministry faculty at the large seminary where I teach, and was sent by four of our top students. While appreciative of what they had learned together the last academic year, they were worried that they had not received enough *practical* "how to" material. I'm sure some of their anxiety was warranted; they would soon be leaving to take jobs in churches where fundraising, recruiting, planning and networking would be very important, so they were right to ask for some help in these areas. However, their letter reminded me how deeply immersed the practice and study of youth ministry are in pragmatic utilitarianism—and therefore why this nascent theological turn Kenda and I are advocating comes up against resistance.

Too often it is assumed that youth ministry is *primarily* about *doing*. Youth ministers *do* things, like visit school campuses, go on trips, plan barbecues, lead Bible studies and play basketball. But of course youth ministry is much deeper than this crust of constant activity. If youth ministry is ministry, it is so because it has joined God's own Ministry in the world. This means that all ministry (youth ministry or otherwise) is only ministry when it adheres to God's continued activity (of revelation, reconciliation and redemption) in the world; for our *doing* to be faithful, in other words, it must follow God's own *doing*. And *this* means that youth ministry is not ultimately about pragmatic utilitarianism but about theological hermeneutics; it's not about *doing* so much as *discerning:* discerning God's will for individuals, communities and creation. So to do theology—to encounter God in the crisis of reality, as we discussed in the last chapter—and to practice faithful youth ministry—to discern God's activity in our own context and then join it—we need eyes to see the activity of God.

Such theological discernment is called for in both the creation and crisis of ministry. As youth workers organize the ministry they are to lead, they must seek to discern God's desire for the ministry, asking, What is God doing in this local context with these people and how might God use us? In addition, youth workers must discern God's desire in the crisis of ministry, in those moments where they seek for God in the crisis of reality: when an adult leader informs you that she is thinking of leaving her husband and asks for your advice, for example, or when a senior with a scholarship to a topflight university informs you that God has told him that he should move to L.A., live on the beach and become an actor instead.

This is all, of course, quite easy to *say*—that youth ministry is about discerning God's continued action in the world—but how do we do this in the midst of the complications of our contexts, our personalities and God's transcendent nature? If we are going to take this theological turn in youth ministry, a theological turn that is committed to the continued activity of God's Ministry, then we must begin to imagine how we actually go about discerning God's action with and for young people.

DOES JESUS STILL DO STUFF?

To see theology as reflection on the continued Ministry of God in the world is to confess that God, through the resurrected Christ, is still moving and acting in our world. This is what makes our experience and our wrestling with the crisis of reality so essential. Theologian Jürgen Moltmann and practical theologians Ray Anderson and Richard Osmer call this commitment to the continued Ministry of God through Christ *Christopraxis*.[1] The word refers to the praxis of Christ's Ministry, which was to serve the Father on behalf of the world. According to these theologians, Christ remains in the world (now as resurrected Lord who is to come), continuing the praxis of his Ministry, which is the restoration of relationship between God and humanity and between humanity and humanity in and through his own humanity. It therefore becomes the church's job, through empowerment of the Spirit, to seek out and then join in Christopraxis—Christ's continued Ministry in the world.

In essence, discerning Christopraxis is discerning God's will. What is God's will for our ministry? we ask. What is God's will for my future? What is God's will in this situation? Such questions are the heart of ministry and yet are difficult to answer. We need help to learn this process of discernment, to learn how we as youth workers might think our way into discerning Christopraxis (God's will) in our ministry context and in the lives of the young people with whom we minister.

THE HERMENEUTICAL SITUATION

The existential line of tragedy and death. Any hermeneutic that is going to be helpful in discerning God's action and our call to join it must be anchored in reality: the reality of our ontological state, cemented in *Sein* and *Zeit* (being and time), which finds its expression in tragedy.[2] In other words, our hermeneutic must see things as they are ("calling a thing what it is," to quote Luther). And the truth, as we examined in the last chapter, is that we are all born and then moved forward by history to our death; there is no stopping the process. Along the way we will of course be confronted by paradoxes of pain and joy, violence and gentleness, evolution and atrophy, love and hate, but eventually all paradoxes will give way to the flow of history; death is our destiny. This fact makes all of life fundamentally tragic.

It is in this tragic flow of history that we need to discern God's action, that we contend that God moves, making one path, decision, action preferable to another. Therefore, all of us are forced into being interpreters of God's action, of God's will for our lives and action in history. If we are asking, Where is Christopraxis? we must also ask, Where is the interpreter?[3] And what is his or her reality?

We start, then, with the assertion that the interpreter is embedded within an existential line of tragedy and death. While this may sound morbid and depressing, it is not completely fatalistic. It's true that this existential reality, while not reductionistic, does point most vividly (and frighteningly) to the judgment of God, which is non-being, or death. But the reality of being and time is still God's creation, even though it's infected with sin and perversion; it is tragic and dangerous but it is not Godforsaken, for in this reality the incarnate Christ dwells. And in the cross of Christ we see that God, in God's own being, suffers this existential reality of tragedy and death; it's significant that the cross appears on this line of history. The interpreter lives and moves in this reality of tragedy and death and must recognize his or her shared solidarity in this state with all of humanity.

Examining the existential. Rudolf Bultmann, the early-twentieth-century German Lutheran theologian and Bible scholar, is most well known for his project of demythologization, which stemmed from his desire for people to

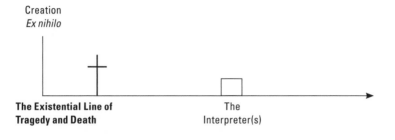

Figure 6.1. The cross, the interpreter and existential reality

be confronted anew by the Word of God. Like many youth workers, Bultmann was less concerned with what happened back in the periods when the Bible was written, calling those times "mythological." Rather, his concern was with how people encountered the living Word of God now, in the contemporary moment.

To support this position Bultmann leans heavily on existential philosophy. Following Heidegger and others he states, "To understand history is possible only for one who does not stand over against it as a neutral, nonparticipating spectator, but [one who] stands in history and shares in responsibility for it. We speak of this encounter with history that grows out of one's own historicity as the existential encounter. The historian participates in it with his whole existence."[4]

The significance of Bultmann's position is that the interpreter never stands outside of this historical existence but rather must give him- or herself over completely to it. To escape wooden historical pontifications, then, we must be willing to be confronted anew by the living Christ in the present moment, to see anew the past, present and future in connection to him. As Bultmann says, "Indeed, the questioning itself grows out of the historical situation, out of the claim of the now, out of the problem that is given in the now. For this reason, historical research is never closed, but rather must always be carried further."[5]

Bultmann's existentialism points to Christopraxis because it assumes that Jesus' life is not just a past event to be exegeted. Rather, what Bultmann tells us is that any hermeneutic that looks to discover the reality of Christopraxis must concern itself with the present historical moment. The reality of the living Christ, the search for Christopraxis, the decision in ministry—these always confront us in the now, the now of our shared existence. So the interpreter—the youth worker, the Christian—can never make any decisions outside the reality of his or her personal and shared existence.

This historically bound reality should color all our interpretations and actions with compassion, since it means there is no elite status: none are outside of history seeing it "clearly," free from its tragic foundations. We all are making our way through history, making sense of the past and peering hazily into the future. What I hope youth workers can learn even more than theological erudition or practical skills is the ability to feel their way into our shared historical reality, into the crisis, to see the mutuality of our suffering.

To help others grasp this, I often use films in classes and presentations, asking people to enter the characters' stories, to recognize how multiple forces are impacting them and to feel the tragic nature of our historical reality—how death appears in rejection, fear, addiction, loneliness. For instance, I've both written about and showed clips numerous times from the movie *Good Will Hunting*. The film's scenes help people see that Will (played by Matt Damon) is the way he is because of the tragic situation of being an orphan and being let down by a number of people. I then help the group I'm with to look for God's presence and absence next to the depth of Will's existence. An exercise like this keeps people from avoiding the tragic reality of existence.

The interpreter has only reality to live in, and if we are honest, we have to admit that reality is tragic, that history has no answers for us and that we are in need of a future hope. Eschatology, a sense that history is moving somewhere, to some end, therefore holds great significance for Bultmann. Yet what Bultmann fails to see is that the *eschaton* is not *only* on the horizon of time but is already breaking in from the future. This breaking in is what makes Christopraxis possible at all.

The eschatological line of hope and promise. The search for Christopraxis can never be found outside time and reality, outside the particularity of each new challenge, choice and action. But this cannot be the whole picture; the hermeneutical situation cannot be only existential. There must also be a christological scaffolding to any truly theologically orientated hermeneutic. In the existential line of tragedy and death we see Christ's connection to us. This reality of tragedy and pain, being in time, is taken up fully by God in the incarnate humanity of God—taken up but not triumphed over. It is taken up and suffered. On the cross, fatalism, tragedy and death are victorious. But in the resurrection they are halted and a new reality is inaugurated. In the resurrected humanity of Jesus, the kingdom of God has broken into our existential reality; the *eschaton* has shown its colors in the empty tomb of Jesus, and they are more beautiful than we could have dreamed. Christopraxis is the in-breaking of the kingdom of God in history, the breaking in of eschatological hope.

In the existential line of tragedy and death, history moves from creation forward, from the past through the present and to some completion, an unknown future that is unforeseeable from the existential line itself (see the gap in figure 6.2 between the existential line and final/complete *parousia*). The eschatological line, however, moves from the future to the present situation and points back to its genesis in the life and resurrection of Christ.[6] History will have its finale in the return of Christ, but even before this culmination the work of Christ is breaking into history.

The interpreter therefore must stand fully embedded in the existential line, but in faith and assurance give heed to the eschatological line. In other words, the interpreter stands in the reality of tragedy but has faith that history has a telos, that in each new challenge, choice and action, God is breaking in. And the hermeneutical situation, while fully existential and bound in history, stands at the same time within the breaking forth of the kingdom of God, which promises the final culmination of history in the hoped-for *eschaton*. It must stand within both an existential line and an eschatological one, balancing the seen reality of history with the unseen reality of hope. To choose one over the other is to give way to either hopeless fatalism or pious mysticism.

Moments before Dietrich Bonhoeffer was hanged in the concentration camp at Flossenbürg, he reportedly said, "This is the end, for me the beginning of life." These final words of his (and his life) demonstrate how to face the darkest realities and yet, in so doing, to utter "Nevertheless, the tomb is empty." A hermeneutic of Christopraxis must likewise see human history

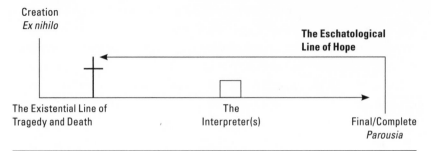

Figure 6.2. Existential reality and eschatological hope

within God's history, never giving one up for the other and understanding that both are linked in the person of Jesus Christ. Theologian Jürgen Moltmann helps us understand how this is possible.

The resurrection. The passion of Christ has initiated a new reality, binding the history of humanity with the history of God. Indeed, the resurrection of Christ has broken into history as a new possibility, asserting the claim that now in connection to the resurrected Christ there is new possibility for all humanity; now, though we cannot avoid history and must face tragedy and death, there is reconciliation of God with all humanity through the passion of Christ. Moltmann explains, "The resurrection of Christ does not mean a possibility within the world and its history, but a new possibility altogether for the world, for existence and for history."[7] It is an eschatological event that has substantiated itself within history but has also transcended and transformed history, allowing the *eschaton* to dawn within history.[8] And this gives us hope—a true hope, because it is a hope that is outside of history but actualized within it.

And as Moltmann states, "The real question [is]: What can I hope for? It is only a future which we are permitted to hope for that gives any meaning to life in history and to all historical experience and action."[9] For this reason the resurrection becomes essential to our hermeneutic, for it is the breaking in of God into history, through which the promise of new creation and new life within a future history is given. Just as meaning cannot be divorced from the existential locus of the individual and community, the eschatological, that for which we hope, is necessary for a meaningful hermeneutic.

So, in our discerning of God's action, in our discerning of how we should act, hope itself confronts us with meaning. This means the interpreter must not only confront history, but also hope; he or she must face not only the historical reality of the present situation, but also the present eschatological reality of hope. Moltmann explains it this way: "We cannot then merely embark on a historical examination of the past that once was, nor yet merely provide an existentialist interpretation of present claims, but we must inquire into what is open, unfinished, unsettled and outstanding, and consequently into the future announced by this event [of resurrection]."[10] Hence, the interpreter, the youth worker, is to stand within history, understanding its impact and force, but never allowing it to pin him or her down, to force him or her into submission. Rather, the youth worker is to feel the full weight of history, never turning from its tragedy, and yet proclaim the inbreaking of the resurrection, stating boldly and confidently, "Nevertheless . . . God is before us, the tomb it is empty!"

As the interpreter discerns Christopraxis, he or she must feel the full weight of the existential situation, but in feeling it must point forward to a future that is on its way. The impact of history cannot be avoided, but in its midst the *eschaton* places another demand upon the interpreter: God is breaking forth, and the kingdom is dawning.[11] The interpreter must see reality, see history, with the vision of the hope of resurrection, through the lens of the kingdom of God. The interpreter is accountable not just to empathy but also to the promise, not just to the seen reality but also to what is unseen, not just to sympathy in tragedy but also to obedience to the command of God. Without this eschatological understanding, history becomes an undefeatable monster, and emancipation and liberation are impossible. But in balancing these two realities, our eyes are opened to see suffering and evil and refuse to stand for it. For we see another reality that meets us from the future, where all are free from death and dehumanization in the arms of the resurrected Christ, in the kingdom of God. Thus, the interpreter is called to confront the present existential reality with the hope of eschatological reality.

Many years ago a dear colleague of mine lost his two-year-old son right before Christmas. And his son had died from an allergic reaction to medicine that he had given him. Drowning in grief and searching for answers, my friend approached his car one night to find a note under the windshield. The note read, "God needed a Christmas present so He took your boy home." This is a clear example of poor ministerial action. The individual who left the note clearly could not face the existential line and therefore defaulted to a kind of eschatological perspective that was disconnected from reality (and therefore could not really be called eschatological).

On the other hand, I know of a youth pastor who stood at the gravesite of a fourteen-year-old girl who killed herself after her boyfriend broke up with her. The pastor, looking at her family and friends, said, "We don't know why Amanda did this, but we can be assured that she was hurting and that we too are hurting, hurting from her loss, hurting for so many reasons. Hurting is part of living. And we have a God who hurts, but a God who also promises us that our pains will not destroy us. They may kill us, but they will not destroy us. For we can be assured that no matter how dark things became for Amanda, there is no darkness, no distance that the light of the empty tomb does not reach." This youth pastor wrote his sermon aware of the hermeneutical situation, and conscious of the need to live between the existential line of tragedy and death and the eschatological line of hope.

THE HERMENEUTICAL METHOD

We have laid out the hermeneutical situation: both the history of humanity and the history of God confront the interpreter, and the interpreter must not give up one for the other. All discernment of Christopraxis must happen within this hermeneutical situation; it's the playing field on which we interpret ministerial action, the situadedness of the youth worker. But now we need some kind of hermeneutical method, some kind of hermeneutical operation. We've acknowledged where we stand (in between tragedy/death and hope), but how do we move in this place, where there are a multitude of possible actions? It is one thing to know that God has acted in such a world, but quite another to claim that your action is the will of God.

Our method must be fully planted within the soil of the reality but must provide direction through a bracketing of possibility and impossibility in discerning God's will and action. This starts with the assertion that God has given Godself both to the social/communal life of humanity and to the normative assertions of the Scriptures; both express God's history with humanity as covenant partner. This understanding, in turn, creates brackets for our action, helping us see a zone of possible Christopraxis. An action or position that falls outside of these brackets is an impossibility for God's will. But those actions or positions found within them can confidently (and yet with a wealth of humility) be asserted as the will of God.

You might feel that, in doing this, we are in some ways boxing in God, bracketing what is possible and what is not. I actually think, though, that this method is an open system that allows for God's complete freedom. It only claims what God asserts of Godself: that in the incarnation God has given Godself fully to humanity, and that in God's history with humanity God will never contradict God's own nature found in the history of God's self-revelation.

The bracket of social/communal experience. The first bracket confronting us in the hermeneutical situation that we will use in forming our hermeneutical method is the bracket of social/communal experience. As we move through history, denial or avoidance of relationship is impossible.[12] Relationship is fundamentally embedded within our humanity. And throughout God's covenant history with humanity, God has continued to call us to the actuality of our neighbor. Love of God and love for neighbor may be different in kind but are nevertheless inseparable.

As figure 6.3 shows, this bracket is grounded within the interpreter, and originates from the existential line of tragedy and death. The other that meets us (as individual or group) shares in a history of tragedy. But the other also, as we have mentioned above, shares in the coming of God, in the universal significance of the resurrection of Christ. Therefore, there is undeniable solidarity between the other and the interpreter; they exist together in the existential line.

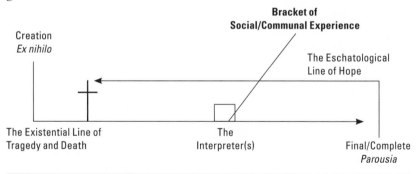

Figure 6.3. The first bracket in the hermeneutical situation

In the United States there are a handful of groups that travel around the country asserting that "God hates fags." Loudly shouting their messages outside of churches, funerals or other gatherings where they sense homosexuality is supported, and armed with biblical texts, they feel they are not only justified but actually obeying the will of God in their actions. But in so doing they deny any common humanity, and reject the fact that through the humanity of Christ all humanity is beloved and accountable to and for each other.

There is an undeniable responsibility for the other we meet, for the eschatological line penetrates through them by the power of the human God found in the resurrected Christ. This penetration assures us that the other, the neighbor, whether far from or near to us, whether similar or strange to us, confronts us with the very presence of God.

For the other, for our neighbor. In the final days of World War II, a truck headed deep into the Bavarian forest, loaded with prisoners on their way to the concentration camp at Flossenbürg. In one corner sat pastor Dietrich Bonhoeffer; next to him was a Russian soldier. As they traveled, the Russian soldier and Bonhoeffer talked, becoming friends as the soldier taught the pastor some words and phrases in Russian. When the truck stopped for the night and it became clear that many of the prisoners would soon meet their demise, Bonhoeffer was asked to administer Communion. He agreed and stood to begin, but the Russian soldier remained sitting, explaining that he was a communist atheist and that it would therefore be hypocritical for him to partake. Upon hearing his response, Bonhoeffer sat back down and reportedly stated, "Then neither will I partake; for how can I be sure that in leaving you for the communion table I would not be leaving Christ?"

Emmanuel Levinas, a Jewish thinker who himself spent time in a Nazi concentration camp, had ideas similar to Bonhoeffer's. Having survived the war, Levinas saw how easily our philosophical and theological perspectives allow us to destroy our neighbor. In exploring this, Levinas put ethics at the forefront of all action, interaction and knowledge. Yet his ethics is not an ethics of absolutes and ideal principles. Rather, for Levinas, ethics is born in the relational connection of I and other. In responsible ethical action, I see the other as a mystery (an infinity) that cannot be captured by my own thoughts, desires or wants. And I experience this transcendent mystery in the other when I see the face of the other. It is in this confrontation that all is changed, for I am pulled from my self-obsession and forced to rearrange my reality; the other must find a place within it. This is most fundamentally a hermeneutical issue, for in every new interaction with an other, I must allow the other's humanity to confront me in such a way that I am forced to critically review what it is that I know and hold to be true.

For example, imagine sitting at a wedding, leaning over to your friend and whispering, "I have no idea what she sees in him." You have only known the groom as obnoxious and shallow. Yet, a few weeks later you are invited to the newlyweds' home for dinner. In their home, through a meal and conversation, you see him differently; you now see him alongside her, in connection to his relationship with her, which allows you to see the depth and wonder of his person. As a result, he escapes your simple categories for him.

But who, concretely, is an "other" to me? We have already mentioned the face as the criterion to see and hear the other. The other, then, is everyone I meet. You can hear in this echoes of the scribe's question to Jesus, "Who is my neighbor?" (Lk 10:29), and Jesus' answer, the parable of the good Samaritan (Lk 10:30-37).[13] The neighbor is the one who confronts me in the now with his or her humanity, and it is in this confrontation that I must act on his or her behalf. When I see someone face to face I have confronted the other and must never turn from him or her. Response-ability is called for.

Even more, though, in the meeting of the other, in seeing him or her face to face, we encounter all of humanity and are confronted by its particularities. Philosopher Adriaan Peperzak draws this out from Levinas: "Other others stand beside and behind this other who obliges me here and now through his/her presence. Since the obligation is not attached to a particular feature of this other but only to his/her entrance into my world, all others oblige me as much as this one. In this one's face, I see the virtual presence of all men and women."[14] The universal principle here is that we uphold the humanity of all by expressing local responsibility for the other we encounter.

What this means is that the Christian, the church, must never endorse or turn ignorantly from the suffering of anyone, far or near, familiar or strange, but must be attentive. Clearly, Christopraxis—the present action of Christ—will never oppose the humanity of another. We can never claim that oppression or abuse is God's will, for where humanity is destroyed and the neighbor beaten, God states only "No." The suffering of the world, however, is vast, and from a universal perspective we are defeated by its enormity. Its enormity must not be our focus, though; our focus is to be the unique particularity of the other that meets us, for it is in meeting him or her that a sacrament of liberation is given to all of humanity.

In this social relation where humanity is upheld and community is formed we can claim the presence of God. And we can claim it only through the life of Christ in which God binds Godself to humanity to be a vehicle of all wholeness and restoration within it. The Spirit of Christ (the work of Christopraxis) is the source of all restoration and healing, all wholeness and vitality. If we are to join in Christopraxis, if we are to claim the will of God, there must be shared relationship where we are free in our humanity to be met by another. The will of God can never be claimed where the other is made into a possession. Rather, all discernment must look to the human other, seeing, speaking to and hearing him or her, understanding that God has bound Godself to humanity in his own humanity. Our hermeneutical method cannot contradict the hermeneutical situation, a situation in which the *eschaton* breaks forth in shared relationship and humanity is upheld and healed.

In the mutuality of shared relationship, the other in his or her openness also confronts me in a way that upholds my humanity but calls me to lay all aside for the good of the other, who speaks to me as Christ.[15] It causes me to see from a new perspective things which I have never seen before, or things about me (my opinions, thoughts, perspectives, presuppositions) that must be changed. This bracket of social/communal experience thus allows our hermeneutic to be both constructive and destructive, productive yet critical.

The bracket of biblical/theological norms. With our first bracket planted in the soil of the hermeneutical situation, we now turn to our second bracket, the bracket of biblical/theological norms. This bracket asserts that there is continuity between the present action and work of Christ in the world and the recorded history of God's self-revelation found in the biblical text. Thus, all present action of Christ will find some continuity in, and cannot contradict, that which is given to the church in the canon of holy Scripture. Scripture itself becomes normative. This bracket has been called "biblical/theological," though, to avoid the misconception that this normative biblical stance allows for some kind of proof-texting, where verses can be interpreted and applied in a way that opposes the larger theological history of the biblical narrative (or the humanity of the other). It has also been called "biblical/theological" because the bracket must encompass within itself the interpretations of past theologians. This is not to say that a new interpretation is not possible, only that, in its possibility, there must be some continuity to the historical understanding of the text. But it must be stated that the text is story (narrative) and not hard principles.

This bracket, like the first one, is embedded within the interpreter as the one who addresses the text in his or her unique context. The existential line runs through it because it is written by human hands, and speaks of the reality of tragedy and death, and the eschatological line penetrates it because it is the Word of God and speaks of God's history with humanity which promises to overcome tragedy, death and sin. It is also embedded within the interpreter because it continues to speak and address the contemporary moment.

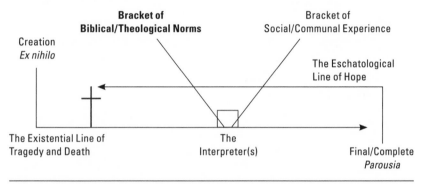

Figure 6.4. The second bracket in the hermeneutical situation

The Word of God as Jesus. Our first question with this bracket must be, What is the Word of God? Karl Barth understood the Word of God in a threefold form. First, the Word of God is Jesus Christ himself, the Word became flesh; the living Christ is the Word of God, moving in the world. Second, the Word of God is the canon of Scripture, which is the Word of God *only* as it leads to Jesus Christ, *only* as it witnesses to his lordship and directs the reader to confession. We will return to this shortly. Third, the Word of God is the preached event.

In Barth's threefold perspective, both the first and the third aspects encounter us in our present moment, within the present reality. The second, the Bible, is not free to confront us as directly, since it is a written document. However, because the Word of God cannot be understood outside this threefold perspective, we cannot separate the three movements. The written Word does meet us and confront us in our present reality, but only as it witnesses to the living Christ, only as it is open to the work of Christopraxis. In other words, the biblical narrative is thrust into our time and discernment not because it is a "playbook" of Christian action but because it witnesses to Jesus Christ, the One who is acting and calls us to follow.

Thus, by the biblical text's inseparability from Jesus Christ, it is given the power to speak to us in our present moments of decision.[16] In its connection to Christ it is resurrected from being merely a lifeless text written in (many) dead languages, millennia ago, and allowed to speak anew; it is allowed to be not only a record of revelation, but revelation itself, found in our time and space. This is its uniqueness. In this understanding there is inseparable continuity between the revelation of the past and that of the present, for the same texts are given new relevance in new moments, not by the church or individuals but by Jesus Christ himself, who is the One at work.

Therefore, any present action of Christ can never contradict the biblical text.[17] He is revelation proper, and revelation cannot oppose itself. The present situation may be critical of past *interpretations,* enlightening us to the deeper meaning and significance of a text, but it can never make a mockery or scandal of the text itself. The Word of God, Jesus Christ, is always pulling us forward, moving and acting in the world.

As the interpreter, then—the youth worker who is left to act in discernment—you can be confident that the present action of Christ will have an antecedent in the past biblical narrative. Ray Anderson explains, "By antecedent, I mean some aspect of God's earlier ministry that can now be seen in a new and liberating way through God's continuing ministry."[18] In reflection on the first-century church, Anderson continues, "As nearly as I can see, for every case in which eschatological preference was exercised by the Spirit in the New Testament church, there was a biblical antecedent for what appeared to be revolutionary and new."[19] In the same way, we can have faith that in every action of Christopraxis there will be a biblical antecedent linking this action of God with that found in the canon of Scripture. This has occurred, for example, in our changed understanding of the roles of women in ministry.

From a philosophical hermeneutical perspective, then, it is, as Paul Ricoeur famously says, "the life in front of the text that is of significance."[20] By this he means that discerning how the text bleeds into our own time, into our own horizon, is the hermeneutical task.

The bracket of biblical/theological norms thus asserts that just as Christ is present in the social relational connection of I to other through the incarnation, Christ is also present in our reflection on the biblical text, because he himself is revelation. Any reflection on the biblical text should therefore always be forward moving, for its vibrancy is found only in connection to Christ who is found in the world, in Christopraxis.

THE HERMENEUTICAL PROCESS: MOVING WITHIN THE BRACKETS

Now that we have placed both brackets within the hermeneutical situation, we can confidently (and yet with humility) assert that the will of God, the action of Christopraxis, will be found somewhere between these two brackets or poles. We'll call this area "the zone of Christopraxis." We've established that any action that would oppose, hurt or destroy the other cannot be the will of God. Any action that is found to be contradictory to the biblical narrative, that has no congruence with the reconciling work of Christ, must be ruled out as well. But we are still left to wonder how one operates within in this zone of Christopraxis. We understand what things are hermeneutical impossibilities, but how do we move hermeneutically within the possibility to finally land on some kind of understanding? Paul Ricoeur and his hermeneneutical arch will give us guidance on how to move within the brackets, therein allowing us to confidently work to discern the will of God in a given situation.

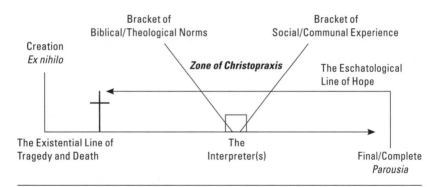

Figure 6.5. The zone of Christopraxis

Swing, swing and swing. Ricoeur, a master Christian philosopher on interpretation, has explained that the process of interpretation is moving back and forth between "understanding" and "explanation." You start with an initial guess of what this event may mean, and what action must be taken. This is what he calls the first naiveté. You then move from this guess, from this hunch, to explanation. In explanation, the first naiveté, the first guess, is placed in dialogue with something to see if validation can be given to the hunch or if it must be revised and then placed in dialogue with explanation again. This second movement (back to explanation) is the second naiveté. This back-and-forth process, which has most helpfully been called "Ricoeur's hermeneutical arch,"[21] continues until the hunch has evolved to a confident assertion. You must then complete the process by stating your interpretation.

Nancy Lammers Gross, in her book, *If You Cannot Preach Like Paul,* has revised this Ricoeurian arch, lifting it, flipping it on its back and calling it a "swing." She explains her reasons: "I propose the image of a swing [because] it has the advantage of the arch in terms of a tensive dialectic [the move from understanding to explanation]. But even more, it has movement, and it holds the possibility that when gathering enough momentum, the swing will go full circle." She continues, "[I]magine a gymnast on the high bar. The gymnast creates an arch, essentially the bottom half of the circle, as the gymnast swings. When enough momentum has been gathered, the gymnast completes 'a giant,' a full circle around the bar."[22] This tensive dialectic between understanding and explanation is what I propose should be our movement within this zone of Christopraxis. Let me explain.

We are always confronted by one of the brackets first. It may, for example, be the social/communal (interaction with the other) when the adult leader comes to your office to explain that she is thinking of leaving her husband and to seek your advice. Or it may be the biblical text when, in studying a passage, you are moved or drawn to the significance of a doctrinal position. From this first encounter, you, the interpreter, will be struck with either confusion or insight; then you'll be pushed from this initial understanding, which comes from confrontation with one of the brackets, to the other bracket, as if on a swing. It is here that you are in a dialogue with explanation. In the counseling situation, for example, you would swing from the social/communal bracket to the biblical/theological bracket; there you would place your understanding (first naiveté), your encounter with the other, alongside the narrative of God's reconciling work of Jesus Christ. Your initial assumptions about the issues and actions must be in dialogue with the biblical/theological bracket. It may affirm that you are right in your thinking, deepening your understanding, or it may remind you of the beauty of the person's humanity and God's love for her.

In preaching or giving a youth talk, on the other hand, you would swing from the biblical/theological to the social/communal. As you prepare your sermon or talk on the text that has moved you, you have to take your understanding of it and put it in dialogue with the community that will hear it and with the larger world that God has given Godself to. You are not free to keep your nose stuck in your commentaries but rather must at least push yourself back from your desk and reflect on the suffering and joy of those who will hear your message.

In this swing from one to the other, the brackets balance and critique each other. After your initial experience with the other, the reading of a biblical text may take on new and different meaning, critiquing your past understanding and leading to new interpretation. In the same way, after reading a biblical text you may be given a new perspective from which to see your fellow human.

After you have swung to the opposite bracket, however, you must return to the first, either in affirmation of your original understanding or with new insight that directs you deeper or sends you in a new direction altogether. At this point you may realize that you must swing again, returning, say, to the biblical text to look deeper by using commentaries and following the discussion of other theologians. Or swinging again may mean returning to the social/communal, asking further questions, sharing more deeply in community, working to see the world through the eyes of another. This second swing would be your second naiveté.

Eventually, the momentum will send you over the bar and you will come to your interpretation. You will make your decision, you will preach your sermon, you will give your diagnoses. When this happens, you will be participating in the will of God; you will have joined in Christopraxis. Through this Ricoeurian swing, then, we are moved from the zone of Christopraxis, from the possibility, to what in faith we assert is the actuality.

The one swinging back and forth from one bracket to the other is the interpreter. It is our responsibility to understand the hermeneutical situation and to be open and ready for movement within the zone of Christopraxis. But the force that moves us, the force that pushes the swing, is the Spirit of Christ. Christ himself confronts and meets us at each bracket, pushing us to the next. When we unite our willingness to swing (to look and look again, think and think anew, pray and pray once more) with our faith that God is acting and calling us to join with him, we participate in Christopraxis. The momentum swings us over and we assert, "It is the will of God."

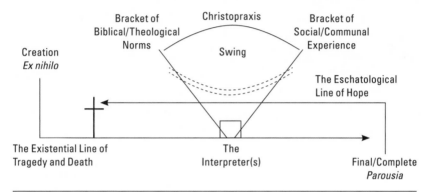

Figure 6.6. Understanding and explanation

We may fear in this process that, upon mounting the swing, we may never get off, always feeling we need one more swing, one more back and forth, to be sure that this action is right, to land on *the* right interpretation. It may be helpful here to return to Ricoeur, who assures us that there is not *one* right interpretation, but rather that, within the swing, within the tensive dialectic, there is a surplus of meaning. This surplus of meaning does not lead to a free-for-all, though; the interpreter has mounted the swing, and in so doing, the plethora of possibilities available is reduced to only a handful. And this handful will never contradict itself. Rather, it will offer differing notes in the same song.

Note also that it is possible, and even common, for us to be confronted with a decision or choice that will give us no time to swing: we will have to act and act now. In these cases, we should feel no paralysis but simply act as best we can. After our actions are complete and the event has passed we will have to ask, "Was what we did the will of God?" or "How do we make sense of our action?" This reflection time is when we will swing, either seeing more clearly than at the point of confrontation that surely God was at work, or coming to realize that we chose wrongly and the action we performed was not right, and therefore an apology and confession is called for.

CONCLUSION

This chapter has sought to present a model or picture to help the minister discern Christopraxis (the will of God). Entering into dialogue with epoch-making theologians and philosophers, I presented a picture of the hermeneutical situation, the hermeneutical method and the hermeneutical process. My hope is that, through this picture, those doing youth ministry will begin to recognize that at its core youth ministry is not about programming events but about discerning God's continued Ministry in the world and then joining it, and that they'll be equipped to actually do this in their ministries.

• DISCUSSION AND REFLECTION EXERCISES
Taking Roles in Discussion

Break into small groups.[23] Each person should be assigned one of the roles listed below. Groups should then discuss the relevance of this chapter for their ministry, exploring issues, perspectives and reasons for the model presented. Each person in each group should operate in their role during their group's discussion.

The roles are as follows:

- *Problem, dilemma or theme poser.* This person's responsibility is to frame the topic of conversation and to draw on his or her own experiences as a way of helping others enter into conversation about the theme.

- *Reflective analyst.* This person is responsible for keeping a record of the conversation's development. Every twenty minutes or so, he or she gives a summary that focuses on shared concerns and emerging common themes.

- *Scrounger.* This person listens for resources, suggestions and tips that participants mention as having been helpful in their efforts to work through a situation or perspective. He or she keeps a record of these ideas and reads it to participants at least once before the discussion is over.

- *Devil's advocate.* This is the person who, as he or she senses a consensus emerging, expresses the contradictory view as a way of avoiding groupthink and helping participants explore a range of alternative interpretations.

- *Detective.* This person listens carefully for unacknowledged, unchecked and unchallenged biases that seem to be emerging in the conversation, such as cultural blindness, gender insensitivity, and comments that ignore variables of power, class or theological perspective.

- *Theme spotter.* This person identifies themes that surfaced during the discussion but were left unexplored and that might therefore form a focus for the next discussion.

- *Umpire.* This person listens for judgmental comments that might offend communicative virtues and/or the ground rules understood by group members.

GOD'S HIDDENNESS, ABSENCE AND DOUBT

ANDREW ROOT

We were all sitting in a circle trying our best to do theological reflection on our concrete experiences in ministry—the issues and forces impacting the young people in our distinct contexts. We had articulated their pains, their moral failings, their family dysfunctions and the societal realities impinging on them. The energy in the small group was palpable. A contemplative silence came over us, but then someone finally said, "Well, then what should we or the church do? What programs or initiatives should be taken?" The group rustled with mounting energy, but as people cleared their throats and prepared to launch in, someone else asked, "But before we get there isn't there another question we should take up? Shouldn't we ask the distinctly theological question? Shouldn't we ask *where* is God?" The palpable energy disappeared, sucked up by the confusion over how (or even perhaps why) to answer, and the group of paid youth ministers and pastors again fell silent.

"Where is God?" Eberhard Jüngel explains, "Whether there is a God at all and what a God is, are decided for contemporary [people] by answering this question: Where can God be encountered and where can he be addressed as God?"[1] This question, *Where* is God? seems to be the very heart of ministry. Where do we and those we minister to encounter the living God? And yet while it is the heart of ministry, the answer seems to escape us. We desire for young people to know, trust and follow God, but few of us have thought about or can articulate where this God is to be found and how this God has made Godself known. Few have placed their actions in ministry in line with their theological conception of God's own action.

In the small group, someone finally spoke into the confused silence that descended after the "Where is God?" question: "Well, I think God is everywhere, so if God is everywhere then God is present everywhere." The group nodded. This nebulous answer seemed to appease us. No more thought was needed on the *where* question; we had decided where God was (everywhere), so now we were free to talk about programs, initiatives and things to be done.

Confusion never really left the group, though. "God is everywhere" seemed both right and yet unhelpful. For example, as we discussed young people's contexts we became very specific, providing concrete stories, examples and anecdotes for the issues they faced, but when it came to giving answers on the location of God in their lives, all we could muster was the very unspecific "everywhere." And in the light of the deep contextual realities of the young people we discussed, in the light of the deep pathos of their pain, to say God was everywhere was in effect to say God was nowhere—which is exactly how many of us in the group felt. "God is everywhere" became the escape hatch that freed us from having to really struggle with the presence of God (or lack thereof).

It seems that in youth ministry we tend to work from this perspective that God is everywhere. This is no doubt a legitimate theological assertion—but only if it is placed in paradoxical opposition. God is present and everywhere, but God is also absent and hidden. We have often been reluctant to allow this paradox to find its way into our theological conceptions of ministry. Sticking with God's omnipresence seems safe; it feels risky to discuss the absence and hiddenness of God. But unless we do so, our theological perspective on ministry doesn't allow for authentic experiences of suffering, yearning and loss.

RAMIFICATIONS OF THE EVERYWHERE-NESS

It was twenty minutes after his bedtime when my then three-year-old son, Owen, had beckoned me from my night of watching TV to his dark room, lit only by the faint blue glow of his nightlight which dimly illuminated the horde of stuffed animals surrounding his body. "Daddy, I'm scared!" he said to me. "I'm scared there is a nightmare in my closet. I'm scared."

Moved by compassion for his fear (and yet also wanting badly to return to the TV), I told him that he need not fear, because Jesus was with him and would protect him.

Frustrated, he shot back, "Where is Jesus? I don't see Jesus." I rambled something about Jesus always being with us, but he wasn't satisfied. With a worried quiver in his voice he said, "Jesus is not here."

I found to my shame that all I could do was provide polemics for my position of Jesus' everywhere-ness. "Yes, Owen he is," I asserted, but he stood his ground.

"No! He is not here!" The objective reality of his fear spoke louder than my Sunday school words.

"Jesus is here, Owen," I repeated, but he could only respond (loudly now, in fear and frustration), "Jesus is *not here.*"

Again, I found myself replying, "Yes, Jesus is. Jesus is with you now."

"Where? Where?" he asked while choking back three-year-old tears. "Where is he? I'm scared!"

"If we pray, he will be here," I said, now starting to distrust myself. Up against his real fear, my affirmation of Jesus' presence was unhelpful. Owen could sense, I imagine, that I was more concerned with getting him over his fear and getting him to go to sleep than I was with acknowledging his deep terror.

It is not that the assertion that God is everywhere is wrong. Clearly God is not bound by time and space; as Creator, God possesses a unique inter-relationship with creation itself (God is omnipresent, to use imported Greek thought). As the one who speaks being out of non-being, God is in a real way present in and through all that is. There is an everywhere-ness and above-ness to God's being and nature. It is from this above-ness that we have tended to articulate our theological conceptions about youth ministry, though, and as a result, three broad theological commitments have too often been overemphasized. This keeps us from being able to richly answer the "where" question.

1. An overemphasis on God as revealed. The church, the youth worker and youth groups as a whole tend to be seen and operate as the unveiler of God. Too often it is assumed that our actions, activities or words—whether the call for personal salvation or the work of social justice—summon or bring forth the unveiling of God. So we tell young people to pray, giving them models and acronyms, telling them that God will be present. But in so doing we never say anything about the silence or absence of God (a theo-logical theme essential to the Reformation, as we'll see below).

Moreover, as part of discipleship, we often push young people to see God everywhere, to interpret every part of their lives as being in line with God.

And we speak as if this is self-evident and obvious. Yet, though we have tried to convince young people that God has revealed Godself, our commitment to God's revealedness has not kept us from falling into broad abstract statements about the "where" of God. Like I did in my conversation with Owen, we continue to insist that God is here, that God is revealed, and like Owen, many adolescents ask (with or without words), "Where?" Up against fear, depression, longing and brokenness, they can only answer our repeated "God is here" with the heartfelt yearning of a three-year-old terrified of a bad dream: "Where is this God? God is not here."

2. An obsession with God as near. It is, of course, true that God is near. In the humanity of Jesus Christ, God is near to our humanity. But if God is person (as both trinitarian and incarnational perspectives claim), then God's nearness must be balanced by absence. We too often abstract God's nearness from God's personhood, talking about God's nearness as God always surrounding us in some amorphous way. Moreover, our clumsy statements about the "where" of God almost always ignore the absence of God. But the presence of a person is determined by absence. We know he or she is here because at other times he or she is not. The theology of Israel, the theology of the New Testament, assumes encounter and being encountered, being struck by presence, presence that is born from absence ("Surely, the LORD is in this place—and I did not know it!" [Gen 28:16]).

We tend to tell young people that God is near to them—that Jesus is like their best friend ("Jesus is just a prayer away!") and God their personal therapist—so faith means living as though God is always near, always watching and surrounding you. But when assertions about God's nearness do not take into consideration God's absence, answers to the "where" quickly lose solidity. When God is always near, God can no longer be one who acts and moves because God can no longer encounter us. Encounter itself demands presence puncturing absence—impossible if God is a substance, a metamorphic reality that is always around but hard to notice, like radio waves. So we explain to young people that if they do what it takes to tune themselves to God's frequency, they will recognize God, for God is near; God surrounds us; God is everywhere. However, just as we are unsure of where radio waves come from and how and when they get through our walls, we're not sure specifically "where" God is either. All we can say is, "God is near." But still, we encourage them to pray more, go to church more, read their Bible more, giving the impression that *doing more* will finally lead them to an understanding that God is on any frequency they tune to—everywhere.

But this can only work if God is found as a substance, as a frequency humming that is nevertheless hard to encounter. My three-year-old's fear, his nightmare, was in his closet. It was concrete; it was *somewhere* in the sense that, even though there wasn't really a nightmare in his closet, he could, without a doubt, name its location. In other words, his nightmare possessed a "where." Knowing exactly "where" his fear was, then, he sought a very concrete location for the "where" of Jesus. But my assertions about the presence of Jesus could not match the concreteness of his fear. I was unable to provide anything other than "Jesus is near," and with no concrete location, he was right to assume that his fear was more real than Jesus.

Like the nightmare in the closet, the suffering, broken hope and yearning of young people are often bound in a concrete "where" (the divorce of my parents, the rejection from my dream school, the shape of my body). We can assert all we want that God is near, but our assertion will be meaningless unless we can help them imagine the "where" of God as concretely as the "where" of their nightmares.

3. A fixation on God as a rational reality and therefore faith as something you must come to know or believe. When God is bound in God's *everywhere-ness,* then faith is bound in rationality. In other words, when we say God is everywhere but cannot say concretely "where," we clothe God in a rational system; we must defend that God is somewhere and fight to provide rational ground that God is not gone, that God exists. Thus, when young people assert that their nightmare is more real than Jesus, we too often seek to defend God and prove God's everywhere-ness, instead of seeking God in the real-ness/reality of fear and brokenness. We make artificial rational systems for God the ground of faith—and, having made these rational systems (or at least living with the residue of them), we then make doubt antithetical to faith.[2]

In his bedroom, though, my three-year-old doubts deeply: "Jesus is not here. I don't see Jesus. He is *not here.*" The tenaciousness of his doubt, alongside the concreteness of his fear, witnesses to a yearning for faith. He wants to believe but has no idea what I am calling him to believe, for though his imagination has revealed the reality/realness of his fear, I cannot articulate to his imagination "where" Jesus is. He wants to believe, but I have given him only a rational ultimatum in which to believe. What he desires is *some kind of framework* in which to make sense of his experiences, but I have not provided one; I have not provided any way for him to understand "where" God is.

So we fight over who is right, and what's more real: his fear or my assertion that Jesus is here. They seem in opposition, with Jesus standing outside fear and doubt. I'm calling Owen away from what he knows is true—that he is scared—to trust in something else outside the fear he concretely experiences. And he is not ready to do that. His fear is irrational, but it is real; if Jesus cannot be found in his irrationality, then he cannot be real. Owen's fear and my position have thus become opposing views. As such, only the more rational view can win (at least, that is the mantra modernity sells us). I therefore turn on the light, open his closet door and show him that there is no nightmare there, and he agrees that he can rationally see nothing. But when the light goes off again, rationality has no say; his fear is more real than his rationality—the nightmare is there again.

Frustrated, I say, "Owen, be logical. There is no nightmare in your closet, so don't be scared. Jesus is here" (as if "be rational" is an incantation that sends fear, hurt and loneliness running). In actuality, rationality cannot battle the reality of fear, for rationality stops at the head, but fear and suffering are borne in the heart (and what is more real in the end, the head or the heart?). My plea for rationality alone to set the terms for reality forces Owen to either deny his fear in order to hold onto rationality and therefore have Jesus, or embrace his fear and therefore lose the everywhere-ness of God that I present to him.

With no concrete way of speaking about "where" God is, we must defend God, and defend that God is everywhere. Moreover, in asking young people to commit to God's everywhere-ness, we are essentially trying to extract doubt from them. Often we treat doubt like a tumor, fearful that, if it's left in adolescents, it will grow and compound like a cancer, eventually killing their faith. But to extract doubt, the vital tissue of suffering, yearning and brokenness must be extracted with it, as though it were all meaningless waste. Doubt, however, may not be a tumor but the very organ of faith surrounded by the tissue of fear, brokenness and suffering. If this is true, we will have to imagine the "where" of God as somewhere other than in rational systems, for suffering, depression, yearning and brokenness do not bow to rationality but, rather, show the folly of rationality's pursuits for the throne of authority.[3]

WHAT IS A TEENAGER?
THE ADOLESCENT'S ONTOLOGICAL STATE

We have often overemphasized the revealed, obsessed about nearness and become fixated on the rational because, at least in part, we believe that this is what adolescents need; our interpretation of their ontological state pushes us to articulate these theological overstatements. We have tended, for example, to view adolescence as a developmental time when advancement, preparation and growth are central, particularly intellectual, spiritual and biological growth. So we see it as a time when the young person is *revealed* to him- or herself as he or she grows toward adulthood, and a time when they advance their identity by discovering their gifts and abilities. It is about young people discovering themselves and making themselves known. Moreover, we assume it is a time for them to be *near* to themselves and others, and that the nearness of friends and lovers, in particular, becomes vital. In addition, we see it as a period of preparation. Education and learning are important, as youth are pointed toward the future. It is no longer enough for them to just be; it is a time for them to achieve and become and develop into something. We perceive adolescence as a time for the young person to *rationally* (through school and achievement) prepare for the future.

Some of these things are no doubt true culturally, but when we assume them ontologically—when we assume that growth, advancement and preparation are the pattern stamped on the fabric of adolescents' being, inseparable from their existence—we easily take on a theological perspective that forecloses and therefore overemphasizes the revealed, near and rational. So as youth workers we try to become the one who reveals God, brings God near and makes a rational case for faith. And the "where" of God itself becomes locked in the growth of the adolescent's faith, in the adolescent's achievement in the Christian life and in the adolescent's participation in godly activities. In other words, the "where" of God becomes bound in adolescent development: God is everywhere, as long as you keep developing and don't acknowledge the nightmare in your closet.

Yet there is a nightmare in our closet, a nightmare that we experience throughout the converging and diverging stages of life, a nightmare that cannot be disentangled from our ontological state.[4] We must always be wrestling with the reality of non-being, with the truth that nothingness is our destiny, as nothingness even now exists within us; we are always pulled into crisis (as we examined in chapter five). Three-year-olds have bad dreams, fathers go through midlife crises and infants yearn for the face of their mother because to live, to be, is always to be close to non-being.[5] We cannot *be* (and sooner or later will cease to be), but nevertheless, we are. If there is anything distinctive about the adolescent's developmental location it is that he or she confronts forcefully the dichotomy and struggle between nothingness and possibility.[6]

The journey of adolescence is not ontologically about growth, advancement and preparation but rather about recognizing (in head and heart) the possibilities for being and yet the thinness of it. Indeed, adolescence may be the time when we become sensitive to (and able to contemplate) our ontological state; we are aware both that there is possibility before us and that this possibility floats on the treacherous rapids of nothingness.[7] For example, the thought and experience of love is rich and the electricity is kinetic in adolescence, making the world's colors brighter. But the possibility of love comes with the awareness and experience that human love so often fails, and when it fails it brings with it a rush of annihilation. Bright colors give way to the gray, overcast burden of death. Life is to be lived, but life must be lived next to death, love must be lived next to hate, hope next to despair, dreams next to disappointment. The reality of truth cannot be avoided: to live is a great joy, but to live is also to encounter death and all its friends around every corner of possibility.[8]

Even more than being the time when we become sensitive to our ontological state, adolescence may be the period when the non-being that is true for us all throughout life seems closest to the surface, as the armor of denial, the armor of societal (and religious) avoidance of nothingness, is still too new, too big and too awkward to protect us from all the arrows of nothingness that never stop their onslaught on our being. As adults, mortgages, careers and 401(k)s have the power to distract us from the nearness of nothingness; they can deceive us into thinking that all that exists is possibility, that we need not dwell on nothingness. Adolescents, no doubt, have their own armor (SAT scores, friendship groups, sports and new jeans), but the young person's armor can feel ever so flimsy in the constant flow of change, with the cultural reality that possibility is ahead and their future is still to be written, yet they are dependent on others. A bad look, a bad grade, a break-up, family chaos and the nightmares in the closet show their face and whisper their threat: "Possibility may be before you, but you will never escape the nothingness."

When we assert that God is everywhere and this everywhere-ness is bound in the revealed, near and rational, then God can only be discovered in growth, advancement and attention to preparation. The perfect shiny kids (those growing, advancing and attentive to their preparation) are the poster children of serious faith. We give them the belief that if they do everything right, then their faith must be strong and true, and they will get what they want in life; in other words, we imply that they can control life. It then becomes our job as youth workers to get young people to grow, advance and be attentive by seeing God, being near to God and thinking correctly about God.

When we do this, though, we ignore that our very ontology is being-toward-death. We ignore that adolescence at its core is an awakening to the fact (the fact that is true for us all) that life is the journey between possibility and nothingness. When God is everywhere, there is possibility (though admittedly abstract), but there is no room for nothingness. And without encountering nothingness, we have little to say about "where," concretely, God is found; all we have are abstractly fluffy words like "everywhere," "here" and "near." In essence, when we say that God is everywhere we refuse to see reality, and fail to stand between possibility and nothingness, to do ministry and theology between them, to name God's "where" alongside possibility and nothingness. And we fail to see that the God of Israel is a God who brings possibility out of nothingness.

In the process, we ignore that young people are exposed to the stiff winds of nothingness, and that a God who is everywhere provides no shelter. For in the end, this God who is everywhere is nowhere; this God who is everywhere has not known annihilation and nothingness and death. So he cannot be here in the swirling fear of a three-year-old, because this everywhere God has not known a moment when nothingness wraps itself around your being and suffocates it in fear, loss or dread.[9] In short, up against suffering, yearning and brokenness, a God that is everywhere is no help, for this God has yet to know, from the inside, the suffering, yearning and brokenness of our humanity.

If God cannot be *here* in fear, then youth ministry is only for those kids who are positive, optimistic and whole. Young people who cannot meet this checklist are inevitably led to believe that, if they can't get better, God is not for them. And there are few (very few) who can meet this checklist and make it through adolescence without experiencing fear or pain. On the contrary, most young people are acutely aware of it. Yet we're not providing theological and practical perspectives that help them confront and seek God in the midst of suffering. Instead, their yearnings are *often* peripheral, not central, in our ministries. And in relegating their suffering, yearning and brokenness to the periphery, we may be keeping them from a faith that can help them face the rest of their lives.

THE EARLY REFORMATION AND THE *VIA NEGATIVA*

In many ways the early Reformation revolved around the question, "Where is God?" Was God, for instance, found in the bureaucratic operations of the church? Was God, and was God's forgiveness, found in the church's sanctioned indulgences? In the period of late scholasticism on into the early Reformation, theological construction of the "where" of God was worked out in dialectics. True statements made about God's "where," like God being revealed, near and rational (or able to be thought of), had to be balanced by looking at their opposites. In other words, you had to go the way of the negative *(via negativa)* to step into the inner reality of the rich theological meaning of these assertions of God's "where."[10] Following this, then, to claim that God is revealed, we must be able to claim that God is hidden; to claim that God is near to us, we must be able to claim God's absence; to claim that faith is a possibility for us, we must claim that it is absurd.[11]

The early Reformers had to do this, for in their context, the revealed, near and rational perspective clearly put the human being in charge of God: it was human action that initiated divine action, the human agent was in control of God, and God was everywhere the church was, even in its corruption. In other words, God was present whenever the coffers of the pope rang with the sound of another coin.

But there was more than just this reason. Luther particularly understood that working the negative, or the opposite, pushes our theological construct into the ontological reality of nothingness. If God is hidden, absent and absurd, then not only can God not be caged in human systems, but also we are directed toward a God who stands between possibility and nothingness, bearing both.[12]

If we take on the *via negativa*—saying outright that God is absent, hidden, *not* there, and that our faith is *not* rational but absurd, which therefore allows us to hold together the seeming opposites of revealed/hidden, near/absent, rational/absurd—then we have a theological imagination that can speak to our ontological struggle between possibility and nothingness.[13] Jüngel says it this way: "The presence and absence of God are no longer to be thought of as alternative in the word of God. Rather, God is present as the one absent in the word."[14] In the midst of the dialectic of nearness and absence, we are forced to look concretely for God's "where" not as a final destination but as an encounter. As Jürgen Moltmann explains, "It is the dialectical knowledge of God in his opposite which first brings heaven down to the earth of those who are abandoned by God, and opens heaven to the godless."[15] It is between possibility and nothingness that we encounter otherness, and it is between possibility and nothingness that we encounter ourselves. And if adolescence is the time when we are sensitive to this reality, sensitive to the possibility that is before us but also oh-so-aware that with possibility comes many forms of nothingness, then working with this dialectic may be how we begin to articulate the "where" of God in young peoples' lives.[16]

The cross. Where then is God, if God is not everywhere? Jüngel reminds us, "Theology can do its assigned task only when, in answering the question 'Where is God?,' it does not refer solely to 'above us.' God is also below us. And that is the very way in which he is God."[17] According to Jüngel, following Luther, God is on the cross. God is on the cross as revealed and hidden, near and absent, rational and absurd. It is God, a crucified God that takes death into Godself, who sinks deeply into nothingness; God as the fullness of possibility completely takes on nothingness, bringing possibility itself out of nothingness. As Moltmann has argued, the fullness of the nothingness of death comes upon the Son, as the soul-tearing loss of one loved swallows the Father.[18] After the crucifixion, nothingness exists in the inner life of the Trinity itself, and it is out of this nothingness that God has made new possibility. It is out of the nothingness and through the nothingness of death that God forms the possibility of community between God and humanity and (as we will see) humanity and humanity.[19] The Trinity, then, exists between possibility and nothingness, and the crucified God reveals that it is out of nothingness that God creates all possibility. Jüngel says it like this: "The fundamental aspect of the victory over death is not the 'standing outside of nothingness' *(extra nihilum sistere)* which flees from nothingness, but rather the creative 'standing into nothingness' *(in nihilum sistere)*."[20]

When we say that God is everywhere we have lost the concreteness of the encounter of God. In other words, we do not have a God who acts. But in the cross, God acts as God encounters death for life; God takes on nothingness for the purpose of new (redefined) possibility.[21] It is the Creator who enters hell and creates out of it. It is the Creator as Reconciler who enters hell and nothingness to bring life and redemption.

The cross, then—the cross as concrete encounter in history—stands between possibility and nothingness and holds in tension the revealed, near and rational with the hidden, absent and absurd. God is revealed through the hiddenness of the peasant from Nazareth;[22] God is near through the absence of death on the cross; God is worth following in the absurdity of his power being born in powerlessness and his kingdom being won in suffering, in the first being last and the last being first.[23] Moltmann states, "When the crucified Jesus is called the 'image of the invisible God,' the meaning is that this is God, and God is like this. God is not greater than he is in this humiliation. God is not more glorious than he is in this self-surrender. God is not more powerful than he is in this helplessness. God is not more divine than he is in this humanity."[24] God is revealed in God's hiddenness through the incognito of humanity, and God is near in his absence in the suffering and nothingness of the cross. In paradoxical nature, then, hiddenness, absence and absurdity are pathways to speak of God's concrete "where," because they directly touch our ontological state—a state that God, through Christ, now shares.[25]

The revelation of God cannot be held within the everywhere-ness of creation or moral orders. It is found instead in the specificity (and yet universality) of suffering, the suffering of hiddenness and absence.[26] Through the cross, God turns suffering and nothingness into the location of God's presence. Thus, it is not growth, advancement and preparation that bring us close to the crucified God (this is the very *theologia gloriae* that Luther opposes). Rather it is in suffering, despair and nothingness that we encounter the actuality of God. But this cannot be a fabricated or produced suffering and despair, or a kind of acetic masochism.[27] It can only be the suffering and despair of the nothingness that exists in our world and touches so deeply the ontological reality of nothingness within us.

In our work with young people, then, we have a clash, because on the one hand we want to hold up and celebrate those youth who are role models of good citizenship, those seen as engaged students and successful leaders. But in truth they are not necessarily role models of faith, for our faith calls us to search for God between possibility and nothingness, between hope and despair (between the existential and eschatological, as we sketched out in the last chapter). In this theological perspective, the supposed loser young people—those invisible adolescents—are the ones where, in fact, God is at work, up against their brokenness and yearning. The incarnate and crucified God calls us to search for God not in the fullness of success but in the emptiness of honest yearning.

So when Owen asks me where Jesus is, I can only answer that Jesus is here if I am able (and willing) to say that he is on the cross, that he is being overwhelmed with the same nothingness that threatens Owen's being. I must answer that God is *not* here like good thoughts, a poem or a word of encouragement; God is absent to such conceptions of Godself, for God is being crucified by death and all its friends, the same friends that now scare Owen.

And what about the cross in youth ministry? The cross has *not* been something that we have forgotten in North American youth ministry. Indeed, we discuss it often, explaining that our sins are forgiven through Jesus' death, and calling young people to claim the significance of the cross for their own lives. They, in turn, wear crosses on their T-shirts, as jewelry or as tattoo art, which somehow makes them representatives for God (their actions become, and can even control, God's presence). Our focus on the cross, however, has rarely set the terms for how we discuss God's "where." Rather, we have seen the cross solely as a sign of victory, as a static reality that provides something—not as the very state of God's being and acting in the world. The problem with viewing the cross as a static sign of victory is that the cross becomes a declaration of control, finality and certainty: God, through the cross, achieves complete control of the sinful world, finally conquering it, and becomes ultimately supreme. In this perspective, the cross is a sign of God's abstract everywhere-ness and has nothing to do with hiddenness, absence and absurdity—which means that, in the end, the cross has little to do with the nothingness of our ontological state, and little to do with a God who joins God's very person with our nothingness.

In truth, the cross is only a sign of victory in that it is a sign of limit and death. It is in resurrection that we see victory and hope, that we see the fullness of possibility—a possibility made actual by going through death. It is in the cross that we see nothingness, that God and God with us comes nose to nose with death and all death's friends. Jüngel explains this powerfully: "Talk about the death of God would then imply that God is in the midst of the struggle between nothingness and possibility. It corresponds to God's deity, and certainly does not contradict it. . . . Of course, the essence of God can no longer be put outside of this struggle, and one can no longer define God as an essence 'above us' *(supra nos)*. Rather, the essence of God is to be thought as being absolutely identical with his existence."[28]

The cross does achieve something. It is the backward battle with nothingness, the battle that overcomes nothingness, by being enveloped by nothingness. And it is a witness to God's economy where nothingness is only beaten by taking on nothingness. Indeed, the cross reveals "where" God is: in places of nothingness, making possibility out of impossibility, making life out of death. God does this making by taking on death so fully that nothingness is drawn into God's history. The cross is the sign that God will make life out of death, but it is just as much a sign that God makes Godself known in the hiddenness and absence of suffering, loss, yearning and brokenness. As Moltmann says, "If one describes the life of God within the Trinity as the 'history of God' (Hegel), this history of God contains within itself the whole abyss of godforsakenness, absolute death and the non-God."[29] When the cross is a sign of limit and death, it is a sign that God has entered fully into our ontological state, that God can now be found between possibility and nothingness.[30] *That is God's very "where"—in those places where the heaviness of nothingness is borne and yet out of the backwardness of bearing comes possibility.*[31]

So then, Where is God? Where do we encounter concretely this God who stands between possibility and nothingness? It is in our suffering and despair; it is within the negation in ourselves and the world that we find the God of the cross; it is up against our ontological reality of nothingness that yearns from the same ontological core for possibility. Hall states, "So, Luther's Christ forever returns to his cross; to his grave, to hell, in order to be 'with us.' He can be for us only insofar as he is with us."[32] Youth ministry, then, can never be about avoiding or ignoring suffering, yearning, loss and brokenness. It can never be about creating a group of model adolescents for our own glory. Rather, youth ministry that seeks to encounter the crucified God seeks for God within nothingness, and stands with young people between possibility and nothingness.

Where is God? God is *not* everywhere, but specifically there, there up against our pain, there up against our questions, there up against our broken dreams. And in that *particular* sense God is "everywhere"—everywhere there is pain and suffering. Anna Madsen writes, "Luther was eager to explain that Christ is *where* any sorrow or suffering exists, both of which . . . concerns death."[33] It is when we encounter the fear, loss, yearning and brokenness that we have encountered concretely the crucified God.

Moreover, when *we* (you and I) bear our nothingness together, God works to bring possibility out of our despair. God is here when I encounter you. In my bravery to stand with you in fear, longing and brokenness, I speak of God's hiddenness, absence and absurdity by bearing with you your suffering. But in standing within it and sharing it we recognize that God is revealed and near in our shared life.

So where then is Jesus, Owen? Jesus is there; Jesus is found at the location of your fear; Jesus is bearing your fear. To claim that Jesus is concretely located next to Owen's fear is to assert that Jesus is on the cross; it is to place the "where" of God at the level of what is concretely real to him, at the place of his suffering, fear, yearning and brokenness. Jesus is here hidden within it, for he is suffering it, so that out of Owen's fear might spring possibility.

Even to this response Owen would have rebutted, "But I don't see Jesus!" And I would respond, "No, but you see Daddy. Look at your Daddy; I see your fear. I feel your fear." When he looks at me, his fear no longer determines his reality, though its actuality is heavy. Rather, our shared life becomes his reality, for I see his suffering, and it is in our bearing of each other's nothingness that we encounter the God of possibility. What Owen was searching for was another to see the nothingness that surrounds him; he was seeking for me to first deny the everywhere God so that a space might be opened to encounter God not beyond, around or outside his fear, but within it. And only after I have joined him in his despair am I ready to see the location of God.

God is found concretely at the place where persons share deeply in the nothingness of each other, for in so doing we follow the One who was crucified and made nothingness. But in shared life through suffering, we also witness beyond the nothingness of crucifixion to the possibility of resurrection, to the hope of restoration, healing and peace. When your suffering is shared in my person—when I see it, name it and open my person to your fear—it has become the suffering of the cross, for I witness in my person that your suffering is shared suffering: God is found in your suffering, bringing life from death.

WHAT DOES THIS MEAN FOR US?

Answering the "where" question in this way forces us to see our ministries and our very selves in ministry differently. We begin to see young people as similar to us in that they, too, have their being between possibility and nothingness. And the nothingness of existence becomes the curriculum for our youth ministry, because it is *both* the call to seek the "where" of God and the way to join deeply in adolescents' lives. Through our shared life, then, we encounter the "where" of God—but only as far as our lives are really shared, only as far as we are willing to see and be near to their nothingness. This can only occur if we see our vocation not as revealing God, bringing God near to them and making faith rational but ultimately as walking near the nothingness of adolescents by being in relationship with them. When we truly share in their lives in this way, we witness to a God who is revealed in hiddenness, who is near in weakness and suffering, and who calls us into the absurd backwardness of following a God who brings possibility out of nothingness.

Ministry, then, becomes seeking God as we share in the longings, fragile hopes and deep doubts of young people. These longings, hopes and doubts are not problems that we need to solve for them so that we can move on to something else. Rather, when God is found between possibility and nothingness on the cross, longings, fragile hopes and doubts become the very curriculum and direction of our ministries. The questions—not answers—borne from our ontological state become the focus of our ministries. Hall asks a helpful question that can easily be directed specifically to youth workers: "Too many Christians seem to feel that their primary calling is to provide answers. Might it not be that our better service is to give a language and a spiritual vantage point from which to explore the great questions of our age? The trouble with most answers . . . is that they are usually provided by persons who have not lived long enough with the questions."[34]

When we share in nothingness as we long for possibility, ministry becomes focused on seeking for the hidden/absent God in the brokenness of our being. Making young people right no longer becomes the goal. Rather, the goal is to share in their impossibility as we await God's possibility, which comes only through nothingness. So we call them to search for God in their wounds and through their doubts. We speak about the absence of God with them, inviting them into a community of shared suffering where they can explore the perplexing nothingness in our societal structures and ourselves. We help them name the absence of God, and see the nothingness within themselves and around them. For only when they can see the absence of God can God become an actual subject to them; only then does God have a "where."

When ministry becomes about proclaiming and joining the "where" of God, we are freed from being either sellers of the faith or the moral police. If God is everywhere, if adolescence is about growth, advancement and preparation, if the Christian faith is about control, finality and certainty, then the practice of ministry revolves around convincing young people to somehow trust in and seek this nebulous God by avoiding things that would hamper their growth, advancement and preparation and by committing to the control, finality and certainty of Christianity. But when the "where" of God is encountered in the nothingness of the cross, which joins our own suffering, yearnings and brokenness, then ministry is, at its core, about being someone who can bear reality with young people. Then it is about being able to "call a thing what it is," being able to see suffering, loss and hurt and not turn from it and, indeed, even join young people in it as we seek for God's possibility.

When we train volunteers and new youth workers we are often concerned about giving them techniques and perspectives that can help them *do* good ministry and be successful. What is central instead is to help budding youth workers be bearers of reality, to help them be able to see, feel and attend to nothingness. We must encourage them to use their theological imagination to become comfortable with the existential anxiety that plagues most of us (themselves included) rather than fleeing from it. We may even need some theological perspective ourselves—perspective that touches our person enough to lead us out to search for God in the heavy nothingness of existence, and that helps us to be people always searching for the "where" of God alongside adolescents. And to see that this is the most beautiful thing that has ever been!

This means that we are the ones who must be able to speak of God's absence, hope with young people in darkness and search with young people through their deepest doubt. And in the paradoxical nature of the cross, by doing this we are able to speak concretely of the "where" of God. For we communicate with our words and with our presence in the adolescent's nothingness that God is there, that God is found in the feelings and actuality of Godforsakenness, that God is near in the midst of yearning that's up against impossibility, that God is found at the place of the struggle between possibility and nothingness.

• DISCUSSION AND REFLECTION EXERCISE
A Quote to Affirm, a Quote to Deny

Choose from within this chapter one quote that you wish to affirm and one quote that you wish to challenge.[35] A quote may be chosen, for example, because you find it insightful or wrong or simply confusing. Then present these quotes in small groups, allowing for discussion after each person presents theirs.

The exercise will help you start reading theology in a way that doesn't demand that you be able to comprehend every element of the argument. Rather, this approach honors ideas, asking each person to find an idea (quote) or two that draws them into thinking more deeply.

PART TWO

THEOLOGY ENACTED

Exploring Youth Ministry Practice

8

IS JESUS MAGIC?

Healing and the Cross in Youth Ministry

ANDREW ROOT

As we read through the syllabus together on the first day of class, it became clear which topic was most significant to Natalie. I had just explained that on Friday of this one-week intensive course we would look at a case study in which someone prays for healing but never receives it. "Great! I can't wait to talk about that," Natalie said. And she said it with a force and engagement that demonstrated that her interest was much more than just intellectual; there was something personal about the topic that she was carrying with her into the course.

That Friday afternoon we began to look in-depth at the case study. It told the story of a high-school girl who was paralyzed at gymnastics camp. As she sat in the hospital unable to move, her father continued to pray for her, convinced that through deep prayer his daughter would be healed. After weeks of (what he interpreted as) failed prayers, he blamed his daughter, rationalizing that she simply didn't have enough faith that God would heal her. At the end of the case study, the students were told that the girl—whose father now refused to see her until she had enough faith—has phoned them and wants to talk. She desires a theological response to her father. Is he right? Does she lack faith? How and why does God heal some and not others?

Halfway through our conversation that Friday, Natalie couldn't contain herself any longer. "Why? Why does God not answer some prayers? I just don't get it! My friend Amanda is just struggling in life. She suffers from crippling depression and nothing helps. She really loves God and my friends and I have prayed constantly for her, but nothing helps. I don't get it! She feels like a failure, and so do we because we can't help her."

Acknowledging Natalie's deep pain and her friend Amanda's as well, I invited the class to look again at Matthias Grunewald's *Crucifixion*, a painting we had been using all week as a window into God's Ministry for the world through the church. We often forget to whom we pray for healing, I explained to them. Too often we imagine we are praying to the Jesus of Sunday school curriculum pictures, one who is clean and powerful, strolling through Galilee as confident as an all-pro football player and as powerful as a ruling politician. But it isn't the powerful, dominating Jesus that we pray to for healing, for this is not the Jesus of the Gospels. Rather, the Jesus to whom we pray is the beaten one; the crucified is the healing Lord. He who hangs on the cross, praying himself for God's rescue and yet hearing nothing, is the God that we come to asking for healing. We plead to the Jesus who himself pleads vigorously for the cup to be removed from him but whose request is met only with silence. The Jesus abandoned on the cross, whose father is witnessing the loss of his beloved son into the dark night of death, is the Jesus we pray to. Amanda and her friends pray to the Jesus who begs for God's intervention and yet is left to die in the vacuum of God's absence.

MAGICAL JESUS

Sometimes I think we imagine that the crucifixion is a ritual (maybe right out of Hogwarts) that earns Jesus the magic to free us from having to live in a world of suffering, a world where pain, brokenness, atrophy and death surround us and cannot be escaped. Or we may believe that Jesus provides a kind loophole of shelter that we can enter when safety from suffering and tragedy is needed. When my wife was a child, the media was, at one point, covering a number of cases of small children being kidnapped. Somehow she came to believe that if she was kidnapped, all she had to do was say to the culprit, "Unhand me in the name of Jesus!" and like a magical incantation, the culprit would release her and she would be safe. After all, she was told in her congregation that "the name of Jesus is powerful." But what kind of power are we talking about: the power of the cross or the power of magic?

A few years ago the comedian Sarah Silverman released a stand-up act in theaters and on DVD called *Jesus Is Magic*. Silverman, both inappropriately crass but also hilarious, explains in one of the early bits of her act how she would explain to her future children the difference between her Jewish religious background and that of her Christian boyfriend. In her deadpan manner she says, "We'll just be honest. We'll say 'Mommy is one of the chosen people, and Daddy believes that Jesus is magic.'" I think Silverman's commentary is right: most Christians do believe that Jesus is magic. Yet if Jesus is magic, then Natalie and Amanda are right to feel abandoned and neglected by God. If Jesus has the potion to shrink the tumor, repair the spine or erase the depression but refuses to use it for us and those we love, then we are left with few conclusions: either we have failed in the technique of our faith or God is a monster (or, at the very least, inconsistent, arbitrary and uncaring).

But Jesus isn't magic. Jesus is human. Jesus is the very incarnation of God; he's God with us—to bring us not magic but accompaniment, not "healing" (a quick solution to a problem) but salvation (intimacy with God and one another). Any healing that is more than a temporary solution—that is, in other words, transformation (and therefore feels like or *is* salvation)—demands deep accompaniment. It demands that another enter into my world and bear my suffering not to magically take it away but to die with me if needed. In my darkest moments, what my heart yearns for more than a solution is a companion, someone who will link their heart to mine and assure me that no matter how ugly or scary things might get, I am not alone. The cross reveals this Jesus: not a magical one but a suffering one, not a God who takes away pain but a God who joins us in it.

WHAT ABOUT THE MIRACLES IN THE GOSPELS?

Stories in the Gospels may be the reason why most people believe that Jesus is magic. Turning water into wine, multiplying fish and bread, raising dead children and friends, and casting out demons all seem like magical acts. The second-to-last act of the story then seems shockingly out of place as this magical Jesus hangs pathetically on a cross.

But most biblical scholars tell us that miracle stories are not stories of magic but rather stories which preview God's future. Jesus proclaims in word and act the future of creation in the future of God. In other words, Jesus declares and then represents in his actions what this future will be, what the world will be like in the end (this end has been called the *eschatos* and the study of it *eschatology*, as I already subjected you to in part one). Every miraculous act of Jesus is therefore a proclamation, a momentary and episodic lifting of the curtain to reveal the future of creation. Jesus states with such acts that in the end, in the future of God, death will have no place, everything will be in its right mind, hunger will be unknown, and all humanity will feast and celebrate without end in the presence of a loving father.

Of course, these acts are only a picture, a representation of the end (the *eschatos*), not its fulfillment. For instance, the raising of Lazarus reveals that one day all will be called from death to life to be embraced by Jesus, but of course Lazarus did die again. In the same way, the bread that was multiplied provided strength and joy to empty stomachs, a sign that one day stomachs will never be empty, but just hours later, poor children who were fed on the hillside returned home with stomachs that ached for more bread. And though the best wine was brought last, pointing to a future where feasting, laughing and worship will never end, that party ended, and the jugs of the best wine made from water lay empty. The miracles of Jesus are not the thing; the acts that look magic are not what is important. What is important is what these miraculous healing acts point to and reveal: they show us who Jesus is; they disclose that he is the fulfillment, that he is the end, that in his person is the future of humanity in the future of God. The miracles are not the thing; Jesus is the thing.

This then leads us back to Jesus on the cross, the beaten one, the one forsaken by God. When we pray for healing we are asking not for magic but for a glimpse, a hint, a limited experience of the end, of what will be in the *eschatos*. We acknowledge that it is only a taste, that even the child cured will one day be the adult buried. And we recognize that in this world (which is not the end), healing, safety and peace are not normative. Rather, the norm—the regular—is sickness, atrophy, danger and violence. Because this is our norm, we need a God who bears it. Because this is the world in which we must live, we need a God who enters it. Because death cannot be escaped, we need a Jesus who is not magic but rather is present, bearing the normative suffering of a dangerous world in his own body. We need a Jesus who pleads for healing and hears only silence.

The beaten and crucified Jesus has entered and made himself known in a world where the norm is suffering and death. Therefore we cannot *solely* equate healing and health with God's presence and suffering with God's absence. For if those who are suffering and receiving prayer experience nothing from God, they may feel like the exception and be led to assume that they have done something wrong spiritually; so many other Christians testify to healing and health, they reason, so their suffering must be abnormal, or somehow their fault. But the God of the cross reveals that it is normal to suffer. God's presence is found first not in acts of healing but in suffering and feelings of abandonment.

As youth workers we must therefore first acknowledge the presence of God not with those who've been healed but with those who are suffering. To be healed in this world is to be abnormal (even in the economy of God). It is neither earned nor normative but rather is simply a gift to the community, a small window into the future. Healing is wonderful, but weird; it is to be celebrated but not glorified; it is to be deeply appreciated, but not overly examined. To suffer, however, is to be embraced by the crucified God; to hear no answer to your pleas for help is to find communion with One crucified. So when someone is healed we can be thankful, but when someone suffers without healing, their perceived Godforsakenness is the very thing that assures us that they are with God and God is for them.

One of my theological mentors, Dr. Ray Anderson, used to describe the following scenario:

> When you're a pastor and someone stands and says, "Last night our daughter was driving home in the pouring rain. She hit a slick spot, slid into the ditch and flipped her car three times, totaling it, but she walked away without a scratch. The officer on the scene said it was a miracle she was alive! We just want to thank God for protecting her," what should you say? You should go over to the couple in the corner who lost their son in a hiking accident two months ago, and standing next to them, you should say, "We praise God that your daughter is okay, but we also remember Jan and Tim, and know that God is with them also as they grieve the loss of Eric."

We might do the same with young people. When Matt stands and announces that his prayers have been answered and he has been accepted to his dream school, we should go and stand with Beth, who has received several rejections, and say, "We praise God for this, Matt, but we also know that God is at work and is with others who have suffered so much disappointment lately." Of course in doing this, *we are not desiring suffering, and never should,* but suffering, as those not healed know full well, cannot be avoided in this world.

FOR THE COMMUNITY

When someone is healed the community must celebrate, thanking and praising God for it. But our praise and thanks is never simply for the individual person, or for the purpose of receiving more healing, as if it were a commodity to be bargained for. Rather, in witnessing healing we thank and praise God and plead with God to bring God's future, to bring the end, to make what is abnormal normal for *all* people. And we can be confident that this future is on the way because the One who was crucified and forsaken by God has passed through death and has been resurrected by God. Jesus was not healed but resurrected; he was not given an extension to his life but new (everlasting) life, and not a repaired body but a new body. Through him this will be our future also: a life beyond all that threatens us.

This is what I tried to say to Natalie that day—that Amanda's feelings of Godforsakenness are the very sacraments of God's presence. And even in the hell of depression she can be assured that she is never alone and that she is embraced by the crucified God who promises a future where depression will evaporate in God's presence. But for now, her struggle and lack of healing do not make her abnormal or point to failed prayers or weak faith. Indeed, in this world suffering and brokenness are the norm. The good news is that her struggle is with the absence of God, which leads right to God's very presence—a presence that accompanies her now and promises a future where her struggles will cease forever in the ceaseless love of the God who overcomes this world by suffering it.

• DISCUSSION AND REFLECTION EXERCISE
Find an Illustrative Quote

Divide into small groups.[1] Each person should read to the group a quote or two they found in their reading of the chapter. These might be quotes they found challenging or helpful, or ones that they see as the key thesis of the chapter. The idea is to get the discussion to focus on the text itself. Therefore, each person should refer directly to the page and place of their quote. Any response to a quote must also refer back to the text itself.

It is important that this time not frustrate participants or keep them from adding their own personal connections, critique or affirmation.

Rather, this exercise helps the discussion focus on the text at hand and not become lost (as too often happens) in anecdotal or tangent perspectives. After each person has had the opportunity to read a quote and responses that refer directly to the text have been shared, allow for more free-flowing conversation and connection.

9

TALKING ABOUT SIN
WITH YOUNG PEOPLE

ANDREW ROOT

There's nothing like a theological conversation with an eighth grader to alert you to the gap in your doctrinal understanding. All of us who have worked with adolescents have had the experience of sitting in a cabin or around a campfire as the discussion progresses from casual and light to an in-depth theological dialogue for which we soon realize we are not prepared. The pimpled-face skater who hasn't sat still for more than two seconds throughout the conversation now seems to take on another personality as he asks intensely, "What really is sin? When do I know I've sinned? How do I keep from sinning? And if I am a sinner, and that's my nature, how is it possible to keep from sinning?"

If you're like me, you may have balked in the face of such questions, perhaps quoting a Bible verse in the hopes that it will distract (or rather "redirect") from the significant questions being asked. Surely we all have some foundational comprehension of what sin is, some scripts to fall back on that we learned in Sunday school (e.g., "All have sinned and fall short of the glory of God" and "All sins are equal"—though note that one of these is a Bible verse while the other is *not*). But if we are honest we must admit that many of those scripts sound hollow and, for the intense inquisitor and his handful of skeptical on-listeners, no doubt banal.

We may assuage our guilt over our ignorance and justify our confusion by claiming that such deep theological conversations are helplessly complex and abstract, and that good youth workers keep abstraction and adolescence in distinct corners—so we are therefore free to ignore the directness of the inquiry.

Yet as theologian Reinhold Niebuhr is credited as saying, "Sin is the only empirically provable Christian doctrine." All it takes is an honest look at society or ten minutes in front of the local news to verify that sin is a real thing. And while acknowledging its empirical existence does not help us—or the young people with whom we work—to understand it, if it is true that "all have sinned" (Rom 3:23) and that Christ died for us "while we were still sinners" (Rom 5:8) then there is great significance in grasping what this opaque doctrine is all about.

So how should we think about sin in light of ministry with young people? Hopefully reflecting on this question will equip us with something to say to our fervent young questioners beyond our old scripts and empower them to see the doctrine's relevance in their lives and the world.

SIN VERSUS SINNING

Original sin, or what has grossly (but no doubt rightly) been called the "total depravity" of humanity, has been a tenet of the Christian faith since the time of Augustine, with strong antecedents going back to Pauline theology, especially the letter to the Romans. This doctrine, rightly understood, makes it clear that there's a difference between *sin* (the state of our being) and *sinning* (the bad or wrong things we do).

We commit sins, of course, but this is because we live in a *state* of sin. Far too often, what adolescents understand about *sin* is only their actions of *sinning*. They fail to recognize that *all* humanity is under the shadow of sin, no matter how good or bad; if you are human, you live in the reality of sin, the reality of brokenness. *Sin* is the name used to describe the state of the broken relationship, at its most fundamental, between God and humanity. Therefore, while sin left unchecked can lead to deep and radical evil, it is primarily a reality born in tragedy.

Adam and Eve were created to be with God and to be for one another, but they chose against God and blamed one another. This destroyed their communion with God, leaving them alone in the world. The rest of humanity, in turn, chose sin over God too—chose to define itself apart from its Creator—therefore tragically breaking relationship with its very source of life.

Karl Barth explains the difference between sin and sinning this way: "Particular sins do not alter the status of a [person]; they merely show how heavily the general dominion of Sin presses upon him [or her]. Sin is the sovereign power in the world as we know it; and it is wholly irrelevant what particular form it takes in the life of each individual."[1] According to Barth, then, we are not sinful because of the bad or wrong things we do; we do bad, wrong and (sometimes) evil things because we live in a reality of sin. Too often in youth ministry we confuse adolescents by making sin a riddle to solve ("How can I live without sinning?") and a problem around which to maneuver rather than a tragic reality of brokenness that is both detrimental and unavoidable. I have sat in small groups with adolescent boys, both as an adult leader and as an adolescent participant, where the conversation centered around Jesus' words in Matthew 5:27-28 that looking on a woman with lust in your heart is sin (adultery). Rather than focusing on how we can live in ways that uphold the integrity and humanity of the women we meet in a culture that frequently objectifies women, we dwelt on the impossible quandary of how to "avoid lusting"—in other words, how to avoid having sexual desire toward women.

When we confuse sin with sinning, adolescents often interpret our message as a reminder of their helpless, constant failure. It rattles around in their ears like the many other messages of failure they hear as they seek to discover who they are ("You're a bad soccer player," "You're weak," "You're fat," "Your grades are not up to snuff," "Those thoughts you have make you a sinner!"). Confusing sin with sinning also often pushes young people deeper into isolation, in an attempt to hide their sinfulness, and rarely toward salvation—confessing their sinfulness and finding grace and for-giveness. This happens because they are told of their sinning (lust, theft, cruelty, bitterness, disobedience, etc.) rather than of the tragic reality of sin, which impacts us all—a reality that reveals our shared participation in trag-edy and culpability. If the larger reality of sin, for example, is that we live in a culture that objectifies women, then simply chastising young boys for lusting, or giving them tools or devices to avoid lusting (such as mental gymnastics, prayers, bracelets and accountability partners), never confronts the real reality of sin and its impact on them. Instead it creates cycles of guilt and failure, all the while perpetuating the reality of sin—boys objecti-fying women by making women something to avoid in order to maintain their own purity.

SIN AS DEATH

What then is the concrete, historical and, dare we say *practical,* reality of sin? It's nothing other than death itself. We see the universal, shared presence of sin in all humanity through the reality of death; we know all are sinners for all will die.

There is nothing more concrete than death, nothing more substantive than the tragic reality of relationships and communities broken by accidents, crime and disease. Death undeniably reveals that humanity is frail and weak, that humanity is not in control or in charge. It is in death that we understand the depth of our broken community with God; it is in death that we see the full weight and consequence of sin. God is life and complete being, but humanity's destiny is death and the sure promise of sliding back into non-being: dust to dust. As Barth says, "Death is the divine command—'stop'—and we cannot disobey it. Through its narrow gate we must pass."[2] This omnipresent reality of death concretely reveals the universal reality of sin.

Death also discloses the great difference between humanity and God. In death we hear God's "No"—a No that places again a boundary between us and God, a boundary transgressed in the beginning through the disobedience of Adam and Eve. Their violation was not in eating the fruit (that would be a moralistic example of sinning, and a weird one at that: "eating fruit!"). Rather, by eating the fruit, participating in sinning and inaugurating a reality of sin, they ignored and denied the concrete command of the personal God who established a boundary (see Bonhoeffer's *Creation and Fall*).

So then when the adolescent asks, What is sin? we must reply, it is death. And what is death? Death is non-being. It is living and operating in the No of God. It is ignoring and denying life, which is found only in God's Yes. Death, no doubt, is the end, the finality of life, but death nevertheless makes itself present, walking on the stage of our lives many times before the curtains are down. It rears its ugly head in moments of depression and disappointment, and may be most fully experienced (before the end) in isolation and rejection. (Ask any adolescent being bullied, rejected or abused if such experiences feel like death.) Death breathes down the neck of the child whose father moves to another state after her parents' divorce, only to send an occasional check on her behalf. Death stares into the face of the boy who can't find a seat in the lunchroom, turned away from table after table while everyone watches him shuffle along with his food tray. Death grips with a cold fist the heart of the girl who leaves the slumber party early because she is mocked by those she had called friends. Death is the reality of sin and death is the consequence of sin because death promises (and never fails) to end community (relationship). Death puts final and complete separation between God and humanity and humanity and humanity (parents from children, friends from friends, lovers from lovers).

SINNING AS DEHUMANIZATION

Sin is not only concrete because it means death (nothing is more certain, they say, than death and taxes) but also because this death terror leads us, whether explicitly or implicitly, into acting on its behalf. In other words, actions that isolate, reject and dehumanize others and us come from the fear of death. This is where sin moves into sinning. For instance, I knew of a straight-A student who was so afraid of being rejected from her college of choice, disappointing family and friends, and losing her stellar reputation that she cheated on her SAT test. I also knew an eighth-grade boy who, to those who encountered him at school, was the frightening guy who lied all the time and incessantly tortured the underclassmen. When he disappeared we found out that he was sent away when his elderly grandmother, with whom he lived, became ill, and that he had been living with her because his mother had abandoned him when he was young. Sin is real because death surrounds us and promises to envelope us, and because death does this, we attempt out of fear to protect our own being, our own humanity, even if it means dehumanizing another. When we take such actions we are sinning. But it is important to see that any single action of sinning has been engendered from fear and from the deeper reality of death (Sin).

Sinning, then, is those things I do that deny God (the source of life) and dehumanize my fellow human being or myself. My sinful actions are not wrong because they deny some perfect law of right and wrong. Rather, my actions are wrong and maybe even evil because they ignore or destroy my connection to God and neighbor in an attempt to maintain myself. In this vein, the Ten Commandments are not simply rigid dos and don'ts but are for covenant living, for loving God and neighbor. We see Jesus himself disobey the fourth commandment when he heals a man on the Sabbath, explaining to the Pharisees, "The Sabbath is made for humanity not humanity for the Sabbath" (Mk 2:27). In this act he reminds us that the commandments exist not to make people "good" or to keep people from being "bad" but to facilitate life in the love of God and neighbor. Actions like cheating, lying, stealing and gossiping are wrong because they presume that by hurting another I can restore my own being (was this not the motive for Cain to kill Abel?). Dietrich Bonhoeffer reminds us in *Ethics* that it is not moral absolutes that put a demand for obedience on us but the concrete humanity of our neighbor. This is why Jesus summarizes all the Law of the Torah to the rich young ruler with one phrase: "Love the Lord your God with all your heart, soul, and mind and your neighbor as yourself" (Lk 10:27).

SIN AND SINNING AS BROKEN COMMUNITY

This all means that we can see the reality of sin most clearly in broken community; we can taste death most fully and painfully in estrangement. Persons were made for God and each other, for community. The reality of the sinful world is the tragedy of broken community with both God and neighbor.

Sinning, then, is not a spiritual state in the sense of there being some kind of metaphysical moral rule book we failed to keep, but rather is a social reality, born from the ever-present reality of impending death. It makes our neighbor a tool for our own use; it causes us to ignore the No of God and act instead as though we are God seeking to save ourselves from our own existential state. Sinning breaks down community, thwarts freedom, and sets people in opposition or estrangement, neglecting their responsibility; it makes death (the state of sin) operational and therefore denies that we are accountable to the God of life and to others who live with us. We do dehumanizing things (sinning things) because we fear! We fear death in its myriad faces and thus seek to protect our being from its promised strangling. Yet the fear of death will not release us even if we sacrifice the humanity of our neighbor to it.

SO WHAT DOES THIS ALL MEAN?

When discussing the doctrine of sin with adolescents we must point them not to their subjective inner state to show the reality of sinning, for this can be manipulated. It is not difficult to make adolescents feel guilty or bad about themselves, to make them feel the need for a savior. Rather we must point them to the objective social reality of dehumanization and broken community that they feel and in which they participate: the state of sin and death. How do we know we are sinners? Not because we don't measure up when we try to compare ourselves to a standard of good and find ourselves falling short (having bad thoughts, not praying enough, lying or disobeying). We know we are truly sinners in the moments when we confront a deep fear and find ourselves acting on death's behalf.

One of the moments in my life when I was painfully aware of my own sinfulness happened one night while I was eating dinner in my college cafeteria with some friends and a few acquaintances. An attractive girl whom I had a crush on walked by our table. My friend elbowed me and gestured to her, teasing, "Hey, there she is!" A girl at our table, mistaking her for someone else, asked, "Is that Tami?" Feeling deeply embarrassed, and terrified of being exposed, I answered, "No! I would never like *Tami*. She's ugly!" A minute later, someone stood up to leave from the table behind me. To my horror, it was Tami, who turned to me with a penetrating gaze before walking away. I was flooded with shame and with the awareness that, because I felt threatened, I was willing to sell Tami out to maintain my own standing among my friends. Because I feared the reality of sin—death, estrangement, humiliation—I sinned. In my own weakness and attempts at self-preservation, I dehumanized another person.

Convincing adolescents that they are sinful and have committed many actions of sinning is unnecessary if we free the doctrine from its opaque theological baggage and see sin as death and sinning as dehumanization. What is needed (and perhaps more difficult to do) is for us to invite young people to face death (sin), recognize their weakness and brokenness, and confess their participation in dehumanization (sinning). We need to be talking honestly about the deep pain in the crevices of human experience, both the pain we feel and the pain we inflict on others.

Seeing the doctrine of sin this way means we free it from abstraction and place it in the consciously concrete reality of the adolescent. There is no hidden mystery about sin and sinning then: sin is death and sinning is that which dehumanizes and breaks relationship with God and neighbor. When we proclaim this message the adolescent is not pushed further into shame and estrangement but rather can find solidarity with us. We too have been dehumanized and have dehumanized others; we too are struggling to confront our own death(s); we too are in need of new community that can extend beyond death.

It is this new community that Jesus Christ offers all humanity by taking death unto himself, suffering its wrath all the way to hell and bearing the dehumanizing actions of his contemporaries. The good news of the gospel is only good news if Jesus is the Christ of God who is at the same time the poor weak human Nazarene who was betrayed, dehumanized and put to death by humanity, only to overcome death with life, thereby breaking the power of sin and sinning, of death and dehumanization.

Sin is not a disease and Jesus' atonement a preventative immunization. It cannot be overcome by us, not by praying or trying or striving to be holy and good. Acknowledging sin (death) and our own participation in sinning leads us beyond pointed fingers and labels of who is righteous and who is not, for none are. Instead it pushes us into the arms of a suffering God and a strong Christ who is only so in weakness and who promises us life beyond death (sin) in his own life.

Christ provides us with a community where dehumanization (sinning) has no value, for death (sin) has lost its power. As Paul wrote, "O death, where is thy victory? O death, where is thy sting?" (1 Cor 15:55). We can only find freedom from sin through community with Jesus Christ who overcomes our sinfulness by bearing it.

I never spoke to Tami about what happened after I saw what my comments had done to her. It would have been so easy for me to have avoided the situation, to simply say, "No, that's not Tami," and leave it at that. But I didn't. I was deceived into thinking that I had to fight to defend myself at her expense, so I betrayed her humanity. And I never had the courage to seek her forgiveness. I wish I had been able to go to her and apologize to her for what I said. It would have required me to admit my own weakness, to tell her that I had felt embarrassed and spoke to protect myself without thinking of anyone else. It would have required me to ask her forgiveness. And it would have invited both her and me into the community of broken, sinful, forgiven people whose life is in Christ. Followers of Christ are not sinless, and are not commanded to be sinless. Rather they are those who by the strength of the Spirit are able to ask forgiveness for their participation in sin and seek reconciliation with those whom they've sinned against. They are those who struggle against that urge to protect themselves and seek to resist the pull to dehumanize others. They are those who strive to live in awareness of their own and others' weakness and share the forgiveness and restoration that God offers us in Christ.

So what is sin? And how do I talk about it with young people? Sin is the tragedy of death and estrangement from God that we must bear. And we talk about sin with young people by acknowledging its inescapable reality in the world, and then sharing together in the hope of a human God who bears this tragic reality with us and promises us life beyond it.

• DISCUSSION AND REFLECTION EXERCISE
Imagine

Imagine at home before the session that the author of this chapter will be with your group the next time you meet.[3] Write down your top three questions that you'd like to ask the author.

Participants should then share their questions on a class LISTSERV, bulletin board or chat room so that the group can begin (at least mentally) to cluster the questions. Right before the discussion time, work together to cluster certain questions (combining or eliminating duplicates). Then break up into small groups, with each one taking a cluster of questions to discuss.

HOLDING ON TO OUR KISSES

The Hormonal Theology of Adolescence

KENDA CREASY DEAN

The teenagers I know are both cynical and harshly passionate. What they want is so big, it's hard to get your eye around it at first. Who would've thought that teenagers talking about sex would end up talking about their souls? For that's what they're talking about, isn't it? Not body heat but life everlasting. Not the adventure of skin on skin, but a dinner table in the skies. They have none of our ambivalence—independence versus love, distinction versus belonging. Their struggle is with the world—will it let them lose their loneliness? And how? They want something bigger than themselves to live for, something steadier and stronger than one-on-one love, something I long for and loathe, something eradicating—a "we" in their lives; a family feast that never ends, a tribe of friends, God's will.

KATHY DOBIE, QUOTED IN *YOUTHWORKER JOURNAL*

When my daughter was in kindergarten her teacher sent a note home. "Shannon has been kissing Ken and Danny," the teacher wrote, implying that we had better lay down the law with our daughter about her budding promiscuity. My husband and I told our puzzled five-year-old, in no uncertain terms, that this behavior was off-limits. "But I like to kiss them!" was Shannon's unrepentant response. She likes Ken and Danny, and they (on most days, at least) like her. They all plan to marry each other someday.

This is the same child who, when our family saw Drew Barrymore's snappy but innocent Cinderella in the movie *Ever After,* turned to me during the prince's first kiss and whispered loudly enough to stop traffic in Buffalo: "Is he sticking his tongue in?" (He wasn't.) I wanted to ask, "How do you even *know* about that?!" although all I actually did was choke on my popcorn. After all, we are a household with more communication degrees than anybody needs. We pride ourselves on critical consumption of media, and we congratulate ourselves every time our ten-year-old son complains about it.

But a more honest reading of conditions—both cultural and parental—forces me to admit: of course Shannon "knows about that," and about many other forms of sexual contact from which we think we are shielding her. In a society that reduces the language of desire to sexual conditions, where the media convinces us that people who want to be near one another must use sexual contact to get there, where consumerism transforms intimacy from a quality of relationship into a commodity for consumption, "desire" finally flattens out into precisely the hormonal forms that titillate teenagers and alarm adults.

In such a social context, churches have tended to treat adolescent sexuality as a Hershey's chocolate kiss, given to teenagers with the instructions: "Unwrap it, and then hold onto it tightly—and much later, when you're ready, you can enjoy it." In the meantime, holding on to our kisses has left both adolescents and the church with a pubescent mess on our hands, and not just resulting from chocolate.

Desire represents the primary theological lens of adolescence. The desire for an "other" implicit in teen sexuality is part and parcel to being human, and not just to being adolescent. But the simultaneous sexual and spiritual longing for relationship that constitutes desire is acute during adolescence, and therefore is more vividly rendered in that life stage. Observers of adolescence have always recognized it as both a highly spiritual and an intensely sexual period in the life cycle. Augustine wrote of his own adolescence, "The single desire that dominated my search for delight was simply to love and to be loved."[1] Despite our sexualized culture, desire is both a sexual and a spiritual phenomenon. Far from lamenting this fact, the twenty-first-century church should be wildly thankful. For adolescents' acute desire for "others" calls the church to rescue desire from popular culture's exclusive rights on the subject and to restore its long-forgotten place in Christian tradition.

Hollywood aside, the human desire for "otherness" is not simply or even primarily the foundation for sexual intercourse. Desire serves as the impetus for life with God, marking human beings among all creation as those God desires for companionship. Desire, therefore, serves as the foundation for Christian spirituality and for the communion that stands at the heart of Christian life. Yet for most of the past five hundred years, Christians became accustomed to thinking about spirituality as an expression of religion's polar extremes: on the one hand, treating spirituality as an inward, individualistic thought exercise, and on the other hand treating it as an outward expression of moral conscience. "The road to holiness," as Dag Hammarskjöld once said, "necessarily passes through the world of action."[2] This chapter in contemporary spirituality recalls the twelfth- and thirteenth-century movements inspired by Francis and Dominic. Less developed, according to historian Urban T. Holmes, "is the realization that the body is involved." He writes:

> A satisfying spirituality of sexuality, which is not tinged by a simplistic *apatheia,* is yet to be written. Perhaps it will emerge in the next generation. Certainly the presence of genital arousal in spiritual experience is common and needs to be acknowledged as a positive element—rather than repressed and made a subject of embarrassment.[3]

Holmes's opinion is that, because northern European males are "culturally retarded in regard to our sexuality,"[4] a non-white male or a woman may be better equipped to develop a spirituality of sexuality. Holmes overlooks the potential of adolescents in this regard, male and female alike. Indeed, after centuries of modern rationalism, youth ministry's legacy to the twenty-first-century church may well be adolescents' insistence that desire matters to Christian faith: our longing for intercourse with others merely underscores our profound desire for communion, "at-one-ment," intercourse with God.

INTERCOURSE: IT REALLY IS A TOWN IN PENNSYLVANIA

Maybe I have shocked you. The double entendre is intended, of course. We cannot shake "intercourse's" genital connotations from our media-drenched imaginations—yet the word actually comes from a Latin root that means "to run between," the way a current runs between two objects, connecting them. If you look the term up in the dictionary, you will discover that the preferred meanings for intercourse are "connection" or "communion." In February, the postal workers in an Amish town near my home are deluged by people who want their Valentine's Day cards to bear the local postmark of "Intercourse, Pennsylvania"—so named not for conjugal pleasure, but for being the connecting point between two roads.

As it happens, the Amish are less rattled by the term *intercourse* than many of us, and in fact link the concept to both baptism and courtship. If an adolescent chooses to be baptized in an Amish community (as 85 percent of Amish teenagers do), he or she becomes eligible for marriage.[5] The period preceding baptism, known as the "run around" or "sowing your wild oats" period, gives Amish youth time to interact with their "English" peers and even have some access to media and technology. Before baptism, Amish girls fasten their clothing with buttons and other "worldly" fasteners, but after baptism Amish women (the change in terminology is instant) fasten their dresses with straight pins as they renounce intercourse with "the world." The pins proclaim, quite literally, that in baptism Jesus Christ holds them together in a new way.

Outside of Amish circles, most of us use the word *intercourse* to describe the "current" that runs between two people in the act of sexual exchange. But intercourse—a relationship that begets—also describes the life-giving current that runs between us and God. By claiming that the church should pay at least as much attention to intercourse as teenagers do, I am not suggesting that we relax standards of sexual restraint among either youth or adults (on the contrary, I will argue that chastity is a time-honored Christian practice that youth ministry stands to reclaim). However, it is also true that our society has confused genital intercourse with sacred desire, and an alarming number of contemporary Christians—including a stunning stream of defrocked clergy—behave as though sexuality and spirituality can somehow be separated from one another.[6] Like their ancient forebears, modern gnostics drain Christianity of a full-spectrum theology of desire by convincing us that the route to spirituality is to jettison our sexuality (or vice versa). Yet the separation of sexuality from spirituality inevitably erodes our ethical footing, because it denies a basic tenet of Christian theology: God created sexuality and spirituality as twin paths to Otherness, divinely appointed routes to the God who desires intercourse, or communion, with us.

If desire represents the primary theological lens of adolescence, then youth ministry becomes the point at which Christians should reclaim a theology of desire—not for the sake of youth ministry, but for the sake of the church composed of people created in the image of a desirous God. Not yet fully socialized into the norms of adult culture, and only recently possessing the cognitive structures that enable self-awareness and reflection, adolescents have never separated sex from spirit: falling in love feels like being on holy ground, just as the spiritual connections common at church camps spawn romantic entanglements as well as conversions. Nor has popular culture overlooked the primal connection between sexual and spiritual desire. Like adolescents, who by virtue of both their hopes and their hormones experience sexuality and spirituality in undiluted measure, popular culture has no qualms about supplying adolescents with a theology of its own that *does* unite sexuality and spirituality—far better than the church—and therefore rings true to teenage consumers.

FULL-SPECTRUM DESIRE:
PEOPLE MAGAZINE MEETS THE DESIRE OF GOD

Stories about intercourse are strewn throughout Scripture, but one will suffice. Mark 5:21-43 offers a kind of typology of desire, as well as a brief glimpse into some of Jesus' own ministry with a youth. As the Gospel writer recounts Jesus' healing of Jairus's daughter, complete with that embarrassing interruption by a bleeding woman, we see Jesus responding to three kinds of desire: *popular* desire, *pastoral* desire and *personal* desire.

The story starts with *popular* desire. A full day of casting out demons already under his belt, Jesus heads for the other side of the lake, only to be mobbed by a crowd. Today it might have been a shot for *People* magazine: the shoving celebrity-seekers, the hungry autograph hounds, the paparazzi and the tourists all clamoring to get a good close-up of the Son of Man on their iPhones and digital cameras. As it is, the scene depicts the raw desire of popular culture, willing consumers of intercourse swayed by the promise that the current of charisma is contagious: a bit of celebrity will rub off on them if only they can get close to someone—anyone—who seems to have it.

Suddenly, a synagogue leader named Jairus throws himself at Jesus' feet: "My little daughter is at the point of death. Come and lay your hands on her, so that she may be made well, and live" (Mk 5:23). Pastoral desire, the desire for Jesus on behalf of another, comes through a blood relative—a father begging Jesus to save his beloved daughter from death. Pastoral desire lies at the heart of ministry where the quest for Christ's salvation takes many forms, but it is always mediated through the loving concern of a third party. The crowd—whose popular desire rises at the prospect of a real miracle—presses in on Jesus even more.

But a third form of desire enters the story at this point, the *personal* desire of a hemorrhaging woman. Her condition has deteriorated after twelve years of fruitless medical treatment, and she knows that even the smallest point of connection with Jesus will restore her health, and with it her place in the community as a person-in-relationship. "If I but touch his clothes," she says, "I will be made well" (Mk 5:28).

Personal desire is for this communion, for relationship, for fulfilling the deep human need for an "other" who loves us for being the person we really are. Jewish law of the time declared menstruating women unclean. Twelve years of bleeding meant twelve years without intercourse, without the current of human interaction, without the relationships that make us fully human instead of merely alive. Isolated from friends, husband, children, the ritual life of the community, she learned to become invisible, to shrink at the approach of others she dare not come near. Her plan, even now, is to remain invisible, to hide in the crowd and only to touch Jesus' clothes. That would be enough.

But no one is invisible to God. As she touches Jesus' cloak, she not only feels herself instantly well, but she also experiences intercourse for the first time in twelve years: communion with God who desires her. At this point, the disciples are apparently anxious to get on with the journey; the real miracle, as far as they can tell, lies farther up the road at Jairus's house, and they are hoping for a miracle that will vindicate their belief in the power of this itinerant rabbi. Jairus himself must have been mad with anxiety, locked as he is in a desperate, not-a-moment-to-lose plan to save his little girl. For all their good intentions, pastoral desire has the disciples and Jairus practically in knots. But Jesus stops. Is he oblivious? Is he cruel? Is he crazy? "Who touched me?" Jesus asks.

The disciples are incredulous. The crowd is immense. They are in a race against time with a dying girl. Jesus, hurry up. Jesus, do our ministry. Jesus, follow our agenda. Jesus, heal this daughter, not that one. "How can you say 'Who touched me?'" they want to know (Mk 5:31). But Jesus ignores the disciples, searching the crowd. Communion has occurred. A current has passed between him and another. A real connection has taken place— God's desire for the bleeding woman has been met by the bleeding woman's desire for God. Jesus is "aware that power [has] gone forth from him" (Mk 5:25). "Who touched me?" he wants to know. And the woman, "knowing what had happened to her, came in fear and trembling, fell down before him, and told him the whole truth" (Mk 5:33). Then Jesus says something remarkable. He calls her "daughter"—the only time he uses this term of familiarity in the New Testament. "Daughter," he says, "your faith has made you well" (Mk 5:34). In this small term of relationship, Jesus makes her human, and not merely disease-free. She is well, not because Jesus has magic clothes, but because communion with God has restored her to rela- tionship. She is, above all else, a "daughter," a child of God.

Jesus might have kept on walking. The disciples were right: it was ridicu- lous to think, in a crowd of so many people, that stopping for one person (an unclean woman, at that) could make much difference. Jairus was right: time was running out. Death pressed in on his daughter even as they spoke; the bleeding woman could have waited. What we have here is a story we know all too well: as soon as we enlist Jesus in some pretty significant youth ministry, some adult comes along and messes up our plans. And yet, God did not call us into youth ministry only for the sake of youth. God called us into youth ministry for the sake of the church, whose ministry involves youth. Jesus did not head to Jairus's house for the sake of one young girl alone; he went to Jairus's house for the sake of the kingdom of God, in which this young girl plays an irreplaceable part. The bleeding woman's interruption should remind those of us in youth ministry that God's desire is not our desire, God's schedule not our schedule, God's time not our time. Jesus' only desire is to love us personally, as the human beings we really are, as children of God.

The word *blood* comes from the same root that means "to bless," making a blessing a blood commitment. To Jesus, the unclean woman—"daughter"— was blood kin. Intercourse is also given to us as a blessing, and it, too, entails blood commitments—something easily overlooked when we spiritualize "true love" to the point that bodies seem irrelevant. Maybe that is why a 2009 United Nations/World Health Organization report found that 40 per- cent of newly reported HIV cases are found in youth.[7] Maybe that is why youth think so little about "exchanging fluids" in the bed of an unsuspecting parent, swapping life for life as they become entangled in one another's bloodstreams. In their potential to beget, they are as close to God as they have ever been, possibly becoming cocreators of life by creating blood kin of their own. Desire is at once sexual and spiritual, and the post-Enlightenment insistence on sanitizing spirituality of its sensuousness—and vice versa—has left contemporary youth a dangerous legacy.

The story of Jairus's daughter has one more chapter. Even before Jesus has finished speaking, people from Jairus's house arrive to say it is too late: "Your daughter is dead. Why trouble the teacher any further?" (Mk 5:35). Still God's desire is not our desire, God's schedule not our schedule, God's time not our time. Jesus has not, as it turns out, ignored Jairus's pastoral desire after all. Jesus has all the time in the world.

He arrives at Jairus's house to find the weeping and wailing at full throttle. The mourners laugh at Jesus' suggestion that the child is sleeping, not dead. In a classic moment of ancient comedy, the text says simply that Jesus "put them all outside," like the cat, and focused on those who really had a stake in this girl's transformation. Bringing only the girl's parents and Peter, James and John into the room with him (the family and the church, even today the two most significant contexts for faith formation[8]), Jesus takes the girl by the hand and tells her to get up. As she does, we learn from the text that she is twelve years old. So astonished were Jesus' onlookers that, weeks and months and centuries later when the story was retold, the only thing anybody can remember Jesus saying is, "Get this kid something to eat." As the curtain falls, popular desire suddenly seems absurd beside the desire of God.

HOLDING ON TO OUR KISSES:
THE DILEMMA OF SACRED INTERCOURSE

Spiritual desire and sexual desire can both be harnessed for popular, pastoral or personal reasons. Unfortunately, by remaining mute on sexuality for several centuries, the church has abandoned it to a media culture that shrinks the spectrum of desire to popular desire alone. For those of us raised in a culture that separates sexual from spiritual desire, associating intercourse with communion seems alien, if not downright offensive. Unfettered by faithfulness to a theological tradition—and, it must be said, unchallenged by the church—popular media creates the impression that desire is a human, not a divine, attribute.

When desire becomes separated from its divine roots, the concept mutates; it becomes viewed as alien to God, reduced to an emotion humans experience when we are not acting like God, when we are "naughty." This view, of course, leaves teenagers with only two options: suppress their desires in order to be more "godly"—or enjoy being "bad." The way out of this dilemma is obvious. Since desire is fundamental to the nature of God and therefore basic to the nature of humans created in the image of God, suppressing desire denies our core humanity. Suppressing desire feels dishonest, and it is no fun—so most of us (youth and adults alike) choose to enjoy being "bad." Without a way to probe desire from the perspective of Christian theology, the tools available to teenagers for exploring their God-given longings inevitably come from the media, and they inevitably reflect popular culture's limited theological imagination.

Meanwhile, the church's de facto decision to let popular culture define desire has had disastrous theological consequences. On the one hand, driving a wedge between sexuality and spirituality forced upon the church a disembodied view of Christian spirituality. Separating sexuality from spirituality reduced sexuality to "parts and plumbing," and equated the human desire for otherness with biological drives and instincts. Christians were thus forced into yet another delicate corner. When sexuality is reduced to "parts and plumbing," affirming sexuality (which Christian doctrine requires) means celebrating body parts and functions—the kind of perspective that creates sticky educational dilemmas akin to unwrapping chocolate kisses and telling teens to just hold on. Every teenager on the planet is programmed for the follow-up question: "If we can celebrate it, why can't we use it?"

RECONNECTING THE DOTS: MADONNA MEETS THE MADONNA

Interestingly, while the church has been busy ignoring the connection between sexuality and spirituality, a theology of desire has been in full swing in popular culture. If the church is squeamish about connecting sexuality and spirituality, the entertainment media is not. As a result, media culture tutors postmodern youth in a theology of desire derived not from the teachings of the church but from the teachings of the marketplace where sensual spirituality sells. Although the media's fusion of sexual and spiritual themes seldom points to anything resembling Christian doctrine, the fusion rings true to adolescents who intuit a deep connection between the two. Yet without a referent, both the sexual and the spiritual images of popular culture remain ambiguous, leaving adolescents to imbue them with content derived from their own experience. As a result, most adolescents' "theology" of desire amounts to a cut-and-paste combination of family values, hormonal urges, social norms and the Jedi belief that faith equals feeling: "If I trust my feelings enough, I will know God."[9]

One of the most dramatic examples, but by no means the only one, of the media's blatant fusion of sexual and spiritual imagery is Madonna's classic *Like a Prayer* video, originally released in 1989 and still considered one of the most controversial music videos of all time (Pepsi cancelled a five-million-dollar contract with her after the video aired).[10] In 1989, *Like a Prayer* was considered shocking for its explicit connection of spiritual and sexual themes. Make no mistake: the purpose of this video is to sell music, as well as to enhance Madonna's popularity as a singer and celebrity. But selling music, it turns out, is infinitely easier when spiritual and sexual desire are involved, and *Like a Prayer* topples barriers to both, like so many dominoes, as the video progresses.

In scope, the *Like a Prayer* video is an ambitious and seductive work, a love song laced with electrical wire. Throughout it, Madonna wears a tight dress with straps that just can't seem to stay on her shoulders. As she intones the song's lyrics and melody, the video's image-narrative broadens the scope of the song's "desire" to include a longing for a multitude of relationships; barriers to relationships of every kind, from racial prejudice to social intolerance, from gender-role stereotypes to sexual inhibitions to religious doctrine, collapse in answer to something "like a prayer."

As the video opens, Madonna seeks sanctuary in a small village church, obviously Roman Catholic, where she gazes upon the statue of a black saint standing behind an altar grate (or is it a prison cell?).[11] She subsequently frees and kisses him. As the saint goes out into the world, Madonna cuts herself; upon reviewing her wounds she discovers that they are the stigmata, bestowing on Madonna the rank of sainthood.

The scene then shifts to Madonna's view of an alley stabbing, where the victim's black rescuer is falsely accused of the crime. Madonna dances seductively in front of a field of flaming crosses, mocking the symbols of white supremacy that led to the racism implicit in his unjust accusation and imprisonment. Then, having mediated the accused man's freedom, Madonna appears liberated herself. Still clad in a cocktail dress, dancing and flying with a Pentecostal choir led by an African American female pastor, Madonna leaves behind what seems, by comparison, to be the rigid liturgy, piety and doctrine of the village Catholic church. Meanwhile, the saint—sad but resigned to his ecclesial incarceration—returns to his place behind the altar grate and once again turns to stone.

Although this video critiques the church's avoidance of sexuality by ignoring a relationship between desire and Christian doctrine, *Like a Prayer* is a triumph of the media's fusion of sexual and spiritual desire. But it is not unique. Sexual and spiritual themes cohabit most entertainment genres. One study of MTV images found that "religious imagery is twice as likely to be found in videos that also use sexual imagery than those without."[12] In fact, Neal Gabler, author of *Life the Movie: How Entertainment Conquered Reality,* argues that celebrity culture is itself a religious phenomenon, as ordinary people turn from religion to the worship of celebrities.[13]

Postmodern youth are deeply suspicious of the institutional church, but they have popular desire to spare for Jesus the celebrity. Adolescents celebrate Jesus the celebrity not for his relationship to the church, but for his independence from it: someone whose ethics are too pure to have been co-opted by institutional religion and who therefore can stand outside as a critic.[14] Jesus the celebrity needs no church building. He goes to the mall and is on sale. Jesus the celebrity appears on primetime in a range of costumes. Jesus the celebrity's footprints mark the music industry well beyond Amy Grant, Jars of Clay and the Jonas Brothers; Jesus is also referenced by Kanye West and Kid Rock.

Such singers are arguably the priestesses and priests of a generation, shaping the religious consciousness of the young in ways the church can only envy. It is catechism writ large, except that the catechist is not the church, but the media; the image of Jesus comes not from the gospel, but from celebrity culture. The tradition being handed on emerges not from the accumulated experience of Christian community, but from the private experience of a handful of commercially successful artists.

So where does the credibility of commercially successful artists come from? Quite simply it comes from the fact that popular culture willingly gives voice to the embodied spirituality of teenagers. Adolescents know that they are at once both body and soul, that they desire both sex and spirit, and that the object of their desire lies both beyond them and within them. They want to express the wholeness of their being so badly that it aches, but without a theological vocabulary they lack a language to fully describe a desire they know is bigger than genital sex and more substantive than vague spirituality. Popular culture's reliance on image, rhythm and melody concretizes adolescents' implicit theology of desire.

CELIBATE PASSION AND EROTIC FAITH:
ANCIENT CONNECTIONS FOR POSTMODERN YOUTH

The irony, of course, is that if we would listen to our own tradition as Christians, we would discover that Madonna, Kanye, Kid Rock and others are exploring an ancient connection, a link between sexuality and spirituality that the church embraced well into the Reformation. Until the corset of modern rationalism squeezed erotic imagery straight out of our theological lexicon, Christians could turn to the teachings of the church to describe the stirrings of desire within themselves, and use these stirrings as a way to point beyond themselves to God.

Until the Enlightenment made passion unfashionable, Christian teaching—where sexual ethics were hardly a fixed code—viewed erotic experience as a helpful tool for learning about God. Steeped in Scripture rife with sexual imagery, medieval mystics naturally thought of God in erotic terms, employing a vocabulary of desire that grew out of the writings of John Cassian and climaxed in the works of Augustine, Gregory and Bernard.[15] In this vocabulary, which became normative for the mystical writers of the early Middle Ages, the free choice of the will differentiated acting in accordance with spiritual desire from being overwhelmed by carnal lust. These early theologians taught that we cannot live without desire (in fact, our human growth is stunted without it), but that the object of our desire determines our moral character. As human beings, we are differentiated according to what we seek. Desire becomes spiritual when directed toward God. Indeed, when a person seeks God, "The very nobility of his purpose has the effect of transforming his life, rendering it progressively more godly and open to the divine."[16] Union with God is realized in desire and becomes inseparable from it.

Consequently, early doctors of the church seemed unconcerned with holding on to their kisses. Kissing, in fact, constituted a major theme in monastic literature, as the ecstasy of communion with God was frequently compared to being passionately kissed by Jesus.[17] By the early seventh century in the Western church, Pope Gregory the Great's practice of using erotic imagery to instruct priests on holiness became a standard mode of instruction for young clerics (youth who undoubtedly found religious instruction more compelling than their contemporary counterparts).[18] Bernard of Clairvaux (1090-1153) encouraged young monks to remember their sexual experiences in order to understand prayer as being kissed by Christ with increasing intimacy.[19] Catherine of Siena (1347-1380) referred to God as being "like one drunk and crazy with love,"[20] while Teresa of Ávila (1515-1582) called all who seek God "God's lovers."[21]

The originators of these themes, of course, lived thousands of years before them. Their legacy is the passion of Israel and the bridal theology of the New Testament.[22] God's desire for Israel is made manifest in God's covenant with her (Hos 11). The desire of Jesus is that we be in communion with him, and God's reign—from the Gospels to John's vision at Patmos—is conceived as a bridal banquet in which Christ is the bridegroom and the church is the bride (Mt 9:15). Jesus' ministry, significantly, begins at a wedding (Jn 2:1-11); the end of history is described as a marriage feast (Rev 19:7-9). The new covenant is a wedding covenant, and all of human history exists in order that the bride can make herself ready (Rev 19:7).

Far from a sign of apostasy, the sensual spirituality of postmodern youth is a sign of their irrepressible longing for the God who loves them. Unlike popular desire, personal desire is often most authentically enacted by those whose humanity has been compromised, those whose bleeding needs blessing, those whose place in the cycle of life renders them "unclean" and marginalized. For all the popular desire that surrounds youth, their personal desire—their desire for identity in relationship to "others," their hunger for full selfhood and humanity—must not be overlooked. Indeed, this desire may point directly to the desire of God.

However, we must also remember that Jesus' mission was not, strictly speaking, to save Jairus's daughter or the youth in our church basement. Jesus' mission is to save the world, including Jairus's daughter and the youth in the church basement, and Jesus calls all of us to get up and walk according to God's plan of salvation. Jesus gave life to Jairus's daughter, but in so doing he also gave a sign to the entire church that, no matter what the mourners may say, salvation is at hand. Jesus' youth ministry included bleeding women as well as dying daughters of noisy parents. So, therefore, must ours. For youth are not the only ones who need Jesus to save them: you and I bleed as well, and our hemorrhages sap the church of life, make the church invisible and marginalize Christianity. If we could just get near enough to touch his cloak, then we would be made well.

Jesus, hold us together. Heal our bleeding. Set us on fire with desire to touch your cloak. And that will be enough. Amen.

• DISCUSSION AND REFLECTION EXERCISE
Statement Worth Making

Break into groups.[23] After reading this chapter, each group should generate three or four "statements worth making" (e.g., "Desire is the primary theological lens of adolescents").

After each group has written down their statements on a sheet of paper, everyone should come back together again and then divide into new groups. Each group receives one sheet of statements. Discuss these statements, with people articulating if they agree or disagree with the statements, and why.

THE ESCHATOLOGICAL SIGNIFICANCE OF SUMMER CAMP

KENDA CREASY DEAN

When our son was sixteen, we informed him that he had to give one tenth of his summer to Jesus. Without batting an eye, he chose the Young Life camp over the high-school mission trip sponsored by our church. This decision had nothing to do with Young Life and everything to do with the fact that Louie was going to camp. Louie, when he was not living at our house, lived three doors down. His parents have unofficially made the care and feeding of Young Life leaders in our area into a tentmaking ministry, and one of them invited Brendan to camp.

"Are you *sure* you don't want to go on the mission trip?" I asked, with just a little too much concern in my voice. It dawned on me that maybe altruism skips a generation.

"No, Mom. I hate helping people," came the unrepentant reply. "I did that *last* year. I'm not doing it again." I noticed that, in the brochure, the Young Life camp quite convincingly described itself as a "vacation."

THE ESCHATOLOGICAL SIGNIFICANCE OF SUMMER CAMP

Forget *Left Behind*, which despite record-breaking book sales is mostly lost on American teenagers (whose intrigue with the end of time is far more likely to be fueled by fantasy novels like *The Hunger Games* and TV shows like *LOST* and *Survivor*). My money is on Christian camps, retreats and conferences as teenagers' introduction to eschatology, though I have never been to one that admitted it. Nearly half (45 percent) of U.S. teenagers have attended religious youth retreats, conferences, rallies or congresses; 39 percent have gone to religious summer camps, and nearly one out of three has been part of a religious mission team or service project.[1] This means that whether we claim, or even recognize, the eschatology informing our approach to these events, they nonetheless leave an impression on significant numbers of American young people who—potentially, anyway—go home with a sense that God's promise includes them.[2]

I have a long history with summer Christian youth programs; I'm in ministry largely because of one of them. That was where, it seemed to me at fifteen, Jesus leapt off the pages of Scripture and into my life, *really,* for the first time. Call it adolescent, call it manipulative, call it finding "my heart strangely warmed"—whatever it was, I went to Lakeside Reach Out as a blasé church kid and came home with a sense of divine purpose that, thirty years later, I have not been able to shake. The revelation that God gave Martin Luther reading Romans in the privy, and John Wesley at the Bible study on Aldersgate Street—namely, the joyous insight that I, myself, am destined for God, that Jesus died for *me,* and me *personally,* and therefore has some kind of bizarre confidence that I can contribute to God's work in the world—God seems to give teenagers, somewhat reliably, in the context of summer camps and conferences.

Why? Why do religious camps and conferences, more than congregations and even more than mission trips, give young people a glimmer of their destiny in God? I have a theory. These events *end.* Mission trips (and let me go on record as a cautious fan) end too, but they end in a radical awareness of here and now, whereas Christian camps, retreats and conferences, by definition and design, traffic in hope. What is left when camp is over is hope—hope for a return next year, hope for a new way of life on the return home, because now we live with a glimpse of what the future holds. These events are marked, from the outset, by a radical finality. The liminal character of camps, retreats and conferences (typically, held in a liminal location like an idyllic patch of nature or a college campus enclave) reminds young people that they are momentarily "suspended" between daily life and eternal promises, and that their time in this place where "the membrane between this world and a reality beyond is especially thin" is temporary.[3] The Christian camp, retreat or conference is less an experience than a pilgrimage. These youth travel together, literally or figuratively, toward a holy destination: life in God.

THE TELOS OF THE CHRISTIAN YOUTH EVENT: THE LAST NIGHT OF CAMP

Consequently, Christian youth events that have existential traction do not meander aimlessly. They aim for a conclusion, with everything structured to honor the event's culminating moments. The "end time" of the event (ordinarily the last night's worship service) ritualizes our understanding of the "end times" described by Christian theology. It is decisive. One chapter closes and another begins. Decisions are made, preparations ensue for a different world—the world that is Not-Camp. In the closing rituals of the last night of camp, we expect Jesus to come. We expect God to act. Furthermore, having had a foretaste of glory divine, young people are sent out from the religious camp or conference, like John of Patmos, as apostles of hope. In short, the condensed week of a summer youth camp or conference enacts an *ordu salutis* (order of salvation), not to manipulate God's saving activity but to dramatize it. Christians are story people, and every story—even God's story with us on earth—has a final chapter. What we do on the last night of camp says a lot about how we think the story ends.

This surprises us. Many of us aren't even aware that we even have a governing eschatology, much less that we enact it with young people. "End time" rhetoric conjures up images of heaven, hell, rapture and the second coming of Christ that have been treated as "the theological equivalent of Timbuktu" in the Protestant church for most of the twentieth century, according to Mark Ralls, writing in *The Christian Century*. "Like a lot of mainline Protestant pastors I know," confesses Ralls, "I'm caught between honest belief and embarrassment."[4] Our way out has been to sidestep any overt discussion of eschatological issues altogether, leaving them to our more literally minded conservative Christian friends. We mainliners prefer transitions to endings, rehabilitation to judgment, regeneration to apocalypticism, phases to finality. But there is a cost to this. Our silence on the subject of eschatology, our reluctance to speak of God's future for fear of boxing in God's expansive grace, has the effect of muting the telos of Christian theology. Youth are thus left to conclude, quite understandably, that the church is literally going nowhere.

BACK TO THE FUTURE: RECLAIMING CHRISTIAN HOPE

Eschatology offers teenagers—and us—the one resource we need in the face of radical finality: hope. This is not an optional doctrine at the end of the Christian story; rather, it is the reason for the Christian story. As Jürgen Moltmann writes, "The eschatological is not one element of Christianity, but . . . the key in which everything in it is set, the glow that suffuses everything here in the dawn of an expected new day."[5] In the Christian view of the end of time lies God's unshakable promise that, though the towers fall, though the economy falters, though the world ends, Christ has died, Christ is risen, and Christ will come again—not in some abstract sense, but to *be with us*. By taking seriously its own "ending," the last night of camp insinuates God's embrace of all of time—the beginnings and the ends. In spite of a radically terminated present, on the last night of camp we enact our belief that Jesus is truly among us, and the finality of the moment does not stop his, or our, return. Through the prayer, sacraments and other means of grace typically offered during the closing worship service of these events, the heavenly life-as-it-should-be briefly merges with the life of a teenager, and young people glimpse, momentarily but significantly, the inbreaking of God.

This is no small thing. According to the National Study of Youth and Religion, many American teenagers inhabit a "morally insignificant universe," in which they perceive no telos, no larger story in which they play a part, no sense that their actions play a notable part in moving the world forward. This was especially true for mainline Protestant, Roman Catholic and Jewish young people in the study, who showed less religious vitality, understanding and hope for the future than their Mormon, conservative Protestant or black Protestant peers.[6] While the majority of the 3,370 teenagers interviewed considered religion "benignly positive," very few could articulate what they believed, or how or why religion made a difference in their lives. Most of them thought about the future in terms of college, marriage or recycling—no further. With rare exceptions, the absence of a meaningful eschatology cut across religious traditions. The study found that even teenagers who attend church regularly live in a world where no ultimacy is assigned to our life together, where God is invoked vaguely and where Jesus primarily wants us to feel good about ourselves.[7]

LIFE BEYOND *LEFT BEHIND*

There is a logic to pilgrimages: altered physical conditions produce an altered—a more alert and sensitive—consciousness.[8] The Left Behind series offers one way for teenagers to imagine the end times, but the small, temporary, God-conscious communities of religious camps, retreats and conferences offer another, and far more young people respond. In these events, teenagers glimpse a future into which they are invited, in which they play a part, in which their actions *matter* because they live in a morally consequential universe. And in the culminating finality of the last night of camp, we ritualize the way God lays claim to them, and we expect Jesus to act—not because this is the way camp is, but because this is the way the story ends. *Come, Lord Jesus, come.*

• DISCUSSION AND REFLECTION EXERCISE
Survival Advice Memo

Imagine it is your last day as a camp counselor or leader.[9] Your replacements are coming next week. You are asked to write these incoming counselors and leaders a memo that articulates what you have learned theologically from your experience.

Drawing from your own experience (and this chapter), tell the newcomers what theological significance camp can have and things that might move it in this direction. The memo should have four parts: (1) what young people experience at camp, (2) how God is active at camp, using a theological motif (e.g., incarnation, Trinity, eschatology), (3) how young people experience God's activity at camp, and (4) what actions camps and leaders should take in light of the other three questions.

After writing this memo, pick what you perceive to be your most insightful remark and construct questions or discussion starters for it. Then, in small groups, each person should share either their memos or their further reflection on the original remark to lead the group into conversation.

WHAT ARE WE DOING IN THESE MOUNTAINS?

The Outdoor Trip and the Theology of the Cross

ANDREW ROOT

As we entered Banff National Park I could feel my breathing quicken and my eyes widen. For a boy from the flat Midwest, the sight of majestic mountains reaching to the sky and covered in snow in late July was breathtaking. The beauty was almost more than I could take. I spent the first few days just staring at them, refusing to take my eyes from them. Little, other than TV, had captured my attention as much as those mountains. As we finished our preparation for our youth ministry backpacking trip into the Canadian Rockies, my high-school anticipation was as high as the mountains themselves. We loaded our packs, parked our vans in some dirt lot and started on the trail, trudging our way into the beauty of creation.

Three hours in, the beauty began to fade, though not objectively, I suppose; the mountains, trees and rocks continued to possess some kind of beauty. But it was the kind of beauty that came with harshness. Three hours in, a tenth-grader had blisters, a junior was dehydrated, and a senior was exhausted from carrying the food pack. We camped the first night next to a glacier-fed pond; it too was beautiful, but unsympathetic. When the sun went down the temperature fell quickly, leaving us shivering in our sleeping bags. In addition, we were told we had to filter the water from the stream, and when getting the water we needed to go in teams, in case we met a bear. The first thing I learned on that trip was that nature was beautiful but harsh.

We spent each morning with our journals, encouraged to depart into creation by ourselves to pray, read Scripture and commune with God. Our morning silence started with the warning not to go too far and ended with us all back together to read Scripture, discuss God's presence in nature and say a final prayer. I began to wonder what it was we were doing out there. It clearly was about being in God's creation, but for what purpose? I guessed that we needed the exercise of hiking, and that the time spent outdoors was a good correction to our hours of playing video games and watching TBS reruns. And the time on the trail did allow us to get to know our leaders better. The God stuff seemed weird, though; we were told that by soaking in God's creation we would meet God, but we were given as many warnings as encouragements: watch out for this, make sure you drink enough water, don't leave any food in your tent, don't slide down the snow on the side of the mountains. We were supposed to meet God in nature, but nature was rugged, dangerous and unforgiving, even in its beauty.

So what are we doing in youth ministry when we take young people on outdoor trips? Do youth encounter God in creation? Is God knowable in the creation? What are we hoping young people will experience on these trips? If, as Kenda has asserted, summer camp has an eschatological dimension, what about youth ministry nature trips? What goes on theologically here?

FOR PERSONAL IMPROVEMENT?

Outdoor trips in youth ministry seem to most often be about a mix of personal improvement and seeing God in nature. We hope that backpacking, canoeing and rock climbing will challenge young people, helping them see what they are capable of doing, so we put them in (controlled) situations that push them beyond what they thought they were capable of. These experiences can no doubt be transforming and significant for a young person's personal development. Overcoming their fear of heights by ziplining, or pushing themselves to walk six miles when they never thought they could, can be very empowering. I don't think we should shy away from admitting that these trips do such things.

But there is a not-so-fine line between bringing together a community of friends who encourage a fellow friend to stretch him- or herself and contending that God will use these trips and their challenges to make young people into what they need to be. I once heard about a youth worker who would tell his young people, in the midst of the exhaustion of building a house or carrying their packs, that God had them on the anvil, insinuating that God was using the experiences, using the heat and pressure of their exertion, to *pound* them into what God wanted them to be. While these trips provide opportunities for young people to grow into their humanity by challenging themselves physically and departing from their normal distractions in the quiet of nature, we may create a problem when we imply that such experiences are the activity of God and therefore *reveal* who God is. Like the youth pastor above, we give young people pictures of a God who is like a personal trainer or Pilates instructor—concerned for them to be all they can be, for them to make themselves into something. When we blend the personal challenge with the direct presence of God on these trips, we not only make self-improvement the goal of God's activity but also, ironically, diminish God's action at the same time, giving young people the idea that it is up to them, up to their effort, to make themselves into something God would be pleased with.

THE GOD OF NATURE

Yet what we most often assume about these outdoor trips is that they will open young people's eyes to see God. We imagine that the beauty of nature can persuade young people of God's presence in the world and therefore of God's presence in their lives; we hope that, as they're away from distractions, nature will reveal God to them. In other words, we anticipate that through these trips young people will know and experience God. So we say things like, "Seeing the beauty of the forest, ocean or mountains, how can you deny that God exists and that God is good?"

Nature is, without a doubt, beautiful. It does possess within it something we might call transcendent; we confess that it is God's good creation. But nature, as my own experience in the story above shows, is just as harsh as it is beautiful. We can experience the beauty of mountains, but if we get lost in those mountains we will die. So while many of us have experiences of dwelling in nature, can we assume de facto that they are experiences that usher in communion with God? After all, nature in itself cannot communicate knowledge of God, and nature in itself gives us experiences of both transcendent mystery and grueling hell.

This may diminish the activity of God, because these trips become about knowledge and experience outside of encounter, outside of God's own action. Nature, in itself, is inert; it cannot encounter us. It can give us moving experiences, experiences that are good and wonderful, but it does not put a direct demand on us and does not encounter us as a person might. Yet when we take young people into nature hoping it will reveal to them that God exists, we tend to imagine that nature itself will mediate knowledge of God. We assume that if young people look deeply at the beauty of nature they will see the fingerprints of God. But even in a bush that burns but is not consumed (a reality that is other than nature since, in nature, all burning bushes are consumed) God calls out, God acts, God speaks with God's Word that, while spoken within nature, is also other than it. It was not the beauty of the bush that Moses attested to but the fact that God spoke to him, acting by revealing to Moses God's very name. God is agent, not a passive reality to experience, which is what God too often becomes in our nature trips. We don't assume God's own action (that God acts to reveal Godself). Rather, we assume that by dwelling in nature we can see God, and though we may not mean to imply it, this assumption can give the impression that God remains passive—something we experience—but does not encounter us. For God to truly encounter us, God would have to be other enough from nature to act for and with us.

In both perspectives (seeing these trips either as opportunities for adolescent self-betterment or as times of nature revealing God) we have conceptions of God that are disconnected from love itself, for love can only be in action; it is never passive but is always an active reality. With the first perspective, we provide pictures of a God who cares about personal betterment, about us stretching ourselves toward excellence, not a God who acts to be near to us in impossibility. There is a fine line between encouraging kids to do things that push them and insinuating that God desires that *they* work to improve themselves. And with the second perspective, we give pictures of a God who is known through nature, which, though beautiful and good, is inert and just as harsh as it is beautiful. Nothing in nature itself engages us out of grace and love. Indeed, nature hides God as much as it reveals God. There is no grace if you fall off the mountain, no forgiveness through the teeth of a bear if you leave an open bag of beef jerky in your tent. When we put these outdoor trips on our calendars, we justify them by claiming that they provide young people with opportunities to challenge themselves and to experience God through nature, but is this even in line with our theological commitments?

THE HEIDELBERG DISPUTATION

In 1518 Luther presented his Heidelberg Disputation to defend his theological breakthrough that would be the impetus of the Reformation. The document not only raises the problem that Luther saw (that all action of the human agent that seeks to justify and make him- or herself good is futile and perilous), but also presents his constructive reimagination of theology beyond the dead end of seeking for God in our own activity and in that which can be easily seen and discerned (like through nature itself).

Luther's constructive reimagination of theology is his theology of the cross (*theologia crucis,* which we focused on a great deal in this book), a theology that asserts that it is God who acts. But this God who acts does so in backward ways, making life out of death and bringing hope from despair by entering death and being found in despair. All theology for Luther therefore begins and ends with the crucified Christ. This does not eliminate for him the importance of the Old Testament or the outpouring of the Spirit; these too are realities that demand deep theological reflection. But, in the end, the crucified Christ is the hinge of history, the hinge of existence itself. The cross of Christ becomes the hidden and backward way that God seeks to act for us, revealing that God's action is never determined by the potency of human action but only by human suffering and impossibility. It is in the crucified Christ, for Luther, that we see the fullness and depth of God's own action for us; it is in sharing our suffering in the cross that God reveals Godself. As Paul says, "The message of the cross is foolishness for those who are perishing, but to us who are saved it is the power of God" (1 Cor 1:18).

For Luther, the cross is the way God reveals Godself most fully, for it is in the cross that we see how fully God seeks to be with and for us. This means the road to encountering God is not in our own action or experience in nature but in God's act of taking on the cross. While nature is good and God is the Creator, nature in itself cannot be with and for us. God chooses to enter the natural world as the God of a people (Israel) and in the fullness of humanity in the incarnation, but in itself nature cannot possess direct knowledge of God, for nature alone meets us as a non-personal reality, not as person encountering persons. By becoming the God of a people, however, by revealing Godself in Jesus Christ, God unveils Godself in the reality of personal encounter, through agency.

Nature can captivate us, can touch some transcendent impulse within us and mediate true beauty, but it has no agency. It can unfold through natural processes and can even adapt to stimulus and threat in the environment, but it cannot encounter our person as person. Nature cannot be with us; it cannot be near to us in our brokenness. And in fact, it can, and indiscriminately will, destroy us. The water that quenches our thirst as a gift can also push our air from our lungs, taking our life.

Thus, God unveils Godself most directly not in nature but in the crucified Christ, Luther believes. To know who God is and where God is found we don't look to nature (or reason, for Luther) but to the peasant man dying on a cross outside the city. The crucified Christ reveals that God is found not in nature, but next to the suffering and longing of persons, next to places of broken searching.

OUTDOOR TRIPS ARE ABOUT SMALLNESS

This, then, is what nature trips are about: *not experiencing God in nature but experiencing our own longings and brokenness.* Why take kids into the mountains or canoeing? What is the point? The point, at least from the place of the early Reformation's theology of the cross, is not because nature mediates who God is or because in overcoming our limitations we become better (better people, better Christians). No, the reason we take kids on these outdoor trips is so that they might experience what is most true for us: that we are caught in discontinuity. In other words, outdoor trips may be one of the most helpful ways to encourage young people to think about the crisis of their very existence. The point of looking at mountains that have been here for a million years and may be here a million more is not to see God in them but to recognize the thinness of our being in their shadow. Outdoor trips are about helping kids ask, What is a lifetime and why do we live it? Who is this God that creates a whole universe of such depth, size, beauty and tragedy and yet cares for me, seeks me? And seeks me not in the majesty and power of the created order, but in the nearness, smallness and closeness of human suffering and love, the cross. We could say that nature is like the Law: it is good and it's a gift, for it reveals to us our limitations. But God in Godself has acted for us in our limitations, taking our brokenness and suffering on Godself through the crucified Christ.

These trips have the power of reminding the ego that it is small, that the self is but a minuscule blip on the screen of time and space. So outdoor trips should call adolescents and their disproportionately large egos to consider their own smallness (like the psalmist in Psalm 8). Where is God present in these trips? If you follow the theology of the cross, God's presence is not in the experience of nature in itself; rather, through experiencing nature, we recognize our own yearnings, longings and brokenness, and next to these yearnings, longings and brokenness, God is found. God is made known as acting through the cross (and now through the Spirit) for us.

Outdoor trips are not, then, about improvement (whether spiritual or personal) but about death, and if they are about death then they are about the cross. Spending time in the harshness and beauty of nature, away from our technological day to day, we witness how near death is to life, how life and death are inevitability connected. The psalmist looked at mountains and realized that he is small, that he is finite, and that beauty and hell are so close together; that which is so beautiful can be so harsh, and that which is so appealing to the eye can destroy us. Sitting with young people on the last day of a trip as the sun comes up over the evergreens, lighting the lake in gold that spreads before our feet, we become aware that our life is so thin, and that in its thinness is beauty. God is there, for God has acted through the thinness of death and brokenness to make our realities of thinness the place of God's very action.

This means that nature is our great gift, a gift we must steward and care for. Not because it possesses knowledge of God, but because it is God's. We care for nature because, in experiencing both its beauty and its harshness (which cannot be untangled from each other), we are reminded that we are dying but also that, in our death, God acts to be near to us. And we care for nature because it is our friend; we are bound to it, for we, like it, are caught in the cycles of moving from life to death. We seek its good not because it reveals God but because, like us, it seeks for new life beyond death through God's own action.

We take young people on outdoor trips not to challenge them to be better or experience God through creation but to help them face the crisis of reality itself, to help them recognize that they are small and near death, that they are in need of a God who acts to cross the abyss to meet them. Outdoor trips have real potential to lead not to personal betterment but to deep reflection on why there is something instead of nothing, on my need, on my questions that have no answers. And when we are willing to face these realities, when we are willing to face the thinness of what is and to reveal our suffering and admit that we are near to death, then the God of the cross stands before us, for the God of the cross has acted for us to be with us by entering our beautiful but harsh world for the sake of love.

• DISCUSSION AND REFLECTION EXERCISE
Sentence Completion

Each person should get a page with the following half-sentences on it.[1] Take a few minutes and complete at least one of these statements. Flesh out as much as possible the one or two half-sentences that you choose.

What most struck me about this chapter for the discussion today is . . .

The question that I'd most like to ask the author of the chapter is . . .

The idea I most take issue with in the chapter is . . .

The most crucial point in the chapter was . . .

The part of the chapter that I felt made the most sense to me was . . .

The part of the chapter that I felt was most confusing was . . .

After taking time to reflect and write on at least one of the half-sentences, break up into small groups to share your thoughts with others.

THE MISSION TRIP
AS GLOBAL TOURISM

Are We OK with This?

ANDREW ROOT

I had just graduated from high school weeks earlier when our family mini van approached the airport. As I entered the terminal, my anticipation gave me the feeling of floating, tethered to the polished floor only by the large bags of luggage I dragged behind me. My eyes scanned the space for a herd of fellow high-school students draped in the same blue T-shirts that read "missions trip '93." Our church, located in suburban Minnesota, was sending a handful of high-school students and their leaders to Trinidad and Tobago, the southernmost islands in the Caribbean. Not only had I never been out of the country, but neither had any member of my family, though we had traveled a lot: to Disney World once and the Florida panhandle most spring breaks. And my dad flew west a few times a month for work. But I would be the first one in our family to leave the U.S.

We gathered to check our luggage with our parents surrounding us; their apprehension and anxiety mixed with our adolescent excitement made the scene electric. I can remember the parents discussing with each other how such a trip never happened in their day and how thankful (though nervous) they were that the church was giving their child such opportunities to see the world. This was something only a stint in the military would have done a generation or two ago.

The trip itself was filled with dichotomies. We left the beautiful, modern Miami airport, where we spent our two-hour layover shoveling cheeseburgers into our mouths, to land in a little rundown airport in Port of Spain. That night we visited impoverished local churches; the next day we walked around the downtown mall. We traveled to a small village, almost untouched by modernization, to run a VBS, then spent the next day bodysurfing and eating shark sandwiches as we baked our upper Midwestern bodies in the Caribbean sun. We sang songs for the poorest of the elderly in the government nursing homes, and then spent our last two days on the resort island of Tobago, sipping (virgin) cocktails under beach umbrellas, buying souvenirs and wasting our parents' spending money. It was a mission trip, mixed with a vacation. It was global service mixed with global tourism.

The short-term mission trip has become a staple of contemporary youth ministry. While camp was the core activity of youth ministry in the 1970s, and the eighties to mid-nineties featured the concert-like big event, today the mission trip has become central. Of course, young people still go to camps—as Kenda's earlier chapter beautifully reflects on—and there are a number of concert-like events still going. But the mission trip, it appears, has become "the" youth ministry activity. Whether it is to Mexico, Chicago, Africa, Appalachia, India or South Dakota, every summer the church sends its adolescent children to the ends of the earth. But to do what? "To serve, to evangelize, to grow in their faith" are usually the answers we give as we raise money for the trips and justify their central place on our calendars. Service and mission seem more noble and, dare we say "holy," than stadium-filled Christian rock concerts sprinkled with funny speakers. And no doubt service and mission happen. But often, for most of us, these short-term mission trips embody mind-spinning contradictions. In living with the poor for a while before hitting the water park, or serving the hungry a meal before shopping for souvenirs, kids learn how to pray together as well as surf; they see poverty and pain as well as the local sights. So why has the short-term mission trip become central to what youth ministries do? And why do these dichotomies exist?

The escalation of short-term youth ministry mission trips has much to do with our cultural and societal transformations, as our parents gave testimony to when my high-school group checked our luggage for Trinidad. It is connected to the arrival of globalization. Globalization has made us all into travelers across time and space. The mission trip appeals to us all because it allows us to enter the streams of a globalized world, to move physically as we do continually through the Internet, satellite television and cell phones. But moving in the strong currents of globalization also thrusts us into what sociologist Zygmunt Bauman calls moving as either tourists or vagabonds. And this might just be a problem, a problem that makes it difficult to extract the tourism from our youth ministry mission trips. So how should we theologically grapple with mission trips that so often can slide into global tourism?

MOVING WITH MOVERS

"Nowadays we are all on the move," Bauman asserts.[1] We are either moving our bodies across miles in our cars or planes, or, if we are not physically moving, the world is moving to us as our devices and technologies broadcast the world into our living rooms. We spend most of our time looking at windows that move us across time and space; with a flip of the channel or a click of the mouse we are moving, and moving quickly. Rarely are we still; our way of being in the world is one of motion, and motion across massive space in a short time. "There are no 'natural borders' any more," states Bauman, "neither are there obvious places to occupy. Wherever we happen to be at the moment, we cannot help knowing that we could be elsewhere, so there is less and less reason to stay anywhere in particular."[2] When time and space can be traversed with such speed, constant movement becomes operative.

But what is the fuel for this constant movement? What propels us and then keeps us moving? According to Bauman, it is consumption. Where past generations were bound to the land or the next turn of the conveyor belt, in our world we are pushed to want and want more, to crave and desire anew in the glare of a constantly available and changing world. Our society is a consumer society; it calls not for duty, service or loyalty, but only for us to want new things and to continue moving to get them. We must move to stay up with fashion, to hear new music, to harvest new experiences, to see new films, to formulate new identities. Moreoever, as Bauman says, the compression of time and space due to technology "takes the waiting out of wanting." We can get whatever we want whenever we want it. Amazon, iTunes and eBay are always open; my credit card limit allows me to get where and what I want now, even if I can't afford it. Thus, as globalization flattens out boundaries, pulling time and space together, consumption keeps us constantly on the move.

It is no wonder then that adolescents are drawn to mission trips. They are movers; every minute they are moving in and out of new space, and the mission trip offers these movers a chance to *go*, to move into a new space and there harvest new and unique experiences. It is therefore not unusual in youth ministry for kids who have had no interest in youth group, Bible study or confirmation to sign up for a mission trip. As constant movers they are adventurers, and little seems more adventurous than going to Mexico or Thailand. The mission trip is an opportunity to live into their cultural way of being; it is a chance to move, and an occasion to consume new experiences in new space. Bauman says it this way: "Consumers are first and foremost gatherers of *sensations;* they are [not *just*] collectors of *things.*"[3]

It is not that young people are not fully invested in the experience; any good consumer is always *fully* invested in the moment of the experience. The problem is that the mission trip is just that—just an experience, a *sensation.* And it is here that the dichotomies that many of us feel reveal themselves. An adolescent fully moved by the poverty of a village, for example, quickly moves on to become the purchaser of a hot new purse. It is not that the moment of encountering poverty was not real and significant; indeed, it was. It is just that she has moved on; the experience of poverty has become just that, an experience. It cannot bog her down; she must keep moving. And while she may go home and start an initiative to help people in that village, she will do this also as a mover, harvesting the sensations of "doing something" and then moving on to prom, choir and SAT prep. After a while, her constant moving and acquiring of new experiences and sensations will encourage her to forget her experience on the mission trip. Again, it is not that it does not matter to her; rather, it has simply become an old experience. The sensation lacks the electricity or flavor it once had, like a piece of gum chewed for too long. She will need a new or similar sensation to remind her of the trip, or else she will spit it out and forget it altogether. For the adolescent mover, the mission trip becomes like the $150 pair of shoes she *had* to have last year that has now been abandoned. It is not her fault; it is just the way of constant moving in a globalized world of consumers.

TOURISTS AND VAGABONDS

Two kinds of movers. For Bauman, this constant moving has changed the very organization of social life. He contends that the days of bourgeois and proletariat (a rigid class system) have disappeared in the transformations of globalization; it makes little sense to speak of a working-class culture anymore. Everyone, he explains, whether rich or poor, must always be moving. So in this consumer-saturated world, all young people are focused on having the same experiences; all desire sensation. A Latino adolescent in east L.A. and a white suburban adolescent in Illinois, for example, are chasing the same experiences (though in many ways, urban youth set the terms for what is "in" for suburban kids): they listen to the same music, idolize the same sports stars and laugh at the same movies. Their worlds are radically different but they are both movers.

Yet by no means does this constant state of movement lead to a kind of cultural equality or a culture without stratification; rather, it is that this stratification has been transformed, like everything else in a globalized world. Instead of seeing the world divided between aristocrats and the working class, Bauman sees our world divided between tourists and vagabonds. Both are propelled to move and keep moving, but their experiences of moving are very different. The tourists are those with means, those who are free to move and who are welcomed by others as they seek new experiences. The world is theirs. Vagabonds, on the other hand, are not welcomed by others. Forced to move, they must hide in the shadows and cross fences and boundaries to find work. Though they want to stay home (and no longer be a vagabond), the globalized world that allows tourists to keep moving and having new experiences and sensations forces vagabonds to *go* in seek of work and sanctuary, all with the hope that one day they too will have the means to be a tourist. And it is in the very places built for tourists—at resorts and airports, for example—that the vagabond finds work as a servant. So the existence of both tourist and vagabond is due to our constant state of motion, but one serves the other. All vagabonds really want, thanks to our shared consumer society, is to be tourists, while the deepest fear of tourists is that they might become a vagabond, an ever-present threat when tourism is achieved through credit.

For the tourist, space is liquid, and easily molded. A tourist can easily jump from one space to the next; it is time that she must concern herself with (hence the need for PDAs, iPhones and conferences on time-management skills). At any given time she knows that she could be in another place if she wished. She is at work, for example, but she could be at home; she is in Baltimore, but she could be with her sister in Baton Rouge.

The vagabond lives the reverse. Space contains *him,* and he cannot easily traverse it. Cemented in his village, borough or project, he is aware, through technology, of a world that *could* be reached, but he has no means to do so. Or, when forced to move to find work, he is aware of every step; every mile hurts. Time does not slip through his hands like it does for the tourist but rather is heavy, slow and often oppressive as he serves.

Tourists go and do things (jet ski, visit museums, get massages, rack up frequent flier miles). Vagabonds go and bear things (the reality of serving tourists, being forced to move when their desire is to stay home, inhospitable places where they hope to find welcome, another long ten-hour shift). When space is easy to jump, *doing* becomes operative; we continue to move so we can do new and more things, so we can have new and unique sensations through new experiences. But when time is stagnant and heavy and space is a cage or a long desert road, we are forced to simply be, to yearn but to be left without. We may want new sensations but we are left with only the place we're in and the many experiences of impossibility.

The tourism trap. Our mission trips are immersed in contradiction (spending the morning serving the poor and the afternoon sipping cocktails) because at their core they carry out the dichotomy between tourists and vagabonds. The mission trip is a tourist event, but one that, most insidiously, uses vagabonds as its activities. We go and do things, like good tourists, but instead of those things being spas and surf lessons (things vagabonds facilitate for us as low-paid employees of our resorts), we enter the villages, homes and neighborhoods of vagabonds to do things for them— things that often seem to be done without conversation with the vagabonds themselves. They become passive and we become active, but we never really meet each other. When the mission trip is global tourism, it is always about *doing*. Our trip brochures therefore explain what we will do, how we will minister and serve, with details about the building project, Bible puppet program or soup kitchen volunteering. And when we come back, we report to the congregation what we *did* and often evaluate our success by saying, "It was a great trip! We built a wing on the church, delivered food, led three worship services, passed out fifty Bibles and put on a VBS for one hundred kids." We could just as easily say, "The vacation was excellent! I played two rounds of golf, saw two shows, rented one paddle boat and ate two porterhouse steaks."

Moreover, when our mission trips are about doing something, then like good tourists we are free to move on and eventually forget them; we did our part and can now keep on moving. The mission trip becomes locked in our digital photos, organized and presented as a great experience, and shown to the congregation through slide shows and music that give them the sensation of being there, of having had the experience themselves. But once the photos are on our hard drive they are labeled as old experiences, worthy of nostalgia but not subject to the judgment of our day-to-day life and our vocational call to open up our being to others.

FROM DOING TO BEING

If we want to avoid the tourist trap on mission trips, we must focus not on *doing* but on *being*. Adolescents and their parents ask, "What will we do?" But if our purpose for going is not first for doing but for being with, the question becomes, "Who will we be with?" "Who will we be encountering?" Our mission trips should be focused on simply being with people. They should be about seeing, hearing and sharing existence with others— others who are living as unwanted vagabonds in our world of tourism.

The way to break the dichotomy of the tourist trap is to enter the perplexity and impossibility of the vagabond: in other words, it's to go to the cross. Global tourism as mission trip lives in the streams of what we do, but a mission trip that breaks the tourist cycle focuses on who God is and what God does. This does not mean there is nothing to be done. Rather, instead of our *doing*—seeking to solve problems which we are, if we are honest, too small to solve—we go and join a people to together yearn, hope and (yes) work for God's future.

In this view, the mission trip becomes as much about confession as action; it is recognizing the impossibility that confronts real people and seeing how we (the tourists) benefit from it. We then invite adolescents not to participate in the sensation of helping others but instead (in fear and trembling) to enter the perplexity and impossibility of others—which, if we're willing to admit it, is similar to the song of our own broken humanity. The mission trip is therefore an invitation to go and seek for God in the hidden, backward, incognito suffering of the vagabond; it's an invitation to go and suffer with others, not solve their problems. Instead of kids feeling empowered because they have done something (what a great experience!), they should return perplexed, recognizing how knotted the world is and how our own advantage as tourists is borne on the backs of vagabonds. They should go home having sought to understand another as near to God and therefore able to see their own lives and recognize their connection and disconnection from others who are forced to live as vagabonds.

At root, mission trips are about accompaniment, not activity. They're about seeing the thinness of our sensationalized, always-moving world through shared life with others. The mission trip, then, is not participating in global tourism but seeking to go and find the crucified Christ who is revealed in the suffering humanity of the vagabond. It is about being with.

WHAT NOW?

But how do we live into this? How do we escape the tourist trap of doing and instead help young people and ourselves simply but profoundly seek the God of the cross by being with others? Karl Barth, in an article called "The Community for the World,"[4] offers three broad assertions about what the faithful community's inclination is to the world. These three dispositions that the church is to take toward the world can help us avoid the dichotomy often present in our mission trips and instead see them as accompaniment.

Barth's first point is that "the true community . . . seeks to know the world as it is."[5] He continues, "To *know* the world means concretely to know [humanity], to *see* with free and unclouded eyes who, what, where and how [humans] exist. It thus means to be constantly *aware*, both as a whole and in detail, both inwardly and outwardly, of what is involved in [humanity's] existence."[6] We might then ask ourselves, How are we preparing young people to *see?* It is not unusual for us to teach them to pound nails or practice skits before going on our trips. But are we taking steps to prepare them to see? Are we asking them to read material from indigenous people, or watch a documentary on a similar village? How are we helping them understand the financial and political situations of the community? Do we do any work that prepares them to recognize their (our) own cultural place and stereotypes? It is more important that we seek to make them truly *aware* than that we make them sensitive travelers, so that they can bear reality with those we meet.

Second, Barth states, "The true community . . . practices solidarity with humanity."[7] It is not enough to just see and be aware. We must also find solidarity; we must find ways to wrap our own humanity around the humanity of these others. It is here that the sensation-seeking tendency is broken, for sensation can become aware but it cannot find solidarity. In finding solidarity our being is changed; because we have entered so deeply into the suffering of the other, our world looks different. How might we do this on our trips? It means going and actually living with the people we encounter. It means that the church enters into a partnership with a community and congregation so that, instead of going to do, we go to be with these partners to share their table, to enter their ministry. It means that we go with *no* packaged ministry (puppet shows, skits, etc.) but instead go to participate in the already active ministry of our partner. In essence, it means that the trip is about learning—learning about a people, learning about the ministry of the church in another place—not about the sensation of doing something.

Finally, Barth asserts, "The true community . . . is given to humanity to be under obligation to the world."[8] In our world of moving, where waiting has been stripped away from wanting, obligation is seen as destroying freedom, and thus tantamount to prison. But when we understand our obligation, we are kept from believing that we have already done our part and can therefore move on. This means there can be no "drive-by" mission trips. Rather, having gone and seen in solidarity, we are called to take these others into our own community and life. In other words, when the mission trip is over we must not only find ways to continue the partnership but must also work to keep bringing the trip back into the life of the community. This can be done by discussing political and cultural issues, and by inviting these others we have met to affect the way we read the Bible and the topics we discuss. It means taking on the obligation to be hospitable to all vagabonds, and seeking to make the world aware of their presence and treacherous movement.

CONCLUSION

As I stood with my youth group in the airport that day just after my high-school graduation, dressed in our matching blue T-shirts, no one mentioned anything like this. No one challenged us to go and for at least one week bear the suffering of others who live so differently from our suburban American way of being. No one told us that God is found on a cross, in places of brokenness and emptiness, or suggested that we go to be in these places, to stare them down and seek God in them. So I boarded the plane and embarked on my great global vacation, all sponsored and made possible by the church. But this church, the church, is a church of vagabonds as well as tourists, and it is time that the short-term mission trip think more theologically about what it is we are sending these (mostly) middle-class young people to experience. I hope we can help them to see!

• DISCUSSION AND REFLECTION EXERCISE
Critical Incident—Thinking Theologically

Think back over the last experience you had on a mission trip (you could have been a participant, a leader or a planner).[9] Describe, in as specific, concrete and honest a fashion as you can, the following details:

1. The incident(s) on the mission trip that you recall as being the most theologically significant/important. In other words, what was the high of the trip? Why was it a high?

2. The incident that you recall as being the most distressing on the trip. Why was it distressing? Does it have any theological significance?

3. What characteristics or actions do you feel have been or could be the most theologically honest in relation to mission trips?

4. What experiences affirmed you on these trips? What experiences affirmed those in the location you served?

5. What did you learn about yourself, others, the church and God on these trips?

After answering these questions, look for themes. For instance,

- What are common themes about the mission trips we go on?

- What common themes arise in relation to our activity with and for other people?

- What common theological themes or issues do you see?

- What advice would you give others (or yourself) as they prepare for their next mission trip?

14

DOUBT AND CONFIRMATION
The Mentor as Co-doubter

ANDREW ROOT

My wife and I boarded the train just after midnight, sad to leave behind the breathless beauty of Venice (and the Italian ice cream sandwiches, of which I had already consumed a half dozen). We were on our way to Nice in the south of France for another adventure on twenty dollars a day. My wife had won a fellowship our final year of seminary, so we chose to stretch the funds to their extreme by traveling the world. (Yes, we chose to enter the stream of global tourism ourselves!)

Hauling our backpacks through the narrow aisles of the train, we found our way to our sleeper car and swung the door open to meet another young couple, also backpackers, from Montreal. After sharing a few travel stories they asked us what we did back home. We explained that we had just finished seminary and that my wife was preparing to be a pastor and I was going to be an academic theologian. "Cool," they said in their perfect English with overtones of a French accent. It was the kind of "cool" that said, "That's surprising and a little weird; I have nothing else to say, soooo . . . cool." After a minute of silence the young woman, realizing that we had hours remaining together, said, "I was kicked out of confirmation when I was in school. The leader thought I asked too many disturbing questions so they asked me to leave." Though I don't often think of the perfect thing to say until *after* a conversation, this was one of those occasions when it came to me in the moment. I responded, "That's too bad, because the best theologians ask the most disturbing questions." She just smiled and we were on to another conversation.

THE STRUGGLE OF CONFIRMATION

When we finally went to bed that night I lay in my sleeping bag as southern Europe raced past the window and thought of the last confirmation class I had taught. I remembered being frustrated by what felt like bipolar meetings with my ninth-grade small group. They never seemed to want to talk about the lesson or faith, preferring instead to rehash school gossip or simply make fun of each other until it was impossible to find our way back to the lesson at hand. But at least a few times a year (and this is where it got bipolar), the conversation would turn from gossip and mayhem and popcorn-throwing to the deepest and most difficult questions. One minute I would be fighting to get them to talk about anything having to do with what I supposed was our reason for being together, and throwing out comments like, "So in reading this Bible passage, what jumps out to you?" Then the next minute I'd suddenly be cornered with something like, "So if God is so powerful and loving, why every minute are children in poor countries dying? And why did my mom's friend who just had a baby get leukemia?" This back and forth made my head spin; what was I doing? I felt like half the time I was taskmaster teacher and the other half I was bumbling defender of the faith, feeling unprepared or inadequate to address these significant questions (and I was a seminary student at the time). So what was I doing as a confirmation leader? Was I to be a teacher, a defender, a mixture of both?

The truth is, when it comes to preparing adults to be confirmation teachers and mentors for students, we often don't know what they are supposed to be doing—which of course means that if we, the paid youth workers, don't know, then surely the volunteer has no clue. Usually, the volunteer is given a packet of lessons and told to get through them, as well as help kids write faith statements and memorize Bible verses. "And of course," they're told, "while you're doing all this essential stuff, stuff that determines whether or not they can be confirmed at all, don't forget to build deep relationships with them." But these goals—passing on the essentials of the Christian faith and tradition to young people while also being in deep relationship with them—seem to conflict.

DOUBT AS OUR CURRICULUM

Maybe this conflicted way of being a confirmation leader is not the best approach; perhaps there is another way. Often we see the confirmation leader as the one responsible for getting kids to know and appropriate the tradition through deep relationship. But what if the objective of the confirmation teacher was not to work to pass on anything but was rather to be a partner and companion in *doubt?* What if, instead of depending on lessons bought from publishing houses, we used our very doubts as the curriculum for passing on the faith? Or to say it another way, what if the best way to actually pass on the faith was not through lessons, certainty and knowledge, but through doubt? What if the confirmation teacher was a convincer and co-doubter with adolescents? What if confirmation wasn't about appropriating a tradition but about exploring doubt, placing it on the table and fiercely seeking understanding through it?

Then the responsibility of confirmation teachers is not to know the tradition in an airtight way, something few to no volunteers can sign off on, but only to be open enough with young people to explore their own doubts as they explore the young peoples'. What energy a small group could have if, for three years or three weeks, they sought to express the depth of their unbelief, working to share it with each other and God! The confirmation teacher then is no longer taskmaster teacher or skilled apologist with defense for all adolescent questions but rather captain of the company of companion doubters. And confirmation would then be the time for students to ask their most disturbing questions about God, self and world and have those questions placed on the table as the group's shared curriculum.

You may be starting to get nervous with my statements (I have to admit that my own stomach is quivering a little as I write this). But our shared nervousness has more to do with misunderstandings than with reality. We wrongly think that doubt is a Trojan horse which, if allowed to penetrate the fortress of our person, will release an army that will undercut our faith and lead us far away from God. And though we may not admit it, we fear that if we allow kids to doubt (even more, if we encourage it!) then they will discover that our faith is only a house of cards that cannot stand up to the winds of their inquisitions. I think this is because we wrongly assume that faith is only faith if it has been immunized from doubt. Yet doubt is not antithetical to faith; doubt is the call to faith. Doubt is the origin of faith, as we saw in part one.

BACK TO THE *VIA NEGATIVA*

As we discussed in chapter seven, the theologians of the early Reformation sought to do theology by discussing the negative or the opposite (the *via negativa*). They believed that it was only by examining the opposite that we could be freed from seeing our common theological language as just that: common, like meaningless phrases plastered on greeting cards that now have no meaning at all. We get back the rich (earth-shaking) meaning by thinking of these realities together in light of their opposite. So, for example, when Paul says that discipleship is encompassed in faith, hope and love, these are not just nice flowery words perfect for church mission statements and Christian college insignias. Rather, in light of their opposites, they are radical assertions. We are to love others in opposition to the will to dominate them. We are to hope in opposition to immediacy. And we are to have faith in opposition to certainty. The call to faith, then, is the call to avoid the temptation of certainty; it is certainty—not doubt—that destroys faith.

Right here is where we usually go wrong with confirmation. Christianity has nothing to do with certainty, and confirmation is not the ritual of claiming that you will, with all certainty, believe the tradition and theology of the church. No, Christianity is about living in opposition to certainty; it is about faith in the midst of doubt. Indeed, Christianity has no room for certainty, for certainty lives by the law of self-protection; its own rightness keeps it from hope and, most importantly (the greatest of these, Paul says), from love. Certainty demands its rightness in the now, even if it means hurting or hating others to maintain its integrity.

Doubt then is not our enemy but our great friend. For it keeps us from the most unchristian of things: assuming that we possess certainty, that we need *not* think about our faith or love our neighbors, and worse, that we need not search for God, for we know this God certainly. Faith that has become certain is no longer (by definition) faith; it has become idolatry, where we no longer seek out a living personal God but make this God into a frozen idol. The truth, then, is that there can be no relationship at all when it is based on certainty. I cannot really love my friend and embrace the fullness of his being if I assume I know him with certainty, if in being with him I keep saying, "I know you; that's not what you think. I don't need to hear you, see you or learn from you. I know you certainly. You cannot change." Faith is about trust. And for trust to be trust, it must always live with doubt. So I say, let us doubt! Let us make confirmation the place of shared doubt. For it is only when we welcome doubt that we are really people who are about *faith seeking understanding* (which the church father Anselm called us to be).

BACK TO CONFIRMATION

The confirmation leader, then, would be committing to affirm that the Christian tradition has something to say to our questions and our deep doubt, something worth exploring, rather than committing to know the tradition perfectly or even accept it fully. It is not important that they have the answers; they only need the willingness to seek God through doubt. This, of course, takes some bravery—much more bravery than going through a lesson handout. But it is a bravery that is borne in the person of the leader. When the group is built around shared doubt, it is constructed around the core of shared humanity. Through doubt the leader is moved to share not simply knowledge or adult wisdom with an adolescent but his or her very person, his or her sufferings and longings. A confirmation small group built on the sharing of doubt embraces the mutual openness of relationship. It is a group of place-sharing.

This means that a good confirmation teacher is not necessarily someone who knows every answer. It is, rather, someone who can create an environment where people feel safe enough to speak their deepest doubts into the life of the group—to speak these doubts and then seek God in them. In other words, the job of the confirmation leader is to invite doubts to be spilled without fear of shock or dehumanizing judgment by others. And the goal is to make doubt shared, and therefore part of a community. When our doubts are shared by others we not only find ourselves squarely in relationship with others but we also discover that our doubts do not alienate us. Rather, they invite us to keep searching, to keep seeking for God with those others. In this we discover that when we cannot believe, others believe for us, and that faith is not a possession or achievement, it is a gift from God.

Thus, confirmation is not the end of a road or a final exam but the welcome and continued encouragement to keep seeking God. Indeed, the lifeblood of faith seeking understanding is confronting and sharing our doubts with others. If confirmation teachers are co-doubters, conveners of the community of doubt, then they are able to do the two things we often ask of them, the two things that often thrust them into an uncomfortable conundrum: they are able to be in deep relationship with young people and, in so doing, explore the tradition deeply.

If relationships are built on mutual identification while respecting the other's difference and otherness, then exploring each other's doubts serves as a road to deep connection through mutual exploration (what more can we want?). Our doubts are usually deeply woven around our being. We doubt, for example, because we have heard that Jesus brings peace, but we have only known the chaos of a drunken father. We've heard that Jesus brings wholeness, but we have only known the emptiness of being out of work. As co-doubters, the small group becomes a deeply woven relational community of shared suffering. But because it has been built around doubt instead of certainty, it is at the same time a group that seeks God, that seeks understanding in the midst of the world's, the tradition's and their own inconsistency. In shared doubt the broken searching of our shared lives leads us into seeking God by asking, Who is this God who joins us in our suffering, who comes near in our doubts? Who is this living God who calls us into relationship, who loves us so that our very unbelief and our willingness to proclaim our doubt, like the father in Mark 9—"I believe; help my unbelief!"—become the invitation to trust, and therefore to have faith in the God made known in Jesus Christ?

I wonder what our sleeper-car companion would have said had she been in a confirmation class that did not kick her out for asking disturbing questions but made her (and the many other unspoken) doubts the curriculum for their time together. My hunch is that she would have said something like this:

> Cool. I went to confirmation. It was one of the most interesting times of my life. I fell in love with those people. We talked about so many crazy, fun and heartbreaking things. I really saw the depth of the Christian life; I tasted it and even now I find myself still searching, always asking big questions, always wondering what God is up to, who I am and what people are dealing with. It was one of the most interesting experiences I've ever had—I discovered life is worth living and God is worth loving.

• DISCUSSION AND REFLECTION EXERCISE
Simulation

This simulation is designed to give you the chance to experience what it might be like to do confirmation or some kind of catechesis around doubt.[1] Therefore, the exercise will work best with people who have led or will be leading some kind of educational dimension within the church with young people.

Break up into groups of three. You will do this simulation in these groups, but you will report back to the full group at the end of the session to share your insight and thoughts.

Background to Simulation

You are three teachers who are coteaching a Wednesday night confirmation small group (eight kids). Due to your busy schedules (something common for volunteers) you only see the class on the week you teach (i.e., every third week).

Situation

Last week you all received an email from students in the small group. Amanda, it seems, has made the rest of the group uncomfortable with her questions. According to the email, the probing and doubt-filled questions she asks disrupt the time and make the others uneasy. All three of you have experienced the depth of these questions, but because you each see the group only every third week, you were unaware of their extent. The kid who sent the email mentions over and over that Amanda is dangerous and that they have to deal with so many people who challenge their beliefs at school that they shouldn't have to deal with this at church.

Your Task

The three of you have now gotten together to figure out what to do. How do you deal with the group's anxiety and Amanda's questions? How do you handle it in a way that honors not only each member's person, but also the objectives of the small group? How can this be an opportunity to shift the group's focus to thinking deeply about their faith? Take your time together to address these questions but also to sketch out strategies of action: ways to keep Amanda's questions from dominating as well as ways to help the other kids open themselves to think deeply and critically about their faith. Sketch out an outline for at least one small group time. Then prepare to report your thoughts back to the rest of the group.

15

ASCENSION DEFICIT DISORDER

Youth Ministry as
a Laboratory for Hope

KENDA CREASY DEAN

If Christianity be not altogether restless eschatology, there remains in it no relationship whatever with Christ.

KARL BARTH

Of course, I was expecting a children's movie. Like countless other families who lined up for Pixar's 2009 animated feature *Up*, Kevin and I had brought our children (okay, they were sixteen and twenty-one, but still), and armed with popcorn, the four of us settled in for another feel-good Pixar adventure.

If you've seen *Up*, you know what happened next. Ten minutes in, we were blowing our noses into our butter-stained napkins, weeping for balloon-man Carl as his beloved Ellie slips from the surly bonds of earth. In mere moments, we had witnessed their long and happy marriage's simple joys and bitter disappointments. Suddenly we shared Carl's desperation, anticipating life without Ellie. We hated those smarmy developers who wanted to bulldoze his home. Our hearts sank when anxiety seized Carl and he whacked a construction worker with his cane. We seethed at the injustice of the court ruling, and despised the laughable aides sent from the

Shady Oaks Retirement Village to fetch him. But above all, we ached for Carl's remorse about never taking Ellie to South America, a promise that he forgot to keep until it was too late. At the movie's ten-minute mark, regret weighs heavily on Carl. "Now what do I do, Ellie?" he sadly asks, leafing through her childhood scrapbook. He can feel—we can feel—his past, his identity, slipping away.

Then he gets an idea.

Spoiler alert: Carl does go to South America, escaping his pursuers by ascending into the heavens—thanks to thousands of helium balloons that lift his house, and his spirits, sky-high. Like all fairy tales, *Up* takes place in a secondary, enchanted universe. Dogs talk and children befriend exotic birds and an old man pulls his past behind him in the form of a floating house. Yet J. R. R. Tolkien insisted that fantasy stories must tell the truth.[1] Because fantasy stories take place in a universe where latent human anxieties are given concrete shapes, these anxieties can be symbolically confronted and conquered. We do children no favors, child therapist Bruno Bettelheim famously argued, by domesticating the evil characters in fairy tales, since confronting and vanquishing evil is necessary to a child's sense of mastery in the world.[2]

THE GOSPEL AS A TRUE STORY

Tolkien maintained that "myths were the best way of conveying truths which would otherwise be inexpressible."[3] Picking up on this theme, Frederick Buechner insists that fairy tales teach us to enter the strange, alternate universe of the gospel on its own terms, so that the death-confounding truth of Christ can reach through the story into our anxious world.[4] Like fairy tales, the gospel communicates truth-beyond-words. The gospel is so universal, so profound, so vital for addressing the deep-seated anxieties of being human, that it defies easy explanation. Yet this does not make it untrue; on the contrary, the deepest truths we know—love, grace, forgiveness, redemption—do not "make sense" by human standards. Love goes beyond all reason, grace goes further than justice, forgiveness willingly suffers for another, resurrection turns death into life. Taken together, these mysteries ground Christian hope. They are signs of the future God has created us for; they point to what the kingdom of God is like[5]—which means that if we preachers tell God's story without its counterintuitive, eschatological promises, we do not tell the truth.

And therein lies the problem. In a church increasingly concerned with self-preservation, telling the truth gets harder and harder to do. Eschatology—the study of God's ultimate purposes for humankind—functions as the church's doctrine of hope, but it gets less attention in most churches than Flag Day, save for obligatory references to heaven at funerals.[6] The link between Christian eschatology and hope is all but forgotten, mostly because (1) we avoid the subject altogether, (2) we dehydrate eschatology to mean God's judgment on the last days (which inevitably winds up looking hopeful for some, and decidedly less hopeful for others), or (3) we convert Christian hope into optimism or cheap cheeriness (making the church look preposterously far removed from real human pain). And no one is more likely to "call us out" on these exclusionary, cheesy interpretations of the gospel than the teenagers, who are the first to accuse Christians of being out-of-touch with the real world because our heads are up in the clouds.

THE PROBLEM WITH LOOKING UP: ASCENSION DEFICIT DISORDER

Anxious people, uncertain about their futures, have always scanned the skies for hope, expecting to find answers in the heavens. Sailors navigated by the stars; wise men interpreted the alignment of the planets; ancient people worshiped the sun. Even among contemporary Christians, the answer always seems to be "up":

> "Lord, I lift your name on high . . ."
> "God will raise you up on eagle's wings . . ."
> "When I fall down, he lifts me up . . ."
> "We will meet him in the air, and then we will be like him . . ."
> "Everybody's gonna have a wonderful time up there, glory hallelujah . . ."

We are not the first anxious culture in history, of course. In the days and weeks following the resurrection, Jesus taught the disciples about the kingdom of God, promised them the power of the Holy Spirit and commissioned them to be his witnesses to the ends of the earth. All the disciples could say in response was, *Are we there yet?* "Lord, is this the time when you will restore the kingdom to Israel?" they asked (Acts 1:6). Lord, does the kingdom of God mean you are finally going to give us what we've been waiting for? Is *this* the time when all our faithfulness and hard work finally pays off? Is *this* the time we finally get the church we want? Lord, are we there yet?

Jesus parries: no, and yes. The future belongs to God, but in the meantime, there is work to be done; God's good news is for all people, but not everyone knows that God's reign has begun to unfold—that "the kingdom of God is at hand." This is where the church comes in:

> It is not for you to know the times or periods that the Father has set by his own authority. But you will receive power when the Holy Spirit has come upon you; and you will be my witnesses in Jerusalem, in all Judea and Samaria, and to the ends of the earth. (Acts 1:7-8)

And with that, Jesus "was lifted up, and a cloud took him out of their sight" as the disciples stood there gaping, gazing up at the heavens, watching him go. Suddenly two men in white robes appeared, and reminded them to stop gawking and trust the future Christ had promised them: "Men of Galilee, why do you stand looking up toward heaven? This Jesus, who has been taken up from you into heaven, will come in the same way as you saw him go into heaven" (Acts 1:11). In other words, "You already know what the future holds. So you can stop worrying, and concentrate on the here and now."

File this under troublesome texts for contemporary Christians. To the ancient Greeks, Jesus' ascent into the clouds would have confirmed his lordship over creation—but to us, it reads more like the floaty exit of Glinda, the good witch in *The Wizard of Oz*. Throughout the centuries, artists have playfully depicted Acts 1:1-11 by portraying the disciples watching Jesus' feet disappear into a cloud. No wonder twenty-first-century churches suffer from what we might call *ascension deficit disorder*[7] (A.D.D.), a tendency to act as though the future God has promised in Jesus Christ is a fairy tale, which shrivels our ability to practice hope. When we don't believe that Christ's promise to secure the future is true, we live as people fearful for our own prospects, protecting ourselves instead of allowing the Holy Spirit to use us as Christ's witnesses. A.D.D. is the reason churches get distracted so easily from the work Jesus commissioned us for: to be his witnesses throughout the earth. Instead, we are stymied and stressed, straining to make sense of the future's cloudy uncertainty. Like Carl (and like the disciples in Acts) we feel lost and alone, missing the implications of the angels' words: Christ is separated from us, but he is not finished with us yet.

If ascension deficit disorder stunts the church's ability to practice hope, maybe the cure lies in developing an *eschatological imagination:* the ability to envision the counterintuitive world God intends, and to live into the fact that this world has already started to unfold. Commenting on the "dystopia"—the sense that things are not as they should be—of global culture, British theologian Ann Morisy says pointedly: "Christians confronted by dystopian perspectives can no longer just *proclaim* or assert the persistence of hope; rather, if confidence in hope is to grow, then hope has to be *demonstrated.*"[8] Churches with eschatological imaginations do not merely cling to hope; they enact it, because the kingdom of God is not just up ahead. The kingdom of God is at hand.

ESCHATOLOGY: THE CHURCH'S ANSWER TO ANXIETY

Nothing rattles a bunch of postmodern, educated, rational Christians quite like talking about the ascension of Jesus. A good deal of our dazed posture toward the ascension story comes from our mainstream allergy to eschatology; surely this isn't a story we are meant to take seriously? Yet eschatology is the church's answer to anxiety, and it is one of Christianity's most practical doctrines. Our vision for the future affects our present choices far more directly than, say, asking "What would Jesus do?" Take the Celts, for example: their vivid sense of God's presence in everyday life gave Christianity "a less imperial feel" than many of its counterparts, which partly accounts for Celtic Christianity's appeal to postmodern young people.[9] The Celts constantly celebrated the interwoven relationship between heaven and earth; indeed, believing that the world is perforated by "thin places"—sites where heaven and earth comingle—Celts viewed their future with God as woven into their daily life on earth.[10]

It's safe to say that most American youth lack the Celts' pragmatic eschatology. Mention "future with God" to most of them, and the afterlife pops up—a subject youth find too distant to be relevant, and the rest of us would just rather avoid. Belief in heaven is growing among Americans (up almost 10 percent from a decade ago, to 81 percent), while the number of hell-believers has remained fairly steady (around 70 percent).[11] More than four out of five (85 percent) think they'll go to heaven.[12] And yet, while the majority of young people believe in an afterlife, few consider it "a life-driver," according to sociologist Christian Smith. In general, young people's religious beliefs amount to abstract agreements, not priorities they organize their lives around, or that guide them as they set their life's goals.[13]

Our reluctance to claim a significant role for eschatology in mainstream Christianity is also due to our persistent misunderstandings about what it is. Eschatology is neither a way to predict the future nor a doctrine about heaven and hell. Rather, eschatology simply means that we know how the story ends—God wins. And because God has bound Godself to humanity in Jesus Christ, if God wins, we win too. Knowing the "end of the story" therefore funds Christian hope, and it profoundly affects the way we live *now*. If we no longer need to worry about the future, we can let go of our survival anxiety. This allows us to live life as it unfolds, one play at a time, without worrying about the score or about running out of time.

Let's try this analogy. Remember the last time you TiVoed a football game and accidentally found out the final score before you had a chance to watch it? Knowing the final score (for better or worse) drains the suspense from the game—suspense that makes gladiator sports entertaining. But if knowing the score in advance makes for boring viewing, it also makes for lower blood pressure and better human relations. When we know how the game ends, we don't sweat the individual plays, even the ones we lose. Life is no longer a gladiator sport. We can approach our teammates *and* our opponents as who they really are, not just as the positions they play. And we can relax a little, since we know a fumble will not cost us our futures. In a similar way, a sturdy eschatology makes the Christian community an "unanxious presence" in the world because we are not obsessed with life's final score. Instead of functioning as a spiritual weathervane, eschatology enables us to read the "signs of our times" in light of an ending God has already written.

ANXIETY IN AMERICAN TEENAGERS: A BARRIER TO CHRISTIAN MATURITY

Unfortunately, young people absorb most of their anxiety from us—and in an era of economic recession, things are likely to get worse before they get better. Youth tend to deal with anxiety the way they deal with many of the traits they get from their parents: through denial. Yet denying the anxiety of the surrounding culture may not prepare them to function in it.[14] With marriage and parenthood receding farther into the future, the first few years after college are often given to "funemployment"—voluntary, transitional jobs that one can easily quit in favor of something else that is more entertaining.[15] However, with unprecedented high expectations for both salary and fulfillment, disdain for work that does not suit their personal needs or lifestyle, and a looming, extended period of national joblessness, American eighteen-year-olds to twentysomethings, according to economist Heidi Shierholz, need to brace themselves for "a big national experiment on stress."[16]

Hope offers an important cushion in stressful circumstances, and its prevalence in religious teenagers is one reason the National Study of Youth and Religion concluded that highly devoted young people are "doing much better" in life, on any number of variables, than their peers.[17] Research consistently finds dramatic differences in the levels of hope expressed by highly devoted teenagers compared to their peers.[18] But even Christian teenagers often have a very simplistic grasp of what hope means, and few relate it to Christian teaching. Take, for example, these hopeful statements gleaned from Christian teenagers in the National Study of Youth and Religion (2004):

"The future's gonna be great, I know it!"

"I just know God won't let me down."

"I hope that there's something after [death]. . . . That's pretty much all. I just hope it's okay, that I don't have to go to hell."

It is unlikely that such simplistic views of hope can be sustained until graduation, much less through a lifetime.

What makes Christian hope different from facile optimism and cheerful determination is its ability to stare down anxiety, the sublimated fear of our own demise. If Christ has secured our future, then this anxiety is superfluous—but in an eschatologically challenged church, anxiety often gets the upper hand. In 1586, the Carmelite priest John of the Cross penned the church's most famous manual on spiritual anxiety, *The Dark Night of the Soul*. But the roots of Christian anxiety reach back for centuries; remember, even in Acts, the disciples fretted over Israel's survival: "Lord, is this the time when you will restore the kingdom to Israel?" (Acts 1:6). We hear ourselves in their concern: Lord, is this the time you're going to fix the church, and make it powerful again, the way it was back when the old pastor was here? Back when 150 teenagers showed up for youth group every week? Back when people cared about church? Back when the people who came to church were like me?

One of the most frequent themes in the Hebrew and Christian scriptures is the anxiety of the people of God, and with it God's repeated efforts to quell this anxiety. Angels appear, and their first words are "Fear not." Jesus urges his followers not to worry, to take their cues from the lilies of the field (Mt 6:28). Again and again Israel is encouraged to step back and wait upon the Lord. In the ascension text, two men (we assume them to be angels) admonish the disciples to stop looking for Jesus in the clouds and assure them of his return.

Today we know that anxiety works against hope for social and biological reasons as well. *New York Times* columnist Kate Zernike dubbed the young people coming of age during the "Great Recession" of 2008-2009 as Generation OMG ("OhMyGod!" for the uninitiated). Zernike cites sociologist Glen Elder's 1974 study, "Children of the Great Depression," in order to compare Generation OMG with those who grew up between 1929 and 1931. In Elder's study, both older (ten and older) and younger (ages two to nine) children internalized adults' anxiety, but the effects of this anxiety differed. Older youth, who had developed a capacity for formal reasoning but were not yet saddled with adult responsibilities, translated their anxiety into resourcefulness. They learned how to survive, make do and solve problems; they grew into resilient adults who were extremely family-centered. However, younger children did not fare as well. Their need for parental care and attention coincided with the worst years of the Depression. They remember feeling bewildered and alone as children, and lacked confidence and direction through high school and beyond.[19]

The verdict is out on whether the "Great Recession" will last long enough to evoke similar responses among today's adolescents (my money is on "no"). But what we do know is that, at any level, the brain's wiring makes us more self-centered when we feel threatened. As Ann Morisy writes, "In the anxious atmosphere of dismal times, generosity of spirit shrinks and the primitive inclination to pursue self-interest increasingly dominates."[20] During the Depression, adversity caused people to pamper teenagers less and depend on them more, which gave youth confidence in their ability to overcome hardship. Today's teenagers, however (with the exception of the very poor), have been protected from real responsibility, and are the products of highly structured childhoods. As a cohort, they act more like the young children in Elder's studies of the Great Depression, dependent on external structures to the point that they grow anxious without them.

In fact, despite their reputation as a generation quick to volunteer and support community causes, research shows that millennial youth actually seldom do either one.[21] Are they an insensitive generation, or has the survival switch been activated in their brains? When we are concerned about survival, we do not think about our neighbors, our communities or important issues in the world. We do not think about Christ, or why he matters. In anxious times, the caretaking hormone, oxytocin, kicks in, motivating us to circle the wagons to protect our own. Our sense of entitlement (or selfishness, if you prefer) goes into overdrive, not because we are greedy but because we are *scared*, which winds up influencing our spirituality as well as our savings accounts. In anxious times we cannot take risks, so we cannot grow, which makes spiritual maturity—in fact, *any* form of maturity—difficult to come by. We cling to what we know, because our entire organism is focused on self-preservation.

ANXIETY IN AMERICAN CHURCHES: A BARRIER TO CHRISTIAN HOPE

Here is the interesting part: systems, also, grow anxious—which means churches can show the same symptoms as individuals. Most American churches are trapped in a rhetoric of decline, and each loss seems to threaten our existence. This is the kind of scenario that sends our brains into survival mode. The creative, problem-solving parts of our brains step aside, so our reflexes take over. Take, for instance, churches' responses to the growing research that identifies emerging adults—young people between the ages of eighteen and thirty—as the least religious cohort in America, and strikingly absent from congregations. Sociologist Robert Wuthnow argues that churches (and American institutions in general) have abandoned this age group, who must consequently make the most important decisions of their lives—decisions with long-lasting consequences about love, work and ideology—without the benefit of traditions or elders to guide them.[22] Living apart from their families, schools, churches and other established structures for community, emerging adults are left to guide one another as best they can.

When institutions are preoccupied with survival, they can scarcely think about nurturing the next generation. *Ephibephobia*—the fear of teenagers—sets in. Rhonda van Dyke Colby, dean of religious life at Shenandoah University, has employed Murray Bowen's classic theory of anxiety to analyze millennial young people, but she might as well be talking about churches.[23] In a state of heightened anxiety, Bowen says, we can't access our entire brains. Our reptilian, survival brain takes over, and instinctively we choose to fight, flee, freeze or protect. The good thing about the reptilian brain is that it is quick—but this speed comes at the expense of the thinking brain's accuracy and compassion.[24] When survival is at stake, there is no time for deliberation or empathy.

Carry this logic over to anxious churches. In anxious churches, our survival skills are on high alert. If your congregation is in survival mode, people are thinking of ways to fight, flee, freeze or protect. They have difficulty reflecting and thinking critically. They lose the ability to perceive humor or paradox. With the exception of protecting their own children, they can't think creatively about young people or newcomers, or anyone else who is not currently part of the congregational system. Those others are intruders, and the church needs to conserve their energy to survive.

Yet young people are notoriously slow to abandon hope. In fact, the age group least likely to develop a generalized anxiety disorder are those between the ages of fifteen and twenty-four.[25] Young people tend to view hope as an ethic, an action as well as an attitude, which serves as a powerful antidote to dystopia. In 2007, Jonathan Reed, a twenty-year-old film studies major at Georgia State University, won second place (and a place in YouTube history) in the American Association of Retired People's "U@50" video competition, in which filmmakers under thirty are invited to describe their lives at age fifty. His video, in which a palindromic poem (a poem that can be read backward or forward) scrolls onscreen, is a manifesto of youthful hope. To date it has received nearly fifteen million hits on YouTube and has inspired dozens of imitations. For the full effect, watch the film version,[26] but here are the words:

Lost Generation
by Jonathan Reed

Forward reading:	*Reverse reading:*
I am part of a lost generation	There is hope.
And I refuse to believe that	It is foolish to presume that
I can change the world	My generation is apathetic and lethargic.
I realize this may be a shock but	It will be evident that
"Happiness comes from within."	My peers and I care about this earth.

Is a lie, and
"Money will make me happy."
So in 30 years I will tell my children
They are not the most important thing in my life
My employers will know that
I have my priorities straight because
Work
Is more important than
Family
I tell you this
Once upon a time
Families stayed together
but this will not be true in my era
This is a quick fix society
Experts tell me
30 years from now, I will be celebrating
    the 10th anniversary of my divorce
I do not concede that
I will live in a country of my own making
In the future
Environmental destruction will be the norm
No longer can it be said that
My peers and I care about this earth
It will be evident that
My generation is apathetic and lethargic
It is foolish to presume that
There is hope.
    And all of this will be true,
    Unless we choose to reverse it . . .

No longer can it be said that
Environmental destruction will be the norm.
In the future
I will live in a country of my own making.
I do not concede that
30 years from now, I will be celebrating the
    10th anniversary of my divorce.
Experts tell me
This is a quick fix society
But this will not be true in my era.
Families stayed together
Once upon a time.
I tell you this
Family
Is more important than
Work.
I have my priorities straight because
My employers will know that they
Are not the most important thing in my life.
So in 30 years I will tell my children
"Money will make me happy"
Is a lie, and
Happiness comes from within.
I realize this may be a shock but
I can change the world,
I refuse to believe that
I am part of a lost generation.

HOMESTEAD ACRES: AN ESCHATOLOGICAL NEIGHBORHOOD

This is the kind of eschatological imagination that enabled saints like St. Francis and Clare, and leaders like Martin Luther and Martin Luther King, to learn to imagine the world as God intended it, and to lean into this vision as it began to unfold. But it's an imagination anyone can develop, even if we are not saints or reformers. I grew up in an intentional community—but the surprising thing is that I was forty years old before I knew that. (In Ohio, if you are up to any good, the worst thing you can do is tell people about it. That might look like bragging, and in the Midwest, bragging comes pretty close to being a mortal sin.) As a result, I had no idea that my neighborhood was any different than any other neighborhood in town. I obviously knew that the Mitchells next door were African American, and that two doors down lived the Lees, and that there were some mixed-race families on the block. It was a fact of life in our neighborhood that people were forever borrowing tools from one another, plowing each other's driveways, mowing each other's lawns. I thought this was how neighborhoods worked.

What my parents never told my sister or me was that Homestead Acres was established in the 1960s by a handful of people who had committed to living together as an interracial community. It wasn't until my dad died—and my mom moved because she remarried a guy down the street—that I learned that the tools in our garage did not all belong to us. Most of the tools and the tractors in Homestead Acres were communally owned. When I read an article in the paper celebrating the fortieth anniversary of the Homestead Acres "experiment," I suddenly realized why so many people in our neighborhood had built their own homes, and why we had a community pond for fishing and swimming. I had assumed that my neighbors built their homes because they were thrifty, and because they were gifted craftsmen and women. I thought we fished and swam in a pond because it was wholesome entertainment. The reality was that, in the 1960s, many contractors refused to build in Homestead Acres because of its interracial stance, and in some parts of the country, pools remained closed to blacks.

In retrospect, I wish my parents had mentioned some of this along the way. On the other hand, if they had, would growing up in Homestead Acres have seemed as natural, as non-anxious? The people of Homestead Acres (many of whom were churchgoing Christians) simply lived as though the reign of God were already unfolding on earth—and if not everywhere on earth, then at least in one tiny corner of Delaware, Ohio.

BECOMING A YOUTHFUL CHURCH

Without attention to the ascension, our imagination as a church grows small and hard. The kingdom of God becomes a platitude instead of a concrete hope we are called to enact. Yet Christians "are called not just to have hope but to perform or enact hope, here and now."[27] Eschatology does not predict the future; it frees us from anxiety about the future, because in Christ, the future is secure. Christ has removed our human time limits by binding our future to his, freeing us to worry less and laugh more. We can stop looking up, and start looking around. As Studs Terkel, the American oral historian, put it, "Hope has never trickled down. It has always sprung up."[28]

This is where youth itself becomes instructive. Theologian Jürgen Molt-mann points out that what makes us "young" is not our age. What makes youth *youth* is its wide-open sense of possibility, the confidence that death is not on the horizon, the exhilarating assumption that the future is wide open and filled with limitless potential. For Christians, this sense of wide-open possibility, the confidence that death poses no threat, that the future is a gift—this is Christ's promise to *all* Christians, not just the young ones. In other words, everyone whose future is bound to Jesus Christ is a youth. In Jesus Christ, the church is inherently youthful—because in Jesus Christ, we are unfettered by death. We are apostles of possibility, with a wide-open future in God. We are participants in the kingdom of God, world without end, not just someday, but now. In Moltmann's words, "It is not that the future belongs to the young. . . . The future *makes* us young."[29]

Moltmann describes how, in August 2002, Pope John Paul II—eighty-two years old, ill and in great pain—visited his hometown of Cracow. He was greeted by cheers of "You are young! You are young!" The pope smiled and denied it, but the crowd was right.[30] For Christians, what makes us young is not age, but hope:

> Even youths will faint and be weary,
>   and the young will fall exhausted;
> but those who wait for the LORD shall renew their strength,
>   they shall mount up with wings like eagles,
> they shall run and not be weary,
>   they shall walk and not faint. (Is 40:30-31)

LOOKING UP: MINISTRY'S OCCUPATIONAL HAZARD

The eschatological message of Pixar is that things are looking "Up." It is true that the image of "looking up" is a powerful one in Scripture as well; as the psalmist sings, "I lift up my eyes to the hills—from where will my help come? My help comes from the LORD, who made heaven and earth" (Ps 121:1-2). But straining to see God's future can never be a permanent posture for Christians. Before long, we begin to feel a crick in the neck. It is easy to convince ourselves that, if we just look hard enough, pray hard enough, stay true enough, some answer from heaven will appear—maybe in the form of a new volunteer, maybe in the form of a pastor, maybe in the form of a youth minister. If we just persevere *long enough*, though, God will send somebody from on high to fix things down here.

But if that were all there were to the gospel, we would be a stiff-necked people. It is understandable that the disciples became anxious at the ascension, when the Jesus they had gotten used to disappeared from sight. And it is understandable that our churches, in a world where God's involvement is often hidden from our sight, and at a time when all we can see of the future is fog, become anxious too. Yet the ascension story reminds us to stop fretting about what lies ahead, and to live as though what Jesus promised is true: the kingdom of God is not up there. The kingdom of God is at hand.

ADVENT: LIVING LIKE PREGNANT PEOPLE

We serve an anxious church, in an anxious culture, that cultivates anxious teenagers, and if we marinate in this anxiety long enough, we become anxious church leaders too. But what if we stopped feeding the beast? What if we began to live as people who believe what we preach—that Jesus is Lord, that his life, death and resurrection binds our futures with his, and that the kingdom of God is at hand? What if our job is not to convince young people that Jesus wins, but to live as though he already has? What if the church were less of an ad agency for Jesus and more a community that embodies the world as God intends it to be? What if youth ministry were a laboratory for developing eschatological imaginations—a place for imagining and embodying God's intentions for the world?

The Christian community has a model for developing such an imagination in an unlikely place: Advent. Some theologians are disillusioned with Advent, put off by the season's cheesy optimism marketed by advertisers through outlets like Hallmark and Hasbro. Yet Advent is a season of hope, and is well-suited for nurturing Christian eschatology. In fact, a case can be made that twenty-first-century Christians are living in one prolonged season of Advent; Advent is the season the contemporary church is in.

Why? Because Advent is a season of pregnancy—a season of expectation, of course, but also a season of waiting, and anxiety, and pain, and risk. New life is coming, but it's not here yet, and our job is to get ready. There is no cheap hope in pregnancy. You can't pass it off as though it doesn't change you, or as if suffering isn't involved. Moreover, with great hope comes the risk of great disappointment, for new life is fragile. It often struggles, and sometimes it emerges in ways we don't expect, or wouldn't wish for. But in new life there is also joy, and as Paul reminded the Thessalonians, joy in the church is a sign of the Lord's coming: "For what is our hope or joy or crown of boasting before our Lord Jesus at his coming? Is it not you?" (1 Thess 2:19).

Advent helps us reframe the anxiety facing the contemporary American church. Yes, our numbers are declining. Yes, our forms are shifting. Yes, Christian communities continue to hemorrhage their youth. Yes, our leadership is in crisis. All of this is true. But what if decline is not a bad thing? What if decline may *save* the church? If, as a church, we have veered into anxious self-centeredness or therapeutic individualism, maybe what we're seeing in our current ecclesial condition is a market correction. Contractions may not be bad; in fact, contractions are *necessary* to new birth. What's more, when we feel these contractions, we know that new life is on the way.[31]

Youth ministers can be midwives for such a time as this. Our ministries serve as signs of God's wide-open future, enacted by young people simply because they are young. If the church has involuntarily entered a new season of Advent, then evoking an eschatological imagination in the faith community is necessary. The church must learn to live like people who are "expecting." We must learn to live like pregnant people. That means several things:

1. Wait. The most obvious thing you do when you're pregnant is wait. As Advent people, we wait, and while we wait, we nourish the vision for the kingdom of God that Christ has planted in us.

Waiting is not doing nothing. During this period of waiting, we are bathing this embryo of new life, this church about to be reborn, in prenatal care. We must tend our own souls so that the Word of God has good soil to grow in. Prenatal care doesn't always feel holy or beautiful; sometimes the vitamins are hard to swallow, and the ultrasound gel is squishy and gross. But just because we cannot see Jesus at work during this incubation period does not mean that he is not multiplying life within us. So we keep hope alive, even when God is invisible to us. We remember the rabbi in Auschwitz who, day in and day out, wailed at God's absence in the death camps. Yet every Friday at sundown, the wailing stopped. The rabbi would say: "Now we must light the candles. It is time to pray."

2. Name our anxieties. New life is scary. There be dragons here—dragons of doubt, disillusionment, uncertainty. So it is even more important that we tell the story of Christ during Advent, mostly because we need to hear it ourselves, as do the young people in our care. As Jacques Ellul put it, we do not need a theology of hope. We need *hope*.[32]

Naming our ecclesial anxieties also means telling the Christian story without rationalizing it or apologizing for it, and certainly without shying away from the parts that bother us. Christian history is filled with advice for addressing the dragons of spiritual anxiety, but none of it advises avoiding them. In 1738, a young John Wesley, already an Anglican priest but in the throes of spiritual doubt, asked his friend, Moravian leader Peter Bohler, whether he should cease preaching, given the depth of his anxiety. "By no means," Bohler said. "But what can I preach?" agonized Wesley—to which Bohler famously replied: "Preach faith till you have it, and then because you have it you will preach faith."[33] In the face of anxiety, we're to tell the Christian story *anyway,* until we believe it.

3. Paint the nursery. Eventually, pregnant people must make room for the new life that is coming, and must brace themselves for the way this new life impinges on their existing reality. In other words, we have to paint the nursery. At some point, the new life Christ promises us must stop being an intellectual possibility and start being an actualized one. We must start enacting God's hope in the world, even if there are times, maybe many, when we will be disappointed, and when we will disappoint ourselves.

A lot of people go into youth ministry—and I count myself among them—partly because we love teenagers, and partly because youth ministry is one of the few places we see real hope for ecclesial change. People who work with teenagers are an irrationally hopeful breed, and because youth ministry serves as the "research and development" arm of the church, it is a place that both generates and test-drives new forms of church life in today's culture. The questions youth ministers wrestle with today will very soon be questions the *entire* church must answer—questions like:

- What does relational ministry look like in a world of ubiquitous connection?

- What is the difference between "pastoring" someone and "friending" them?

- What makes small, face-to-face Christian communities matter, when teenagers are already networked online with thousands of friends who already share their most intimate hopes, dreams and fears?

- Can the church offer a richer slice of reality than a virtual one, a taste of communion beyond community?[34]

When the church does start asking these kinds of questions, the go-to people in the Christian community will be those who work with teenagers.

IMAGINEERING THE KINGDOM OF GOD: LESSONS FROM IMPROV EVERYWHERE

There are many metaphors that describe the role of the youth minister in a pregnant church. We are ecclesial lab technicians, vocational "test rats," maybe even pastoral "crash dummies"—pick your image—as we learn, trial-and-error, to represent Christ in a world that young people will not let us avoid. Perhaps a more apt description comes from Disney: youth ministers serve as the Christian community's "imagineers." It is our job, to the best of our ability, to imagine the world the way God imagines it. It is our job, to the best of our ability, to treat young people as the people God made them to be instead of as the people they have become. It is our job, to the best of our ability, to live alongside young people as though we believe what we preach—as though the kingdom of God, strange as it sounds, really is at hand.

This is why it is not enough for Christians to have hope; we must enact hope, in every corner of the earth, in every crevice of human life. Pope Benedict XIV makes the case eloquently:

> The Christian message was not only "informative" but "performative." That means: The Gospel is not merely a communication of things that can be known—it is one that makes things happen and is life-changing. The dark door of time, of the future, has been thrown open. The one who has hope lives differently; the one who hopes has been granted the gift of a new life.[35]

In truth, what drove this point home for me was not a church, but a group of young adults whose sole purpose is to give people, in their words, "the story of a lifetime." Improv Everywhere is a New York–based improvisation troupe that invites ordinary people into "missions" that enact a reality that does not yet exist—until the actors insert a small but noticeable change into a present situation.[36] One of their most famous stunts involved two hundred "agents" (volunteers) who entered Grand Central Station and simultaneously "froze" on cue. For schedule-crazed New Yorkers, the stunt was a humorous, disorienting masterpiece. After a few moments the agents "unfroze" and everyone went about business as usual.

I became acquainted with Improv Everywhere by accident. A friend sent me a YouTube clip of a free wedding reception, thrown for a random couple as they exited a courthouse in New York City.[37] "Do you want a free wedding reception?" a man, dressed for church, asked the couple—and the bride said, "Sure." The man escorted the couple to a park across the street where a tent was waiting with bridesmaids and groomsmen, in full regalia, along with a wedding cake, a dance floor, a band, guests and even presents. As the bride and groom laughed, danced and cut the cake, the change in their expressions—from skeptical curiosity to unbridled joy and appreciation—was unmistakable. "What church does this?" I wondered, anxious to discover the community that had come up with such an incredible ministry.

Then I learned that the wedding reception was not the ministry of a church, but a "mission" (their word, not mine) sponsored by Improv Everywhere. I was crestfallen . . . and a little angry. Why *hadn't* a church thought of doing that? Why were we Christians leaving mission to young people who just want "to see what would happen" if they introduce extravagant hope into ordinary human situations? Why wasn't it the church giving people "the story of a lifetime"? The young people in Improv Everywhere, of course, gave no thought to participating in God's reign; they would not recognize the parallels between my job and theirs. And yet they too were on a mission of hope—and it occurred to me that they might be better at fulfilling their mission than I am at fulfilling mine.

THE BEST GAME EVER

Fun, of course, goes a long way toward dissipating anxiety, and working with teenagers offers ample opportunities for playfulness. Yet without the gospel to inform such play, Christian hope goes unproclaimed, and in some cases it is clearly absent (Improv Everywhere's "pantless subway ride" comes to mind). Yet Improv Everywhere has captured something that churches have forgotten: the ability to enter a situation assuming that there is a different game to be played in human time than the one that is scripted. My favorite Improv Everywhere mission is called "The Best Game Ever," in which several dozen agents infiltrate a Little League game, unannounced, and treat it like the World Series. The "fans" cheer for each player by name, wave team posters, dress like mascots and broadcast plays on a JumboTron. Even the Goodyear Blimp ("Go Mudcats!") makes an appearance, coming out of the clouds over the game. At first, players and parents greet the hoopla with disbelief, but soon the boys are thinking of themselves as champions. I am willing to wager that the kingdom of God is like that: every player feels like a champion, because this is how God views each and every one of us.

Jesus calls us to be a youthful church, not because we are young but because we are his. Nothing is more important for a youthful church than developing an eschatological imagination, which allows us to wait with confidence, to name our anxieties without fear, and to make room for new life and new possibilities as Christ works, unseen, to usher us into an unknown future. Young people's sense of open-ended possibility, their candid rejection of the fear of death, remind us that youthfulness is built into Christian eschatology. It is not age that makes us young. The future makes us young, and the future belongs to Christ. Fear not.

• DISCUSSION AND REFLECTION EXERCISE
Hat Full of Quotes

Choose quotes within the reading that you find interesting or challenging—ideas that get you thinking—and come to the discussion with one or two of these quotes typed out.[38]

When you all arrive, place your quotes in a hat. Then break up into small groups. Each group should choose two or three quotes out of the hat. Allow these quotes to become the starting point of discussion.

Postscript: REFLECTING ON METHOD

Youth Ministry as Practical Theology

ANDREW ROOT

*WITH **BLAIR D. BERTRAND***

eleased from its long incubation as a subdiscipline under Christian education, where it received its essential theoretical nourishment from the social sciences, American academic youth ministry has slowly matured over the last two decades. Like coming out of a cocoon, youth ministry scholarship has begun not only to recognize its limbs and its ability to create and move in new directions, but also to see that it has wings, and colorful ones at that. And it is realizing that these beautifully colored wings are its essential theological nature, that reflection on the practice of youth ministry is a fundamental theological task. Thus, recognizing its freedom from the incubating cocoon and the colorful theological wings it possesses, youth ministry scholarship has begun to see itself as a practical theological activity.

This has led to a fresh theological turn for youth ministry; drawing from practical theological and missiological perspectives, youth ministry scholarship has sought to give attention to the activity of God in distinct local communities of practice. Therefore, youth ministry, like many of the practical theological disciplines, has turned to ethnography and other qualitative research methods, seeking to thickly describe and interpret contexts as places of theological action. In addition, youth ministry has followed (and therefore placed itself within) the larger field of practical theology by seeing its core activity as reflecting on concrete/present situations for their theological depth.

Yet something has been missing in this significant turn, and missing not only in youth ministry but in practical theology more broadly. I contend that this something is essential for helping those preparing for (and already in) ministry think theologically about their actions and identity. In all the constructive work in youth ministry and practical theology, there has been little systematic attention given to how divine action and human action (or divine praxis and human praxis) relate one to another, to how and where they actually associate. So while we have sought to articulate theological issues and perspectives in connection to concrete communities and practices, we have not yet sought to articulate how to go about discerning the activity of God from the place of human action or how human action is participation in the action and being of God in the world. And though we have turned our attention to local practice for its theological depth, we have not articulated clearly how our actions are associated with our conceptions of how God acts and moves in human history—at least, not clearly enough to impact local practitioners' views of how their action is associated with divine action. Yet it seems, at least to me, that this association is the heart of ministry itself. Ministry at its core is human action that participates in divine action.

If practical theology, and youth ministry following it, is concerned with the theological activity of local communities of action, then youth ministry imbedded within practical theology is fundamentally about the articulation and association of two distinct forms of action (praxis): God's and humanity's. James Loder called this "the generative problematic of practical theology."[1] It is problematic because divine and human actions are distinct and different—or, at the very least, we must admit that divine action is hidden directly from the human knower. But it's also generative, because although these forms of action (praxis) are distinct, they nevertheless do relate. God does act with and for us within our local communities, as our ethnographic studies have uncovered. But how do we understand this, and how can it help us do ministry and practice our faith in a way that is congruent with our understanding of how divine and human actions associate in our local concrete histories?

This postscript explores this question. Drawing from the work of Richard Bernstein and his book *Praxis and Action,* I will seek to articulate how certain forms of human reflection have understood how the divine and human forms of action find association. In *Praxis and Action* Bernstein shows how four significant philosophical streams of thought have all provided unique ways of understanding action (praxis) within human history. All four streams, Bernstein believes, find their energy in conflict with Hegel's system. I will push Bernstein's thesis beyond its philosophical perspective into the theological, asserting that the forms of human action he teases out have been methodological pathways of relating divine and human action for theologians.[2]

This article will thus place the philosophical in conversation with the theological. While twentieth-century theology has warned us against the dangers of doing so (dangers that I consider significant), Dietrich Bonhoeffer, a great proponent of revelation-centric distinctiveness, nevertheless maintains that philosophy cannot be obliterated from the theological. Rather, if God has not only entered into human history through act but also through action has impacted our very being-in-the-world (as Bonhoeffer argues in *Act and Being*), then the philosophical must be considered as helping to give perspective as the human seeks to discern and participate in divine action.

Bernstein contends that Marxism (critical theory), pragmatism and Kierkegaardian existentialism (the three streams from Bernstein that I will consider) can all be understood as philosophical projects about action or praxis. In opposition to a Hegelian method, each of these philosophical perspectives seeks to reconceptualize human action. But because of Hegel's extensive and all-encompassing approach (e.g., *Geist* not only being the flow of history but also the activity of God), Bernstein contends that these perspectives give attention to ultimacy (communism's political perspective shows the form of ultimacy in Marxism, even in relation to its atheism).[3] Therefore, due to their attention both to action (praxis) and to ultimacy, it is no wonder that these philosophical streams have provided intuitive direction in practical theological methodological construction. Clearly, critical theory, pragmatism and a Kierkegaardian existentialism are not the only philosophical perspectives worth considering, but as I will argue, they have been the most consistently and generatively drawn upon by practical theological perspectives on ministry. Bernstein, however, did not give attention to all the significant philosophical perspectives drawn on within practical theology. Rather, more recently a recovery of Aristotle through the lens of the work of philosopher Alasdair MacIntyre has pushed forth a neo-Aristotelian perspective in practical theology.

This postscript will examine each of these four perspectives (neo-Aristotelianism, critical theory, pragmatism and a Kierkegaardian perspective) to explore their understanding of praxis/action, how this understanding has been appropriated within practical theology, and where divine and human action find association from within this perspective. To give these conversations flesh, I will then provide an example from within youth ministry of how a thinker has drawn from each of these perspectives. We will see Kenda Creasy Dean as an exemplar of the neo-Aristotelian perspective, David White in relation to critical theory, Chap Clark in light of pragmatism and myself (through the writing of Blair D. Bertrand) in connection to Kierkegaardian existentialism. While some of these thinkers work explicitly from these perspectives and others more intuitively, I will seek to show how their understanding of divine and human action leads them to argue for a distinct understanding of where and how human agents encounter the activity of God.

Each thinker makes a case that youth ministry should revolve around certain actions, because each thinker believes that divine and human action come together in certain ways. While I have placed myself (through the hand of Bertrand) in this article, I will *not* make the case that one perspective is better than the others; I leave evaluation to the reader. Like Osmer's description of practical theology, this article provides a heuristic or descriptive map.[4] In addition, the fact that I have placed a thinker in one stream does not mean that they do not also drink from others. For instance, while I will argue that Dean is deeply imbedded in a neo-Aristotelian perspective, she does at many points drink from Kierkegaard,[5] and White much more than superficially draws from the practices discussion of a neo-Aristotlianism. Nevertheless, I will argue that each of these thinkers draws *mostly* from one stream in constructing their commitments to how young people encounter the action of God in their concrete lives.

This, then, is the ultimate significance of this postscript for the reader, to explore the essence of ministry: to understand and articulate how concrete people encounter the action of God, and to therefore construct their ministries in such a manner.

FORMS OF DIVINE AND HUMAN ACTION

Neo-Aristotelian. If there were a father of "praxis" as a concept, it would be Aristotle. Aristotle sought to tease out how the actions of *praxis* were different from those of *poesis*. *Poesis* is an action that has its telos, or end, as a final product, but in praxis the telos is in doing the activity well in itself.

Therefore, the practical life has its own telos and therefore its own distinct form of knowledge. These forms of knowledge were essential for life in the polis, Aristotle believed, contending that the practical life resulted in a good political life for the polis. Praxis as practical forms of knowledge was participated in through practice or action itself. As one engaged in praxis, one did practices that held within them knowledge and virtues that transformed individuals. And if these practices were practiced together, which most practices demand both in their operation and historical form, then communities themselves would be transformed. These practices, because they were grounded in praxis, were not about utilitarian function—getting to some simple end—but about being in community. So praxis was lived out as a set of communal practices performed by members of a group for the sake of being in community well. The understanding was that people form excellence not by seeking a final goal but by reflecting on their journey, on the practices that they use to form their life together.

Alasdair MacIntyre has revived Aristotle's philosophical perspective, applying it to our late modern post-industrial times. Seeking to move past frozen principles as the ground for ethics, MacIntyre turns to virtue. He argues that it is through habits and knowledge of a good life—thus, through character and virtue—that one learns to act ethically. However, character and virtue are learned through the practices of a community. As one lives in a community of practice, one is drawn into the community's habits, taking on its virtues. It is therefore through practice that we learn how to act in the world.

This perspective has been ripe for practical theological reflection. Dorothy Bass and Craig Dykstra have been two of the greatest proponents of reflecting deeply on the practices of communities as *the* task of practical theology. They define Christian practices as "things Christian people do together over time to address fundamental human needs in response to and in the light of God's active presence for the life of the world."[6] This rich definition reveals that a neo-Aristotelian perspective sees divine and human action coming together in the practices of a community of faith. When a community engages in the practices of faith they encounter God. The human action of practice aligns the community with divine action. However, it is not just any practice that matters; rather, it is practices that have been built up over time, practices that are imbedded in the tradition of Christian faith. These practices connect reflection on faith with experience and action, making faith a passionate engagement with self, world and community and, through this, passionate engagement with God. *Therefore, we encounter God as we practice our faith together.*

In *Practicing Passion* Kenda Creasy Dean richly places youth ministry within a neo-Aristotelian perspective. While her overall argument pushes beyond one category, when it comes to the connection between divine and human action she proposes that practices in a passionate church are the place of encounter with God. Dean is adamant about the independent and dynamic activity of God; she returns repeatedly to this reality. Nevertheless, Dean also seeks to explore how human beings, particularly young people, encounter this dynamic action. She contends that this action of God is so dynamic that it can be understood as pure passion; God acts in the world from God's passion for God's creation. The goal of her project is to articulate how the human agent can encounter this passion. Dean asserts that adolescents are the perfect people to make the central focus of this pursuit, because adolescents, in her definition, are ontologically passionate, though she sees their present passionate action as misdirected toward consumer over-attention. She doesn't necessarily blame adolescents for this (nor the system, as some of our thinkers below will); she blames the church. Dean grieves that the church has lost passion and as such is unable to connect to the ontological passion of young people. The church, in her view, has ceased expecting to encounter God, has ceased placing a theological emphasis on a lived experience of soteriology as the natural extension of God's passionate engagement with the world. This loss of passion, she believes, has much to do with misdirected human action. The church has failed to make God's passionate action central to its life. Her book, then, is ultimately about a church that is failing to engage the ontological passion of people, which is seen most directly in the apathy of young people toward it.

How, then, do we encounter this dynamic action of the passion of God in the world? Dean turns to human action, believing that the church can reignite its passion by reviving its practices, thereby inviting young people to also passionately practice their faith in a passionate community. Thus, in neo-Aristotelian form (though Dean pushes the dynamic independent activity of God more than most), she asserts that it is through practices that the passion of human action is taken into the passion of the activity of God.[7] "Spiritual practices," Dean states, "did not eliminate human passion, but refocused it on its proper object: God. Especially among inexperienced

Christians, spiritual disciplines became the tools that loosened young people's grip on lesser loves so they could freely accept and respond to the passion of God."[8] As human agents take on the practices of faith—the practices embedded in the tradition of the faithful community—they encounter the activity of God. Dean notes, for instance, that "in worship, our lives become signs of God's passion as we take part in holy practices, human actions that God uses to infuse creation with grace, wonder, and love."[9]

Thus, we engage the passion of young people by inviting them into practice, into taking on the virtues and habits of the faithful community—but these practices, for Dean, are only virtues, and are therefore only transformative because they are infused with God's very presence. The ultimate objective of youth ministry is to ignite young people's passion in Godself, but the way to do this is to move them into practice. *Practice is the ground of divine and human encounter.* It is through practice that young people are given an identity as Christian, an identity that invites them to passionately practice their faith in the activity of God, to practice their faith in passion as opposed to giving their action and their identity to other cultural realities. Dean asserts, "In spiritual disciplines that imitate Christ [in practices], God imparts the grace that 'detaches' adolescent passions from the therapeutic gods of consumer culture."[10] Holding to the dynamic activity of God, she continues, "Christian practices form identity in Christ not because of what young people do in these practices, but because of what God does in them."[11] Practices in good neo-Aristotelian perspective form young people, transforming their very action in the world, as they are invited deeper into the practices of the life of a community.

Therefore, a youth worker's job is to form his or her ministry around faithful and rich practices, not only because they lead to virtue and Christian habits (a Christian identity, Dean would assert), but more importantly because they are the place young people are drawn into the passion of God. She explains, "What I am suggesting . . . is that the practices of the Christian community should comprise the core of Christian curriculum for young people."[12] Young people are drawn into this passion not as an individual reality, however, but as a communal one. Practices engage the young person in the presence of God within and through a community of action, and therefore young people are immediately called out into the world as they practice their faith with others over time. Dean sees this as the heart and soul of passionate action—action that is missing in most churches. The human action of practice is the container God fills with God's very presence; the practice itself becomes the place to encounter God.[13]

Critical social theory. It is commonly cited that there are two Karl Marxes, the early one and the mature one. While the mature Marx of the *Capital* is known for his economic theory and political ideas, which served as the soil for communism, the early Marx is considered to be a philosopher and thinker. After Aristotelian praxis lost its magnetism within philosophical reflection, it was the early Marx who revived and added to the concept of praxis. Having studied Hegel, the early Marx contends that it is not the philosopher's job to simply describe the world (Hegel had done a good job of this) but to change it. Therefore, the job of philosophy is not found in simply constructing theory but in propelling people out into action, to change what is wrong with the world. And the young Marx, writing from a nascent industrialized nineteenth century, believed there was much wrong with the world.

Marx felt that it was wrong, for example, that people were disconnected from their labor, and not engaged in their own action—that people were no longer in control of what they produced—which meant that what they produced was no longer an expression of their self but rather dominated them. This happened because of the system, because the structure of society embedded in its intuitions functioned (acted) to estrange people from themselves for the sake of their own power. Marx believed that society is therefore constructed in a manner that leads to alienation.[14] For Marx, people are what they do, so if their work estranges them from themselves, if their action has nothing to do with their very person, then people are alienated by the very structures they live in. In other words, people are alienated because they have become objectified, turned into cogs laboring, which keeps them from participating in their own action. Marx asserted that the very structures and institutions of society are wrapped together in such a manner that people are estranged from their own action, which therefore means that people are forced into contradictions: they are free (ontologically) but bound practically and societally.[15] As Bernstein explains, "At the heart of Marx's theorizing is a 'radical anthropology' which seeks to overcome the dichotomies that have plagued modern thought and life."[16]

This estrangement is *not* an ontological reality but a *historical* one, since people are not meant to live in contradiction, to be alienated as objects from the world. Rather, they are meant to be agents, to be actors, to be people of praxis. They are meant, from their ontological core, to live beyond contradiction. Much like Hegel, Marx sought to overcome all contradictions, but unlike Hegel, Marx believed that what is needed to overcome contradiction is action to rework the historical flow of society and its institutions. Hegel interpreted the world, but Marx sought to change it, to rework and remodel the structures of society by tearing down the old. Thus, for Marx, the only way to overcome contradiction is to engage in revolutionary praxis, to overcome the estranging, alienating systems with new ones.

The chief task to bring forth revolutionary praxis, Marx believed, is educating the people, and awakening their consciousness so that they might see and understand the alienating conditions of their world that thrust them into contradiction. It is, in other words, about educating them to recognize that they are being exploited for the gain of the structures of society. For revolutionary praxis to happen, people must be taken to a place of consciousness raising. While the historical system seeks to wash our very selves from our action, revolutionary praxis places consciousness back within our action, leading us to act beyond contradiction and in unity of ourselves. But for this to reach its needed end, the telos of its praxis, the systems and institutions themselves must change. Revolutionary praxis is thus praxis with the goal of changing the historical unfolding of the world from within human action. Consciousness raising begins, for Marx, with "'relentless criticism of all existing institutions.' A criticism that demands a correct theoretical analysis of existing institutions and the contradictions inherent in them."[17]

A number of practical theologians, especially those in education, have drawn from the wells of Marx, most often following thinkers who have constructed theories and praxis from within Marx's theory (Paulo Freire would be an example of a Marxist thinker who has had great impact on practical theologians in education). As Bernstein notes, "Marx's [and those like Freire who follow him] fundamental conviction . . . is that the situation in which we find ourselves is not ultimately an ontological or existential one from which there is no escape. It is an historical state of affairs, which while it has its 'own necessity,' is nevertheless the resultant of human activity and can be changed by revolutionary praxis."[18]

The praxis of practical theology that follows from this, then, is engaging historical alienating forces of society and opposing them with actions of liberation. The practical theologian seeks to raise people's consciousness of their estrangement and oppression by criticizing deeply the societal functions that they live within. In so doing, human action participates in divine action by pushing out the oppression of the present historical structure and replacing it with God's reign of humanization, freedom and wholeness. Divine and human action thus find association (often through the motif of God's reign) as an alternative *historical* reality that can be brought forth through human action. Where oppressive systems are put down for the sake of liberation, God is active. *God can be found in acts of liberation.* Therefore, divine and human action come together through the critique of systems that oppose us in which our consciousness is raised so that we might act beyond our bondage and toward unity of self and world. God stands on the side of the oppressed, so in acting for them we encounter the action of God in the world, and our action ushers in the reign of God.

In the context of youth ministry, David White and his book *Practicing Discernment with Youth* is a good example of a social critical perspective on divine and human action. Throughout the first chapters of the book, White makes the argument that adolescence is a social construction that itself thrusts contradiction on young people, alienating them from their true selves by disconnecting them from family in peer units that quickly become infused with consumerism. White states, "The social institution of adolescence, like Frankenstein's monster, is not natural. It was constructed from a conglomeration of ideas and practices that served the interests of marketers, employers, labor unions, educators, politicians, and the middle class— yet remained oblivious to the yearnings of youth to contribute their gifts to the common good, and the church that sought to call forth these charisms."[19]

Much like for Marx, the very structures of society are the enemy for White; a consumerist fetish has kept young people from recognizing that they are agents, that they can act.[20] And, like Marx, White gives sharp attention to the historical, asserting that "over the last thirty years the opportunities that once made adolescence bearable have become limited, leaving young people with fewer ways *to act upon history.*"[21] In other words, in the flavor of social critical theory, White sees the structures as opposing and alienating young people from their true selves, which is the ability to act upon history. According to White, adolescents have been estranged from acting upon history by becoming overly concerned with commercial and popular culture. These systemic realities subvert the adolescent's greater will.

In the second half of his book White provides a way for adolescents to raise their consciousness and escape the contradiction by engaging in reconstructing a historical reality beyond the oppression of their condition. The youth worker becomes their teacher and model for revolutionary praxis, or what White would call "the reign of God."[22] In this, then, the youth worker's job is to take adolescents into a process of discernment, leading them to see how the system thrusts them into contradiction and how their action is estranged from them through the alienating forces of society. White explains, "Youth do not need more activity or more entertainment; they need ministers who dedicate whatever resources they already have to understanding and resisting the distortions of culture and living into the way of Jesus—and helping youth to do the same."[23]

For White, adolescents themselves are oppressed peoples,[24] meaning that divine action can be encountered when these oppressed people act for the sake of their liberation. This also means that, when these oppressed people are alienated and silenced, God's reign is opposed. White states, for instance, that "when youth's gifts are not respected and cultivated, the beauty of God is limited and the reign of God is postponed."[25] Moreover, when these oppressed people find unity in their action by overcoming oppressive structure, they are participating in the action of God. White has a potent understanding of divine action, which is that human action can participate in divine action and that human action is essential for the dynamism of divine action.

Therefore, youth workers who want their young people to participate in God's action in the world would, according to White, call young people into the historical to engage the structures (most directly consumerism). In other words, they would help young people move beyond their oppression by practicing all new actions in the world, actions that are congruent with God's own action of liberation. White sums up what he sees as discipleship—how he sees divine and human action coming together in the life of young people—this way: "Discipleship requires attentiveness to the holy, that is, to God's ongoing activity in the world. It requires prophetic social critique, engendered by seeing the world as God sees it and speaking out for that vision. Discipleship in its fullest sense also requires justice-seeking action in the world on behalf of 'the widows and orphans' and the neediest of God's children."[26]

Pragmatism. American pragmatism was a philosophical position born through the work of William James, Charles Sanders Peirce and John Dewey (to name a few). At its core, pragmatism sought to make philosophy a practical force for change within society. Moving beyond what it saw as the abstract epistemological obsessions of continental thought, it gave total attention to action. John Dewey, for instance, believed that philosophical attention on education could produce a greater democratic society.

Like Marxism, pragmatism gives attention to the social and historical, but unlike Marxism, it refuses to see the systems and structures of culture as fundamentally corrosive. So, while human action in Marxism seeks to overcome oppression by ushering in a new historical epoch, pragmatism sees human action as a way to convert certain elements in society to function for the greater good. In other words, it sees no real reason to overthrow the present system but rather seeks to work within it, believing that the present historical situation can be transformed with proper inquiry; human action is an operation of reflection rather than revolution. Indeed, the heart of pragmatism is the belief that "a primary characteristic of human experience is its purposiveness. We are creatures who can imaginatively construct new possibilities and by intelligent inquiry we can reconstruct our experience so that the goods that we most deeply desire can be achieved and made stable."[27]

For Peirce, this form of action is contingent on a community of inquiry— a community that gives attention to the present situation by turning to the tradition of thought for resources to lead the community into inquiry that can bring about changing praxis.[28] As Bernstein elucidates, "The community of inquirers, which is ultimately the basis for distinguishing the real from the unreal, and the true from the false, functions as a regulative ideal in Peirce's philosophic scheme."[29] Therefore, human action in pragmatism has much to do with moral/behavioral ethics: with seeking what the necessary or needed action is within the existing systems of history to bring about the greater good. Thus, it is not only action that matters, but action that has connection to conduct, action that has reflected upon and therefore impacted our very behavior in the world. The action desired here is action that is primarily about how we "behave" in the world. It seeks a new horizon for the historical (like Marxism) but sees this new horizon in continuity with—not in opposition to—the present historical reality, believing that with the right action that affects our conduct and behavior, much can change.

Practical theologians working from a pragmatist perspective give significant attention to the community of inquiry, seeing communities as places of investigation, places to discern and hone human action by influencing conduct and behavior. To discern divine action, the practical theologian turns to the tradition, with its wealth of knowledge for action in the now. Thus, the community of inquiry reflects on the tradition to discern the necessary actions to take. Don Browning, perhaps the most famous practical theologian working explicitly from a pragmatist understanding of divine and human action, sees the job of the practical theologian as mining the tradition in communities of inquiry to formulate new ethical actions of practice within our present historical situation.

In youth ministry, one of the greatest *implicit* pragmatist thinkers may be Chap Clark. His work has a significant ethical dimension. For instance, he sees a considerable piece of youth ministry as working to "right wrongs,"[30] and in his most methodological piece, "Youth Ministry as Practical Theology,"[31] he presents the sexual practices of students as his central problem, asserting that practical reflection must help students (and young people) make good decisions for behavior and conduct through appropriate information. We can see how deeply this runs in his interpretation of practical theology as a whole when he says, "As practical theology has developed, virtually every model is designed to ultimately *influence behavior.*"[32]

While Clark is more conservative than Browning or even than pragmatism in general, his understanding of divine and human action and their association is deeply pragmatist in nature; he attempts with his work to bring forth change within the existing system. Like White, he sees a number of threatening cultural realities confronting young people, but unlike White, he is less willing to wipe away the system that is. Where White is happy to abandon technology and return to a premodern concept of young people, Clark seeks to bring reform by abandoning only some of the elements of the system (not the whole thing), and converting other elements toward the goal he seeks.

The goal he seeks, the telos of human action, is aligning oneself with the biblical text. He asserts, "The goal of our teaching must be to equip our students . . . to guide the believing community where they are called to serve in making kingdom-driven decisions and choices as they live in a complex and changing world."[33] Keeping, then, with the pragmatists who seek to acquire new action in the present historical moment through reflection on the classic tradition, Clark turns to the Bible, not as the witness to God's story and continued action but as a tradition that sets the terms for action (conduct and behavior) in itself and therefore demands complete assimilation to its perceived wishes.[34]

Thus, in pragmatist fashion, divine and human action come together as the human agent reflects on the classic (God-given, even) tradition and then applies it to the case at hand for changed conduct and behavior. From Clark's perspective, the divine and human come together when the human acts, through his or her behavior, in congruence with the Bible, specifically, for he believes the Bible is God's action in the world (for Clark, God's kingdom and the Bible are nearly inseparable). While Clark has room for other traditional elements as resources for reflection, it is ultimately the Bible and the way the Bible directs us that bring divine and human action together.[35] Clark says it this way: "What practical theology offers is a focused and deliberative process for discerning how biblical and theological insights apply to the challenges of applied faithful action in a changing culture. Practical theology begins with a specific reality, or context, and moves from there to a reflexive conversation with the Scriptures that leads us to new action."[36]

Like in social critical theory pragmatism provides a significant theological motif to think about divine action (White likes "the reign" and Clark "the kingdom" of God). But for both what is important is attending to the historical; human action possesses the power to bring forth the very activity of God, either through consciousness-raising action against the system (White) or by attending to biblical truth and applying it to conduct and behavior (Clark). For both, divine action can be thwarted if young people are oppressed or ignore (deny) biblical truth. In Clark's words, "The goal . . . of practical theology is to arrive at a biblical theology of an issue (and related questions) in order to determine an applicable biblical theology, or theologically-derived and biblically-defined praxilogical response to the context and issue at hand."[37]

Where Clark may have the most resonance with pragmatism is in the function of communal decision-making. He understands that his biblical-centric perspective, his reflection on the classic for molding present action in behavior and conduct, holds within it hermeneutical problems; he recognizes, for instance, that the human knower may get the biblical meaning wrong and therefore miss divine action. So, like Browning, who seeks a rich conversation with hermeneutical theory (mostly Gadamer) to assist his reflection on the tradition, Clark provides a hermeneutical perspective. In pragmatist fashion, he places a community as central.[38] For Clark, the community functions like Peirce's community of inquiry, attending to the classic (the Bible) by reflecting on actions in the present historical. Thus, he holds up the Bible and the community as leading to human ethical actions that participate in God's activity. Yet, unlike pragmatism in general, Clark has little discussion on how the community itself could be sinful or prone toward evil. Rather, for him, the community alone serves as an antidote for corrupt (or simply wrong) biblical interpretation.

For Clark then, the job of the youth worker is to help young people act in a manner congruent with the Bible so that they might, in their individual lives and for the good of society, glorify God. Their actions assimilate them to the classic as they trust the biblical perspective. Therefore, divine and human action come together in the pragmatic activity of the human agent; the human agent encounters divine action not necessarily in its independent dynamism but in the human agent's assimilation to the biblical through the community, which points toward correct action through behavior and conduct.[39]

Kierkegaardian. Søren Kierkegaard wrote in opposition to the Hegelian system. Hegel had seen great possibility for human action to bring the world, through the unfolding of history, to a great synthesis. Kierkegaard was never convinced. He believed there existed *within* persons and within society as a whole far too much impossibility to take any hope in the idealist vision of the unfolding of history that Hegel and others presented. Kierkegaard contended that human action itself was bankrupt because human action existed next to an abyss: the abyss of infinite freedom, a freedom that forced human action to crash on the rocks of anxiety.[40]

Kierkegaard showed that all forms of action, whether aesthetic (seeking beauty), ethical or even religious, fall short of reaching their objective.[41] And it takes little jostling to connect Kierkegaard's three failed actions with neo-Aristotlianism, pragmatism and Marxism: all these forms of action ignore the fact that there exists an ocean of impossibility in the human condition, that suffering and death are operative realities. No matter how we might act, no action can save us from a world in which we die and return to non-being. All actions that don't take this into consideration ignore that our actions are always actions near death.

Kierkegaard believed that his perspective followed the tradition of Luther, who saw human action as an impossibility to save itself, and sought for

God, the very activity of God, in and through impossibility (the cross) as our hope. Therefore, Kierkegaard contends that divine and human action are completely distinct, one in heaven and the other on earth. The only action that the human agent can take is to face the abyss, to admit the impossibility of action and, in the midst of the impossibility, to trust in the utterly absurd.[42] Trusting that God has acted, and acted in the absurd paradox of being human, places the action of heaven within reach of the human. Therefore, the only action possible from the human side is the action of the knight's move: the action of faith; it is to trust in God's action in the midst of the futility of human action.

There are few practical theologians who have worked from a Kierkegaardian perspective. Because practical theology is fundamentally reflection on human action within the scope of divine action, it is no wonder that most have found little help in Kierkegaard's position of the impossibility of human action itself. James Loder is the practical theologian who has most robustly turned to Kierkegaard, constructing a method of practical theology which sees divine action and human action coming together in negation. He contends that the Spirit of God negates the negation (death and the abyss) in the human spirit, therefore allowing human action to be taken up into divine action.

While Loder's work has deep wells of significance for ministry in general, he mainly sticks with Kierkegaard himself. In *Revisiting Relational Youth Ministry,* Andrew Root[43] pushes past Kierkegaard back to Luther and through Luther to the early Moltmann, Eberhard Jüngel and Douglas John Hall. Specifically, Root draws on the words of German Lutheran theologian Dietrich Bonhoeffer to tease out what it means to be in relationship with another human in light of the absurdity of the human condition. Following Kierkegaard, Root contends that human action is an impossibility; it cannot be a means of transformation or salvation. Human action is too close to death and death is too operative in our realities to maintain that practices, critical engagement or corrected behavior can mediate the presence of God. None of the above perspectives contend with death and suffering directly; none place being as central within human activity, let alone being-toward-death. As opposed to seeing adolescents as fundamentally passionate, oppressed or in need of ethical conversion, then, Root contends that adolescents are awakening to the existential state of their existence—awakening to the tragic core of human existence—and seeking to discover who they are next to impossibility and limitation. They are confronting the reality that their own actions cannot give them answers to the question, "What is a lifetime and why do we live it?"[44]

Yet unlike a strictly Kierkegaardian perspective, as a practical theologian Root still believes that humans need to act. The human action that is needed, though, is action that reveals and dwells in impossibility, a human action that unveils what we already know: that we are stuck and that death is operative in our lives. This action of articulating and facing a reality of impossibility, Root contends, is where divine and human action associate. When we invite young people to face their impossibility, the God of the cross encounters them. Divine action envelops them, calling them to a new and whole life that seeks God in death and brokenness, a new life that seeks God's future in backwardness and brokenness, a new life that goes out into the world in search of God in the brokenness of existence as God is near in the brokenness of our own being. It is going out into the world to proclaim that we can find God on the cross, always with those facing suffering and death. And it is through bearing this paradoxical impossibility that human action and divine action are associated. In Root's view, God is concretely present in the human action of facing impossibility, for in facing impossibility we encounter the God who brings life and possibility out of death and impossibility by taking on the cross and overcoming it through resurrection.

This impossibility becomes most clear for Root "within personal encounter, shared relational bonds of I and other."[45] Jesus Christ, as the one who has taken the impossibility of the human condition into himself and negated the negation, stands with us and for us; as fully human and fully divine, Jesus Christ stands with each person. Therefore, "to be in relationship with another is to encounter Jesus Christ who is beside and for us."[46] Over and against any conception of relationship that denies the very presence of the fully human and fully divine Christ, Root proposes that Christians must encounter each other in our reality.

This means that we should not cajole each other into participating in practices, educate so that we might change the world or debate about ethical action, because each of these actions denies the human condition in some subtle way. Practices purport to get it right, to actually make something other than humanity the vehicle of God's presence in the world. Yet practices still deny the fact that no action that we take can ever get it right enough to act as a vehicle for God because each action is an action at the edge of an inescapable abyss. Education, in turn, does not go deep enough to reveal that not only are systems oppressive to us but also the very human condition is absurdly oppressive. And ethical action in the pragmatist tradition can descend to mere utilitarianism, treating humans as ends unto themselves; even at its best, it does not fully take into account the depths of our mortality. The "good enough" action, the stable system that promotes the good for many are ways of denying the absurdity of the human condition by putting a thin veneer of respectability over the truth. Each of these approaches attempts to move a person away from the truth of the matter.

Real relationship then, for Root, is a relationship that fully acknowledges and in fact reveals the human condition by fully acknowledging and revealing the living Christ. In encountering the other as other, we begin to see the absurdity of our common condition; as we see others, hear them speak, delight in their existence and serve them with our actions, we see the human condition—and we also see that God in Jesus Christ has worked to redeem us. We are not trying to influence each other but rather to see the reality of God in the relationship. This reality will prompt us to do certain things together—it will spur us on to help others and will suggest ethical ways of acting—but the relationship itself always remains the primary place of divine and human encounter. At times, this reality will call us simply to share the place of the other, to sit in the absurdity of the human condition without the intention of doing, freeing or fixing anything. This place-sharing itself can be a moment of revelation when we gain a glimpse of the place-sharing that God accomplished on the cross through Jesus Christ.

The objective of the youth worker, then, is to be a bearer of reality, to walk deeply into the suffering, doubts and yearning of young people, being with and for them in the midst of their impossibility. The youth worker thus claims the presence of God, the encounter of divine and human action, in being found deeply in the lives of young people, in being their place-sharers.

SUMMARY AND CONCLUSION

All four of these conceptions of divine and human action have their advantages, and each has its own overlap and nearness to one or two other perspectives. For example, a neo-Aristotelian perspective, like a Kierkegaardian one, sees divine action as connected to the core of the human agent. Yet, like pragmatism, neo-Aristotelianism sees the function of the community as essential. Pragmatism, in turn, seeks the historical, just as social theory does. These perspectives should therefore be interpreted not as fundamentally opposed but as distinct, though related, fields of reflection on divine and human action.

In this postscript, I did not seek to state that one perspective is better than the others. Nor did I want to imply that any of these thinkers can be completely bound in only one of these perspectives. Indeed, placing myself in one of the categories made me aware that I work from more than just the Kierkegaardian perspective. Yet, with that said, I am arguing here that each of these thinkers has a particular primary understanding of how divine and human action come into association. This descriptive offering may therefore be of help to youth workers as they read youth ministry texts and seek to understand the author's position. But more importantly, it may help them begin to conceptualize for themselves how and where human action connects to divine action, so that they might then mold their ministries in ways that fit their theological perspectives.

• DISCUSSION AND REFLECTION EXERCISE
Critical Debate

After you've taken some time to discuss the differences and tensions in the understanding of divine and human action as a large group, pick the one that you are most convinced by.[47] The leader will then frame a statement that has some tension to it, like, "When it comes to how pop culture functions in young people's lives, only a _____ perspective is worth considering in youth ministry, for it articulates that God meets young people by _____."

At this point, participants should take on a different perspective than the one they relate to most. For example, the leader may ask those identifying with neo-Aristotelianism to take the perspective of a social critical Marxist, the social critical Marxists to take on pragmatism, the pragmatists to become Kierkegaardians and the Kierkegaardians to become neo-Aristotelians.

Break into small groups with others who've been assigned the same perspective as you. Fill in the blanks of the statement, but in discussing why your group's position is most helpful, also explain why the others are not. This will allow you all to try to defend a position that you do not hold emotionally, which will get you to indwell the ideas more fully.

The objective is not to get to one right perspective but to try on each of these perspectives, whether in affirmation or critique.

NOTES

Introduction

[1]L. Gregory Jones, "Learning Curve," *The Christian Century,* May 18, 2010 <www.christiancentury.org/article.lasso?id=8444>.

[2]See Kenda Creasy Dean, *Practicing Passion: Youth and the Quest for a Passionate Church* (Grand Rapids: Eerdmans, 2004) and *Almost Christian: What the Faith of Our Teenagers Is Telling the American Church* (New York: Oxford University Press, 2010); also see Andrew Root, *Revisiting Relational Youth Ministry: From a Strategy of Influence to a Theology of Incarnation* (Downers Grove, Ill.: IVP Books, 2007) and *The Children of Divorce: The Loss of Family as the Loss of Being* (Grand Rapids: Baker, 2010).

[3]See Christian Smith with Melinda Denton, *Soul Searching: The Religious and Spiritual Lives of American Teenagers* (New York: Oxford University Press, 2005), and Christian Smith and Patricia Snell, *Souls in Transition: The Religious and Spiritual Lives of Emerging Adults* (New York: Oxford University Press, 2009).

[4]C. S. Lewis, "Christian Apologetics," in *God in the Dock: Essays on Theology and Ethics* (Grand Rapids: Eerdmans, 1970), p. 101.

Chapter 1: The New Rhetoric of Youth Ministry

[1]Scholars who overlook the church or religion as possible responses to adolescent problems include Kenneth Keniston, *The Uncommitted: Alienated Youth in American Society* (New York: Delta, 1960); Francis Ianni, *The Search for Structure* (New York: Free Press, 1989); Joy Dryfoos, *Adolescents at Risk: Prevalence and Prevention* (New York: Oxford University Press, 1990); Reginald Jones, ed., *Black Adolescents* (Berkeley, Calif.: Cobb and Henry, 1989); Mary Pipher, *Reviving Ophelia* (New York: Ballantine, 2002); Lyn Mikel Brown and Carol Gilligan, *Meeting at the Crossroads* (Cambridge, Mass.: Harvard University Press, 1992); Patricia Hersch, *A Tribe Apart* (New York: Fawcett Columbine, 1998); Thomas Hine, *The Rise and Fall of the American Teenager* (New York: Perennial, 2000); and Ron Taffel, *The Second Family* (New York: St. Martin's, 2001). Two important exceptions were the Carnegie Corporation's research and the ongoing research of Search Institute (cf. *A Matter of Time* [Washington, D.C.: Carnegie

Corporation of New York/Carnegie Council on Adolescent Development, December 1992]; Dale Blythe and Eugene Roehlkepartain, *Healthy Communities, Healthy Youth* [Minneapolis: Search Institute, 1993]).

[2]See Stuart Cummings-Bond, "The One-Eared Mickey Mouse," *YouthWorker Journal* 6 (Fall 1989): 76-78; Mark Senter, *The Coming Revolution in Youth Ministry* (Wheaton, Ill.: Victor, 1992); Milton J. Coalter et al., "A Re-Forming Agenda," *Presbyterian Survey* 82 (July/August 1992): 12-13.

[3]Albert van den Heuvel, *The New Creation and the New Generation: A Forum for Youth Workers* (New York: Friendship Press, 1965).

[4]Kenda Creasy Dean, "A Review of the Literature on, and a Descriptive Overview of, Protestant, Catholic, and Jewish Religious Youth Work in the U.S." (technical paper, Washington, D.C., Carnegie Council for Adolescent Development, 1991), p. iv.

[5]Ronald White, "History of Youth Ministry Project" (unpublished midproject report submitted to the Lilly Endowment, Indianapolis, Ind., August 20, 1994), p. 7.

[6]As of this writing (March 2003), Lilly funds implementation grants for youth and vocation in eighty-eight U.S. colleges, for youth and theology programs in forty-eight U.S. seminaries, and for seven multi-institution research projects on youth ministry, youth and religion, and related subjects.

[7]See Peter Berger, "Epistemological Modesty: An Interview with Peter Berger," *The Christian Century,* October 29, 1997, pp. 972-78.

[8]These themes are not new in adolescent research; G. Stanley Hall's tome *Adolescence* (1904) gave a prominent place to conversion, defined psychologically (*Adolescence* [New York: Arno Press, 1969]), and Erik H. Erikson's research on adolescent identity formation in the 1950s and 1960s describes the adolescent search for ideology in explicitly religious terms (see *Youth Identity and Crisis* [New York: W. W. Norton, 1968]). For approaches to secular research that reclaim a place for spirituality in the healthy development of children, see Robert Coles, *The Spiritual Lives of Children* (Boston: Houghton Mifflin, 1990); Robert Kegan, *In Over Our Heads* (Cambridge, Mass.: Harvard University Press, 1994); and James Gabarino, *Lost Boys* (New York: Free Press, 1999), to name a few.

[9]Thanks to Dave Zimmerman for this anecdote. Personal correspondence, January 26, 2011.

[10]The first of these won small but influential followings as early as the 1960s; Sara Little's *Youth, World and Church* (Richmond, Va.: John Knox Press, 1968) and later David Ng's *Youth in the Community of Disciples* (Valley Forge, Penn.: Judson Press, 1984) stand out in this regard. Attempts to couch youth ministry in terms of practical theology have been uneven, in part because no consensus exists on the nature of practical theology itself.

[11]Laying much of the intellectual groundwork for this perspective were Sara Little at Union Theological Seminary, William Myers at Chicago Theological Seminary,

Michael Warren at St. John's University, Robin Maas at Wesley Theological Seminary, Richard R. Osmer at Princeton Theological Seminary and, above all, Craig Dykstra at the Lilly Endowment.

[12]See Miroslav Volf, "Theology for a Way of Life," in *Practicing Theology,* ed. Miroslav Volf and Dorothy C. Bass (Grand Rapids: Eerdmans, 2002), pp. 250-51.

[13]James Coleman, *The Adolescent Society* (New York: Free Press, 1961).

[14]For examples of this new rhetoric's approach to culture, see Tom Beaudoin, *Virtual Faith* (San Francisco: Jossey-Bass, 1998); Tony Jones, *Postmodern Youth Ministry* (El Cajon, Calif.: Youth Specialties, 2000); Evelyn Parker, *Trouble Don't Last Always: Emancipatory Hope Among African American Adolescents* (New York: Pilgrim, 2003); Pete Ward, *Liquid Church* (Peabody, Mass.: Hendrickson, 2003).

[15]Once again it was the Lilly Endowment that helped translate this renewed interest in Christian practices into ministry with young people. Thanks in large part to a fertile partnership between Christian educator Craig Dykstra at Lilly and church historian Dorothy Bass of Valparaiso University, multiple efforts to make the practices of the church the primary curriculum for youth ministry sprang up in the 1990s and 2000s (see Dorothy Bass's *Practicing Our Faith* [San Francisco: Jossey-Bass, 1997] and the subsequent volume for teenagers, Dorothy Bass and Don Richter's *Way to Live* [Nashville: Upper Room, 2002]).

[16]This exercise is greatly adapted from Stephen Brookfield and Stephen Preskill's *Discussion as a Way of Teaching* (San Francisco: Jossey-Bass, 1999), pp. 77ff.

Chapter 2: God Is a Minister

[1]As a side note, this has been true for mostly all of the meaningful theological perspectives that have moved the church in a new direction; the monk, Luther, and the pastor, Barth, were far from the center of respected academic work, but through their construction the church responded with attention.

[2]Understanding and reflecting on the Scriptures and tradition of the Christian faith no doubt takes some work and skill. But this reflection is done with the conviction that it will point us to the living God, who gives us the Scriptures and tradition in order to understand and join in his continued Ministry today. We'll get into much of this shortly.

[3]See Sara McLanahan and Gary Sandefur, *Growing Up with a Single Parent* (Cambridge, Mass.: Harvard University Press, 1994); Robert Putnam, *Bowling Alone* (New York: Simon & Schuster, 2000); and Don Browning et al., *From Culture Wars to Common Ground* (Louisville: Westminster John Knox, 1997).

[4]Laura Sessions Stepp, *Unhooked: How Young Women Pursue Sex, Delay Love and Lose at Both* (New York: Riverhead Books, 2007).

[5]This exercise is adapted from Stephen Brookfield's *Becoming a Critically Reflective Teacher* (San Francisco: Jossey-Bass, 1995), p. 77.

Chapter 3: Youth Ministry as an Integrative Theological Task

[1]Karl Barth elicits further what I mean (though perhaps with harsher rhetoric than is helpful): "If [theology] is ranked as a science, and lays claim to such ranking, this does not mean that it must allow itself to be disturbed or hampered in its own task by regard for what is described as science elsewhere. On the contrary, to the discharge of its own task it must absolutely subordinate and if necessary sacrifice all concern for what is called science elsewhere. The existence of other sciences, and the praiseworthy fidelity with which many of them at last pursue their own axioms and methods, can and must remind [theology] that it must pursue its own task in due order and with the same fidelity. But it cannot allow itself to be told by them what this means concretely in its own case. As regards method, it has nothing to learn from them" (*Church Dogmatics* 1.1, trans. Geoffrey Bromiley and Thomas F. Torrance [Edinburgh: T & T Clark, 1936], p. 8).

[2]"Theology cannot be classed under a 'universally valid' concept of *Wissenschaft* but, like other subject matters, has its own internal logic, or, as Barth put it, its own consistent path to knowledge in accord with its own specific object of knowledge" (Hans Frei, *Types of Christian Theology* [New Haven, Conn.: Yale University Press, 1992], p. 104).

[3]Douglas John Hall, *Thinking the Faith* (Minneapolis: Fortress, 1991), p. 402.

[4]Ibid., p. 412.

[5]Hall provides a full summary of why theology is contextual, which, because of space constrictions, cannot be unpacked above. Here's a very brief synopsis: "We must now attempt to say why this theology is contextual, that is: what is the rationale of theological contextuality? Three fundamental reasons can be adduced: (1) Theology is a human enterprise, (2) theology attempts to speak of the living God and of God's relation to a dynamic creation, and (3) theology exists for the sake 'of the church's confession'" (ibid., p. 93).

[6]Ibid.

[7]Even Barth, with his heavy rhetoric on the needed distinction between theology and all other systems and fields of thought (as we will see below), agrees that theology must be contextual: "The [theologian] . . . must think and speak in a particular age and should thus be a man of his age, which also means a man of the past that constitutes his age, i.e., an educated man" (*Church Dogmatics* 1.1, p. 284).

[8]Hall, *Thinking the Faith*, p. 91.

[9]"The church [or the theologian] has the function of answering the question implied in man's very existence, the question of the meaning of this existence" (Paul Tillich, *Theology and Culture* [London: Oxford University Press, 1959], p. 49).

[10]Tillich's correlational method was picked up and revised by David Tracy who, while holding to the same Tillichian unity of theology and culture, pushed the task further, allowing culture not only to ask questions but also to provide answers. Instead of theology and culture in a one-way conversation, where culture asked and theology answered, from Tracy's perspective both culture and theology could ask and answer, allowing for a true dialogue. According to Tracy, then, not only did culture need theology but also theology needed culture in order to exist at all. See David Tracy, *Blessed Rage for Order* (Chicago: University of Chicago Press, 1996).

[11]James McClendon, *Witness* (Nashville: Abingdon, 2000), p. 37.

[12]Hall, *Thinking the Faith*, p. 358.

[13]See George Hunsinger's *How to Read Karl Barth* (New York: Oxford University Press, 1993) for a discussion on how Barth's theological method is constructed around the divine/human perspective.

[14]See also James Loder's *The Logic of the Spirit* (San Francisco: Jossey-Bass, 1998) as an example of this method. Loder uses the same Chalcedonian pattern, though with a number of distinct Loderian contributions. See also "Normativity and Context in Practical Theology" in *Practical Theology: International Perspectives,* ed. Friedrich Schweitzer and Johannes van der Ven (Berlin: Peter Lang, 1999).

[15]See Deborah van Deusen Hunsinger, *Theology and Pastoral Counseling: A New Interdisciplinary Approach* (Grand Rapids: Eerdmans, 1995), p. 65, for a nice definition of these three terms.

[16]See the epilogue of Hunsinger's *How to Read Karl Barth* for a discussion of secular parables of the truth.

[17]"Chalcedon's resolution of this biblical problem, insightful as it was in some respects, created other, lasting problems for the church whenever it applied to its theology the rule of Scripture; for it substituted for the relational language of the Bible a substantialistic language that, while perhaps comprehensible within the Hellenistic framework, is no longer helpful even if it can be made to overcome the basic ontological leap—which is doubtful. We have seen that the 'two natures' Christology never has been an adequate positive statement of the biblical witness to the Christ, and today it is usually falsely scandalous and a barrier to faith" (Douglas John Hall, *Professing the Faith* [Minneapolis: Fortress, 1993], p. 513). Hall continues, "What I mean is that the historic church's adherence to Chalcedon, while it has made possible a modicum of consensus with respect to the central figure of Christian belief, has also encouraged a faith that is more nearly assent to doctrine . . . than trust in the one to whom doctrine tries feebly to testify. . . . The internal question in the process leading to and following Chalcedon is whether it does not signify a quite different kind of interest in the Christ—different, that is to say, from what is present in the witness of the newer Testament itself" (ibid., p. 401).

[18]"For Luther, the sole authentic *locus* of [humanity's] knowledge of God is the cross of Christ, in which God is to be found revealed, and yet paradoxically hidden in that revelation" (Alister McGrath, *Luther's Theology of the Cross* [Malden, Mass.: Blackwell, 1985], p. 149).

[19]"Representing the God of the Scriptures, Jesus moves toward humanity in unqualified commitment and love. Representing humanity, Jesus moves toward God in trust, obedience, and expectation" (Hall, *Professing the Faith,* p. 526).

[20]Ibid., p. 514.

[21]This representative perspective, I believe, also opens up conversations about ecclesiology. Neither the correlationalist nor the Chalcedonian method give much attention to the church. Hall explains how a representative Christology does this: "The church is not a substitute community but a representative community. It does not take the place of the world, it exists in behalf of the world. It is not an elite but an elect community: that is, it is chosen for service and as a means, not an end. It is the world that God loves and wills to engage, embrace, and heal. The church as means to that end is brought to appear before God, in and through Jesus Christ, to represent creaturely being" (ibid., p. 524).

[22]This exercise has been greatly adapted from Stephen Brookfield and Stephen Preskill's *Discussion as a Way of Teaching* (San Francisco: Jossey-Bass, 1999), pp. 57-60.

Chapter 4: Proclaiming Salvation

[1]Lance Morrow, "Just a Routine School Shooting: Special Report," *Time,* May 31, 1999, p. 110. Citations from J. D. Salinger, *The Catcher in the Rye* (New York: Back Bay Books, 2001), p. 30.

[2]Mark DeVries, *Sustainable Youth Ministry* (Downers Grove, Ill.: InterVarsity Press, 2008), p. 92. For a more extended discussion of professional trends in youth ministry, see Kenda Creasy Dean et al., *OMG: A Youth Ministry Handbook* (Nashville: Abingdon, 2010), pp. 107-27.

[3]These statistics may be found in Dean R. Hoge et al., *Vanishing Boundaries: The Religion of Mainline Protestant Baby Boomers* (Louisville: Westminster John Knox, 1994), p. 75; Richard R. Osmer, *Confirmation: Presbyterian Practices in Ecumenical Perspective* (Louisville: Geneva Press, 1996), p. 4; Peter Scales et al., *The Attitudes and Needs of Religious Youth Workers: Perspectives from the Field* (Minneapolis: Search Institute, 1995), p. 13; Philip J. Murnion et al., *New Parish Ministers* (New York: National Pastoral Life Center, 1992), p. 52, cited by Mark A. Lamport, "The Professionalization of Youth Ministry," *The Edge* 3 (April 1999); Kenda Creasy Dean, "Overview of Protestant, Catholic, and Jewish Religious Youth Programs in the U.S." (technical paper, Washington, D.C., Carnegie Council for Adolescent Development, 1991).

[4]Walter Kirn, "The Danger of Suppressing Sadness," *Time,* May 31, 1999, p. 48.

[5]"Mass Shootings at Virginia Tech," *Report of the Virginia Tech Review Panel,* April 16, 2007, p. 33 <www.governor.virginia.gov/TempContent/techpanel report.cfm>; also, Amy Gardner and David Cho, "Isolation Defined Cho's Senior Year," *The Washington Post,* May 7, 2007 <www.washingtonpost.com/wp-dyn/content/article/2007/05/05/AR2007050501221.html>.

[6]Salinger, *Catcher in the Rye,* p. 204.

[7]James E. Loder, *The Logic of the Spirit* (San Francisco: Jossey-Bass, 1998), p. 204.

[8]For a full explanation of Loder's theory of adolescence and the relationship between theology and the gain and loss of self, see *Logic of the Spirit,* chaps. 9-11.

[9]Erik H. Erikson, *Identity, Youth and Crisis* (New York: W. W. Norton, 1968), p. 233, italics mine. Erikson called the search for "fidelity" the most urgent striving of youth, and believed that the ability to give and receive fidelity marks the conclusion of adolescence (p. 265). Feminist psychology has nuanced Erikson's theory by noting that girls tend to develop identity in the context of relationships. Erikson describes a pattern more common to boys in which autonomy may precede intimacy. Feminist psychology does tend to avoid virtue theory; however, fidelity is the signature strength (virtue) to be developed by both boys and girls during adolescence if identity is to be achieved. For theories of identity formation in girls, see Carol Gilligan, *In a Different Voice: Psychological Theory and Women's Development* (Cambridge, Mass.: Harvard University Press, 1982); Judith V. Jordan et al., *Women's Growth in Connection* (New York: Guilford Press, 1991). For a theological interpretation of theories of girls' development, see Carol Lakey Hess, *Caretakers of Our Common House* (Nashville: Abingdon, 1997).

[10]Roberta C. Bondi, *To Pray and to Love: Conversations on Prayer with the Early Church* (Minneapolis: Fortress, 1991), pp. 121-22.

[11]The story of Christian martyrs at Columbine quickly became exaggerated urban legends; still, no one disputes the fact that many students responded in the crisis with courageous Christian conviction and charity. Two girls who were fatally shot, Rachel Scott and Cassie Bernall, were explicitly held up by their families and friends as Christian martyrs. Cassie's life was chronicled by her mother, Misty Bernall, in *She Said Yes: The Unlikely Martyrdom of Cassie Bernall* (New York: Plough, 1999).

[12]Patricia Hersch, *A Tribe Apart* (New York: Ballantine Readers Circle, 1999), pp. 10-30.

[13]John Cloud et al., "Just a Routine School Shooting: Special Report," *Time,* May 31, 1999 <www.time.com/time/magazine/article/0,9171,991076,00.html>.

[14]Author unnamed, *Life,* July 1999, p. 18.

[15]See Kenneth J. Gergen, *The Saturated Self: Dilemmas of Identity in Contemporary Life* (New York: Basic, 1991).

[16]James Fowler, "Perspectives on Adolescents, Personhood, and Faith," in *Christ and the Adolescent: A Theological Approach to Youth Ministry*, 1996 Princeton Lectures on Youth, Church and Culture (Princeton, N.J.: Princeton Theological Seminary, 1996), pp. 1-12.

[17]Communitarian responses to youth work span secular as well as theological sources. See for example cognitive psychologists David Elkind, *The Hurried Child: Growing Up Too Fast Too Soon* (Reading, Mass.: Addison-Wesley, 1981) and *All Grown Up and No Place to Go* (Reading, Mass.: Addison-Wesley, 1984); James Fowler, *Stages of Faith* (San Francisco: Harper & Row, 1981); Robert Kegan, *The Evolving Self: Problem and Process in Human Development* (Cambridge, Mass.: Harvard University Press, 1982) and *In Over Our Heads* (Cambridge, Mass.: Harvard University Press, 1994); sociologist Francis X. J. Ianni, *The Search for Structure: A Report on American Youth Today* (New York: Free Press, 1989); and public policy advocates the Carnegie Corporation, *A Matter of Time: Risk and Opportunity in the Nonschool Hours* (Washington, D.C.: Carnegie Corporation of New York/Carnegie Council on Adolescent Development, 1992); Peter Benson, *The Troubled Journey* (Minneapolis: Search Institute/Lutheran Brotherhood, 1990); and Dayle Blyth and Eugene Roehlkepartain, *Healthy Communities, Healthy Youth* (Minneapolis: Search Institute, 1993). A journalist's account of adolescence that has received enormous media attention is Patricia Hersch's *A Tribe Apart* (see n. 35). To sample a range of theological perspectives that come together around communitarian concerns for youth ministry, see David Ng, *Youth in the Community of Disciples* (Valley Forge, Penn.: Judson Press, 1984); Duffy Robbins, *The Ministry of Nurture* (Grand Rapids: Zondervan, 1990); and John H. Westerhoff, *Will Our Children Have Faith?* (New York: Seabury Press, 1976). Ng, for example, belonged to the Presbyterian Church (U.S.A.); Robbins is United Methodist; Westerhoff is Episcopalian; Maas is Roman Catholic.

[18]Like their communitarian colleagues, liberating individualists have supporters across the disciplines of social science as well. Feminist psychology, for instance, despite its emphasis on the centrality of human relationality, seeks to develop skills of resistance in young girls so that they are not co-opted by patriarchal communities (see Lyn Mikel Brown and Carol Gilligan, *Meeting at the Crossroads: Women's Psychology and Girls' Development* [Cambridge, Mass.: Harvard University Press, 1992]; Hess, *Caretakers of Our Common House*). See also Ronald L. Koteskey, "Adolescence as Cultural Invention," in *Handbook of Youth Ministry* (Birmingham, Ala.: Religious Education Press, 1991); sociologists Mihaly Csikzentmihalyi and Reed Larson, *Being Adolescent: Conflict and Growth in the Teenage Years* (New York: Basic, 1984); and educator Paolo Freire, *Pedagogy of the*

Oppressed (New York: Seabury Press, 1973). A recent journalist's account of American adolescence from this perspective that has received much attention is Thomas Hine, *The Rise and Fall of the American Teenager* (New York: Avon, 1999). Again, the range of theological perspectives clustered around the liberating individualist approach to youth ministry is impressive. See World Council of Churches publications Albert van den Heuvel, *The New Creation and the New Generation* (New York: Friendship Press, 1965); Ars J. van der Bent, *From Generation to Generation: The Story of Youth in the World Council of Churches* (Geneva: World Council of Churches, 1986); Sara Little, *Youth, World and Church* (Richmond: John Knox Press, 1968); Mary-Ruth Marshall, "Precedents and Accomplishments: An Analytical Study of the Presbyterian Youth Fellowship of the Presbyterian Church in the United States, 1943-1958" (Ph.D. dissertation, Presbyterian School of Christian Education, 1993); William R. Myers, *Black and White Styles of Youth Ministry: Two Congregations in America* (New York: Pilgrim Press, 1991); Maria Harris, *Portrait of Youth Ministry* (New York: Paulist, 1981); and Michael Warren, *Youth Gospel Liberation* (San Francisco: Harper & Row, 1987). Little, Marshall and Myers belong to the Presbyterian Church (U.S.A.); Harris and Warren are Roman Catholic. For a more detailed summary of both the communitarian and liberating individualist approaches to youth ministry as we enter the twenty-first century, see Kenda Creasy Dean, "Research Report: Practical Theology and Adolescence in America," *International Journal of Practical Theology* 2, no. 1 (1998), pp. 132-54.

[19]H. Richard Niebuhr, *The Meaning of Revelation* (New York: Collier, 1941), pp. 52, 59.

[20]Ibid., p. 57.

[21]This exercise is almost completely taken from Stephen Brookfield's *Becoming a Critically Reflective Teacher* (San Francisco: Jossey-Bass, 1995), p. 150.

Chapter 5: Walking into the Crisis of Reality

[1]This anecdote has been significantly changed from what really happened, and "Ryan" is not this person's real name.

[2]Ray Anderson says it like this: "As a theological discipline, the hermeneutical task of the Church is to continue to search out and seek to be conformed to the hermeneutical structure of revelation itself, as given in Holy Scripture. Thus, the ministry of the Church necessarily involves theological reflection and a correction of its own inevitable tendencies to create ministry for its own justification" ("A Theology for Ministry," in *Theological Foundations for Ministry,* ed. Ray Anderson [Edinburgh: T & T Clark, 1979], p. 19).

[3]In the postscript of this book I present a deeper understanding of divine and human action and articulate how different youth ministry thinkers (sometimes

innately) bring divine and human action together in their thought. If you really want to see how Kenda and I are different, turn to the postscript.

[4]Karl Barth, "The Place of Theology," in *Theological Foundations for Ministry*, ed. Ray Anderson (Edinburgh: T & T Clark, 1979), p. 22.

[5]"Theology itself is a word, a human response; yet what makes it theology is not its own word or response but the Word which it hears and to which it responds. Theology stands and falls with the Word of God, for the Word of God precedes all theological words by creating, arousing, and challenging them. Should theology wish to be more or less or anything other than action in response to that Word, its thinking and speaking would be empty, meaningless, and futile" (ibid., p. 30).

[6]See Robert Kolb's "God Kills to Make Alive: Romans 6 and Luther's Understanding of Justification (1535)," *Lutheran Quarterly* 12 (1998): 33-56.

[7]Douglas John Hall says it this way: "Revelation is not . . . the communication of ideas about God and the things of God, even though ideas are included in the experience of revelation, as they are included in the experience of meeting another human being. Revelation, however, is the 'divine-human encounter' (Emil Brunner)" (*Thinking the Faith* [Minneapolis: Fortress, 1991], p. 407).

[8]Ibid., p. 286.

[9]Even Karl Barth, who is known for his tenuous assertion that theology is speaking of God by the way God has acted, reveals the need to attend to the crisis people confront in existence as a place for theological fodder: "There is no man who does not have his own god or gods as the object of his highest desire and trust, or as the basis of his deepest loyalty and commitment. There is no one who is not to this extent also a theologian. There is, moreover, no religion, no philosophy, no world view that is not dedicated to some such divinity. . . . There is no philosophy that is not to some extent also theology" (Barth, "The Place of Theology," p. 23).

[10]This is Kierkegaard's move against the Hegelian system.

[11]Douglas John Hall, *Bound and Free: A Theologian's Journey* (Minneapolis: Fortress, 2005), p. 45.

[12]Anthony Giddens argues that we are not so much in a postmodern time, but a time of late modernity, a time when tradition has collapsed. He contends that if we are "post" anything we're post-traditional people. See his argument in *Runaway World: How Globalization Is Reshaping Our Lives,* rev. ed. (New York: Routledge, 2002) for a short discussion of this point.

[13]Hall says, "The substance of belief, in other words, is not that the Bible is true, but rather that that towards which the Bible points us is true. The truth as such is incapable of containment in words, even the inspired words of the Bible." He continues, "Certainly neither Zwingli nor Calvin were prepared to equate the Bible—with revelation. For them, too, revelation is a dynamic and personal encounter. All the same, their humanistically grounded respect for 'the sources' led

them to place much more faith in the Word written than the still-medieval man Martin Luther could ever have done" (*Thinking the Faith,* pp. 120, 406).

[14]There is an element (maybe even a significant one) of critical realism in my perspective.

[15]Hall says it this way: "What is important . . . is neither a priori approval nor a priori disapproval of society but (as we have put it in the foregoing) the engagement of society. It is dialogue that is called for—a dialogue in the course of which the disciple community may learn to 'discern the signs of the times,' and thus be able to bear testimony to a hope which both incorporates and transcends the possibilities and rim possibilities inherent in the situation" (ibid., p. 115).

[16]"Meanwhile, a great many novelists, dramatists, and filmmakers showed me our world in nonideological terms, causing me to remember Tillich's dictum that Art can depict three states: hope, false hope, and hopelessness (and, he said, art in our time overwhelmingly depicts hopelessness). I learned more from the artists and writers of novels than from the social scientists, whose testimony has always seemed to me too easily tainted by ideological interests" (Hall, *Bound and Free*, p. 47).

[17]Ray Anderson, maybe more than any other theologian, has sought to articulate how ministry precedes and produces theology. He says, "One fundamental thesis will control this discussion—the thesis that ministry precedes and produces theology, not the reverse. It must immediately be added, however, that ministry is determined and set forth by God's own ministry of revelation and reconciliation in the world, beginning with Israel and culminating in Jesus Christ and the Church." Anderson continues, "Theology, thus, serves as the handmaid of ministry, proclaiming it as God's ministry and making known the eternal being of God. This knowledge of God, as Calvin reminds us in the opening paragraphs of his *Institutes,* leads us to a knowledge of ourselves. We cannot contemplate the nature of God in his revelation without contemplating our own nature and purpose" ("A Theology for Ministry," p. 7).

[18]Martin Luther, *Werke* (Weimar: H. Böhlaus Nachfolger, 1883-2009), 5.163.28. See also Douglas John Hall, *Remembered Voices* (Louisville: Westminster John Knox, 1998), p. 42.

[19]This exercise drew slightly on Stephen Brookfield's "learning journal" idea in *Becoming a Critically Reflective Teacher* (San Francisco: Jossey-Bass, 1995), p. 97.

Chapter 6: Youth Ministry as Discerning Christopraxis

[1]See Jürgen Moltmann, *The Way of Jesus Christ* (Minneapolis: Fortress, 1990); Ray Anderson, "Christopraxis: The Ministry and the Humanity of Christ for the World," in *Christ in Our Place: The Humanity of God in Christ for the Reconciliation of the World (Essays Presented to James Torrance),* ed. Trevor Hart and Daniel

Thimell (Exeter, U.K.: Paternoster, 1989), and *The Shape of Practical Theology* (Downers Grove, Ill.: InterVarsity Press, 2001); and Richard Osmer, *The Teaching Ministry of Congregations* (Louisville: Westminster John Knox, 2005).

[2]Moltmann powerfully points to this reality: "'The tragic sense of life' is a fundamental existential experience, for it is the experience of the death of human existence. 'Life is a tragedy, and a tragedy is a perpetual struggle without victory or hope of victory—simply a contradiction'" (*The Trinity and the Kingdom* [Minneapolis: Fortress, 1993], p. 36).

[3]For the remainder of this chapter, I will be using "the interpreter" to refer to not just an individual but also a group or community who functions as the interpreter. I have chosen the singular construction for grammatical flow only.

[4]Rudolf Bultmann, "Hermeneutics and Theology," in *The Hermeneutics Reader,* ed. Kurt Mueller-Vollmer (New York: Continuum, 1994), p. 246.

[5]Ibid.

[6]"God's future is not that he will be as he was and is, but that he is on the move and coming towards the world. God's Being is in his coming, not in his becoming" (Jürgen Moltmann, *The Coming of God* [Minneapolis: Fortress, 1996], p. 23).

[7]Jürgen Moltmann, *The Theology of Hope* (Minneapolis: Fortress, 1993), p. 179.

[8]"Christ's resurrection is therefore not a historical event; it is an eschatological happening to the crucified Christ and took place 'once for all' (Rom. 6.10)" (ibid., p. 69). My point here is that it is an eschatological event, yet one that took place within history.

[9]Jürgen Moltmann, *God for a Secular Society* (Minneapolis: Fortress, 1999), p. 11.

[10]Moltmann, *Theology of Hope*, p. 188.

[11]"The hope of resurrection does not overcome the deadliness of death by regarding living and dying as mere summary expressions for the transience of all things and as such important, but by proclaiming the victory of praise and therewith of life over death and over the curse of godforsakenness, by announcing the victory of God over the absence of God" (ibid., p. 210).

[12]Moltmann highlights the systemic nature of our humanity: "For nothing in the world exists, lives and moves of itself. Everything exists, lives and moves in others, in one another, with one another, for one another, in the cosmic interrelations of the divine spirit. So it is only the community of creation in the Spirit itself that can be called 'fundamental'" (*God in Creation* [Minneapolis: Fortress, 1993], p. 11). He continues pointedly, "To be alive means existing in relationship with other people and things. Life is communication in communion. And, conversely, isolation and lack of relationship means death for all living things, and dissolution even for elementary particles. So if we want to understand what is real *as* real, and what is living *as* living, we have to know it in its own primal and individual community, in its relationships, interconnections and surroundings" (ibid., p. 3).

[13]See Luke 10:25-37.

[14]Adriaan Peperzak, *To the Other: An Introduction to the Philosophy of Emmanuel Levinas* (West Lafayette, Ind.: Purdue University Press, 1993), p. 31.

[15]"God or the Holy Spirit joins the concrete You; only through God's active working does the other become a you to me from whom my I arises. In other words, every human you is an image of the divine You" (Dietrich Bonhoeffer, *Sanctorum Communio* [Minneapolis: Fortress, 1963], pp. 54-55).

[16]Anderson, drawing from Moltmann, adds to this point: "Jürgen Moltmann suggests that a 'hermeneutics of origin,' which grounds theology in scripture alone (*sola Scriptura*) must understand that Scripture is grounded in Christ, not only historically but eschatologically" (*Shape of Practical Theology*, p. 37).

[17]Barth continues this thought: "The witness of Holy Scripture to itself consists simply in the fact that it is witness to Jesus Christ. And the knowledge of the truth of this self-witness, the knowledge if its unique authority, stands or falls with the knowledge that Jesus Christ is the incarnate Son of God" (*Church Dogmatics* 1.2, trans. Geoffrey Bromiley and Thomas F. Torrance [Edinburgh: T & T Clark, 1956], p. 485).

[18]Ray Anderson, *The Soul of Ministry* (Louisville: Westminster John Knox, 1997), p. 22.

[19]Anderson, *Shape of Practical Theology*, p. 109.

[20]"You will recall my insistence on defining the hermeneutic task not in terms of the author's intention supposedly hidden behind the text, but in terms of the quality of being-in-the-world unfolded in front of the text as the reference of the text" (Paul Ricoeur, *Essays on Biblical Interpretation* [Philadelphia: Fortress, 1980], p. 108).

[21]See Theodoor van Leeuwen, *Surplus of Meaning: Ontology and Eschatology in the Philosophy of Paul Ricoeur* (Amsterdam: Rodopi, 1981).

[22]Nancy Lammers Gross, *If You Cannot Preach Like Paul* (Grand Rapids: Eerdmans, 2002), p. 115.

[23]These roles are taken from Stephen Brookfield's *Becoming a Critically Reflective Teacher* (San Francisco: Jossey-Bass, 1995), p. 153.

Chapter 7: God's Hiddenness, Absence and Doubt

[1]Eberhard Jüngel, *God as the Mystery of the World* (Grand Rapids: Eerdmans, 1983), p. 49.

[2]Douglas John Hall drives this point deeper, saying, "In short, there has been little space for not-knowing (agnosis) and for 'existential doubt' (Tillich) in the dominant traditions of the faith concerning the knowledge of God. Or, to speak more accurately, these traditions have too categorically celebrated the victory of knowledge and certitude over ignorance and unbelief. They have not been content to

engage in an ongoing dialogue with the antithesis, but have presented the knowledge of God as a finished accomplishment for those who could profess the faith" (*Professing the Faith* [Minneapolis: Fortress, 1993], p. 93).

[3]Hall explains this overemphasis and points us in the direction we will be headed: "As we have seen, all three conventional paths to the knowledge of God have stressed the positive element to the virtual exclusion of the negative: (1) God is Self-revealing, but few have explored the depths of the concealment that is entailed in every profound self-revelation. (2) God is the counterpart of our human being and quest, but few of those who formulated for the church the normative outlines of its Theology have pondered how such knowledge of God is affected by our real alienation, our sense of being-alone and being-against. (3) God is the conclusion our minds must reach if they observe the cosmos rationally, but few have struggled with the irrational, the absurd, the contradictory and chaotic dimensions of our human experience of the cosmos, which, at least today, can hardly be ignored." Hall, continues, "Thus (1) the revealing God has been presented too consistently as one in whom the (negative) dimension of concealment is lacking; (2) God as counterpart of the human spirit has taken too little account of the human sense of 'being alone'; and (3) God as the reasonable consequence of thought about the world has not been sufficiently cognizant, at least for our epoch, of the unreasonable, disjointed, and absurd world, the world that would hardly lead anyone to the splendid conclusion that it is the beloved of a Creator" (ibid., pp. 93, 136).

[4]This is the very argument that James Loder makes in his book *The Logic of the Spirit* (San Francisco: Jossey-Bass, 1998). Loder seeks to explain how negation is a driving force in human development—or to say it another way, how the human spirit seeks for the Spirit of God as the human spirit recognizes its negation.

[5]Hall explains this using Tillich: "Children, as Paul Tillich never tired of insisting, instinctively ask ontological questions. It is instinctual with them because, in their earliest stages of self-awareness, their very survival and growth depend upon their coming to terms with the consciousness of their own being—and with the prospect of not being. What Tillich called 'the shock of non-being' is perhaps a greater shock to the five-year-old than to the thirty-year-old, who has already learned subtle psychic techniques for repressing it. Very young children have been known to be so obsessed with death, despite the relative absence of actual death from their experience, that they could overcome it only with the help of skillful and sensitive adults" (*Professing the Faith*, p. 315).

[6]I am borrowing this struggle between possibility and nothingness from Eberhard Jüngel. It will be a theme throughout this chapter. John Webster further explains Jüngel's position: "Jüngel seeks to suggest that transience is 'in being': it is not itself nihil but rather it demonstrates 'a tendency towards nothingness.'

Transience as it were straddles being and non-being: 'Transience is the struggle between possibility and nothingness, the struggle between the capacity of the possible and the maelstrom of nothingness. . . . And insofar as we have understood possibility as ontological more primary than actuality, we may also say: transience is the struggle between being and non-being.' If the negativity of transience is its 'tending towards nothingness,' its positivity consists in the possibilities it contains; for possibility is not merely that which is unrealised (and so lacking in 'being'), but much more 'the capacity of becoming'" (*Eberhard Jüngel: An Introduction to His Theology* [London: Cambridge University Press, 1986], p. 70).

[7]"Becoming is suffering. One must 'suffer' one's becoming . . . from childhood to adolescence," Hall says (*God & Human Suffering: An Exercise in the Theology of the Cross* [Minneapolis: Fortress, 1986], p. 65).

[8]Hall beautifully states my point here: "Because in this social context people have lost the sensitivity to recognize the sometimes subtle ways in which children and adolescents (as well as the aged and the dying) raise ontological questions, such questions are regularly transmuted by parents and teachers (and by physicians and others who serve humanity at the other end of the life-span) into technical questions. For example, the child asks, 'How did I get here, Daddy?' and the modern father, elated at the precocity of his offspring, proceeds with his son's first sex lesson. But the child is not asking for technical information about the intricacies and delights of reproduction, most of which he could not possibly grasp anyway; he is asking about 'being-here.' He wants someone to explain, or at least to listen to, his new and unsettling sense of existing, of being different from other existing things, of being, however, like the dead bird he discovered among the flowers, impermanent, subject to overwhelming change, the plaything of time" (*Professing the Faith*, p. 316).

[9]For clarity, I am arguing that hiddenness is part of God's very being. I am not arguing that absence is, however. Absence is not part of God's nature, but because God has gone to the cross, absence is a part of God's being (and therefore good), as we will see, in the sense that God being absent to Godself assures us that God will meet us in our own experiences of absence.

[10]I am using the *via negativa* in a very specific way. Late scholasticism tended to use it as a method to help them more faithfully speak of God's nature. Luther, drawing on this perspective, used the dialectic to speak of how God encountered us. He knew God was present; his great breakthrough was how. So, recognizing that the "where" question is a question born after modernity, I am following Luther in his articulations, but doing so by placing them alongside the "where" question.

[11]"Martin Luther, who understood well this dialectic of revealing and concealing—

Deus revelatus/Deus absconditus—regarded it as the cornerstone of the *theologia crucis*. Luther learned this dialectic, not only from the Scriptures of Israel and the church, but from the whole submerged tradition of Christian mysticism" (Hall, *Professing the Faith*, p. 140). Jürgen Moltmann continues, "The dialectical principle of 'revelation in the opposite' does not replace the analogical principle of 'like is known only by like,' but alone makes it possible. In so far as God is revealed in his opposite, he can be known by the godless and those who are abandoned by God, and it is this knowledge which brings them into correspondence with God and, as I John 3.2 says, enables them even to have the hope of being like God" (*The Crucified God* [Minneapolis: Fortress, 1974], p. 28).

[12]"If the mode of knowing God is one that discourages the contemplation of God's actual hiddenness and inaccessibility, this already contains a decisive statement about the nature of the Deity. What it precludes is the ineffable otherness of God. Only faith—that is, faith understood as trust within the context of relationship—enables the disciple community to preserve a Theology that takes seriously the mystery and livingness of God" (Hall, *Professing the Faith*, p. 95).

[13]"The hiddenness of God under its opposite, as Luther called it, cannot however mean that in this particular hiddenness God contradicts himself, but rather must mean that God corresponds to himself in this hiddenness. Even in the greatest of all imaginable contradictions, even in the contradiction of eternal life and earthly death, God corresponds to himself. The being of God is capable of this contradiction. Indeed, God's being is realized in this contradiction without being destroyed by it. God endures it. And this endurance of the contradiction of life and death is God himself, it is the depth of God's glory" (Eberhard Jüngel, "The Revelation of the Hiddenness of God: A Contribution to the Protestant Understanding of the Hiddeneness of Divine Action," in *Theological Essays II* [Edinburgh: T & T Clark, 1994], p. 130).

[14]Jüngel, *God as the Mystery of the World*, p. 166.

[15]Moltmann, *The Crucified God*, p. 28.

[16]Jüngel asserts, "Based on the word of the cross, which emphatically proclaims that the one who was raised from the dead is the Crucified One, we answer that the being of God is first revealed as creative being in the struggle with the annihilating nothingness of nothing" (*God as the Mystery of the World*, p. 218). Jüngel continues, "God's being does not first become love because love is necessary to counter nothingness. Rather, because God is love as he is himself, he counters nothingness and its power. Because God is love, this is then God's being: to be related to nothingness" (ibid., p. 222).

[17]Jüngel, *God as the Mystery of the World*, p. 197.

[18]This is the very argument of Moltmann's beautiful book *The Crucified God*, in which he states, "In the passion of the Son, the Father himself suffers the pains of

abandonment. In the death of the Son, death comes upon God himself, and the Father suffers the death of his Son in his love for forsaken man. Consequently, what happened on the cross must be understood as an event between God and the Son of God" (p. 192).

[19]One of the major advantages of this perspective is that it keeps Christology and soteriology together. Too often, both in theological discourse and ministerial conceptions, Christology and soteriology fall into distinct categories. The cross achieves some soteriological effect, but it has little to do with the very person of Jesus Christ. Here, the very person of Jesus as incarnation God who comes to us as hidden, absent and absurd achieves our salvation by so being. Salvation is won not by beating nothingness but by being overtaken by nothingness.

[20]Jüngel, *God as the Mystery of the World*, p. 224.

[21]We could call this vocation.

[22]Alister McGrath says it this way: "God is revealed in the *passiones et crucem*— and yet he is hidden in this very revelation. In the very things which human wisdom regards as the antithesis of deity—such as weakness, foolishness and humility—God stands revealed in the humility and shame of the cross" (*Luther's Theology of the Cross* [Malden, Mass.: Blackwell, 1985], p. 149).

[23]Jüngel (as Luther) argues that this theology of the cross is Pauline: "For Paul, the Crucified One is weak, subject to death. But Paul does not celebrate this thought with melancholy, but rather thinks of it as the gospel, as a source of joy. What is joyful about the weakness of the Crucified One? The weakness of the Crucified One is for Paul the way in which God's power of life is perfected (II Cor. 13:4). Weakness is then not understood as a contradiction of God's power. There is, however, only one phenomenon in which power and weakness do not contradict each other, in which rather power can perfect itself as weakness. This phenomenon is the event of love" (*God as the Mystery of the World*, p. 206).

[24]Moltmann, *The Crucified God*, p. 205.

[25]So then there is not an *analogia entis* between humanity and God, but an analogy of nonbeing. Humanity is bent toward nonbeing, and in God's freedom (for encounter with humanity), Godself takes on completely nonbeing.

[26]"What, then, is the theology of the cross? The theology of the cross announces that God is found in death, for it is there that boundaries disappear. In the death of sin, of suffering, of uncertainty, and marked by service, Christians are assured that God is present. The theology of the cross is therefore a theology of grace, a theology of freedom, and a theology of trust. These are words of hope and promise that are vital and indispensable regardless of history or context" (Anna M. Madsen, *The Theology of the Cross in Historical Perspective* [Eugene, Ore.: Pickwick Publications, 2007], p. 241).

[27]"It is not a heroic suffering to which we are called, but only a suffering that be-

longs to our creature hood. We have long been acquainted with it—though we have avoided, repressed, and resented its reality" (Hall, *God & Human Suffering*, p. 133).

[28]Jüngel, *God as the Mystery of the World*, p. 217.

[29]Moltmann, *The Crucified God*, p. 246.

[30]"What is most significant for our present concerns in all of this is that the theology of the cross as Luther elaborates it is a theology that determines to take its stand within the experience of negation" (Douglas John Hall, *Lighten Our Darkness: Toward an Indigenous Theology of the Cross* [Lima, Ohio: Academic Renewal Press, 2001], p. 114).

[31]"For this theology, God and suffering are no longer contradictions, as in theism and atheism, but God's being is in suffering and the suffering is in God's being itself, because God is love. It takes the 'metaphysical rebellion' up into itself because it recognizes in the cross of Christ a rebellion in metaphysics, or better, a rebellion in God himself: God himself loves and suffers the death of Christ in his love. He is no 'cold heavenly power,' nor does he 'tread his way over corpses,' but is known as the human God in the crucified Son of Man" (Moltmann, *The Crucified God*, p. 227).

[32]Hall, *Lighten Our Darkness*, p. 116.

[33]Madsen, *The Theology of the Cross in Historical Perspective*, p. 155 (italics mine).

[34]Hall, *God & Human Suffering*, p. 90.

[35]This exercise is adapted from Stephen Brookfield and Stephen Preskill's *Discussion as a Way of Teaching* (San Francisco: Jossey-Bass, 1999), p. 74.

Chapter 8: Is Jesus Magic?

[1]This exercise is adapted from Stephen Brookfield and Stephen Preskill's *Discussion as a Way of Teaching* (San Francisco: Jossey-Bass, 1999), p. 73.

Chapter 9: Talking About Sin with Young People

[1]Karl Barth, *Epistle to the Romans* (London: Oxford University Press, 1933), p. 167.

[2]Ibid., p. 169.

[3]This exercise is taken from Stephen Brookfield and Stephen Preskill's *Discussion as a Way of Teaching* (San Francisco: Jossey-Bass, 1999), pp. 68-69.

Chapter 10: Holding On to Our Kisses

[1]Augustine, *Confessions,* trans. Henry Chadwick (Oxford: Oxford University Press, 1992), p. 24. G. Stanley Hall, whose 1905 tome *Adolescence* more or less christened the twentieth century as the "age of adolescence," viewed psychology as a new theology and based his theory of adolescent psychology around the close

relationship between sexuality and spirituality during adolescence. Hall hypothesized (incorrectly) that puberty signaled a period of "storm and stress" caused by budding sexual maturation and that this turbulence was best resolved by adolescent "conversion" (defined not as reconciliation with God, but as a harmonization of drives and instincts). See G. Stanley Hall, *Adolescence: Its Psychology and Its Relations to Anthropology, Sex, Crime, Religion, and Education,* vols. 1 and 2 (New York: D. Appleton, 1908).

[2]Dag Hammarskjöld, cited in Urban T. Holmes, *A History of Christian Spirituality: An Analytical Introduction* (New York: Harper and Row, 1980), p. 150. I am indebted to Christian educator Korey Lowry for pointing out this excerpt.

[3]Ibid., pp. 150-51.

[4]Ibid., p. 151.

[5]Information provided by the guides at the Amish Farm and House, Lancaster, Pennsylvania, via phone interview (August 30, 1999).

[6]According to *Christianity Online,* 12 percent of pastors have had sexual intercourse outside of their marriages, and 18 percent have had other sexual contact with someone besides their spouse. Cited in "Avoiding an Affair," *Vital Ministry* (September/October 1999): 19.

[7]UNAIDS/World Health Organization, "Global Facts and Figures 2009" <www .unaids.org/en/dataanalysis/epidemiology/2009aidsepidemicupdate>.

[8]Robert Wuthnow, "Religious Upbringing: Does It Matter and If So, What Matters?" in *Christ and the Adolescent: A Theological Approach to Youth Ministry* (Princeton, N.J.: Princeton Theological Seminary, 1996), p. 79; also Peter L. Benson and Carolyn H. Elkin, *Effective Christian Education: A National Study of Protestant Congregations—A Summary Report on Faith, Loyalty, and Congregational Life* (Minneapolis: Search Institute, 1990), p. 38. For the relationship of this research to youth ministry, see Mark DeVries, *Family-Based Youth Ministry: Reaching the Been-There, Done-That Generation* (Downers Grove, Ill.: InterVarsity Press, 1994), and Kenda Creasy Dean and Ron Foster, *The Godbearing Life: The Art of Soul-Tending for Youth Ministry* (Nashville: Upper Room, 1998).

[9]Star Wars creator George Lucas told Bill Moyers that Luke Skywalker, the Star Wars protagonist, must learn "not to *rely* on pure logic, not to rely on the computers, but to rely on faith. That is what 'Use the Force' is, a leap of faith. There are mysteries and powers larger than we are, and you have to trust your feelings in order to access them" (Bill Moyers, "Of Myth and Men," *Time,* April 26, 1999, p. 94).

[10]Mark Bego, "The Madonna/Pepsi Controversy," *The Eighties Club: The Politics and Pop Culture of the 1980s* (New York: Cooper Square Press, 1992) <http://eightiesclub.tripod.com/id135.htm>. The popularity of the video remained unabated; more than twenty years later, producer Ryan Murphy reintroduced the song to a new generation of listeners on the teen TV series *Glee*—and explicitly

recalled the 1989 version by placing a gospel choir in the performance in ways reminiscent of the original video.

[11]For a provocative and slightly different exposition of the *Like a Prayer* video, see Tom Beaudoin, *Virtual Faith: The Irreverent Spiritual Quest of Generation X* (San Francisco: Jossey-Bass, 1998), pp. 74-75 and 90-92. I think Beaudoin overexegetes the video; for instance, he cites media analysis suggesting that Madonna's natural brunette tresses in the video symbolize a return to her Catholic "roots" (M. Rettenmund, *Totally Awesome 80s* [New York: St. Martin's, 1996]). This may be more likely than Beaudoin's suggestion that Madonna's hair color honors the Afro-Peruvian saint portrayed in the narrative, Martin de Porres, patron saint for the poor, interracial justice, daily work and (according to Beaudoin) hairdressers. My own exposition of the video is more cynical, but no less admiring, than Beaudoin's: I maintain that Madonna's artistic decisions, like those of other commercially distributed musicians, are ultimately made for marketing more than for symbolic reasons. Obviously, seamless storytelling is an element in good marketing.

[12]Beaudoin, *Virtual Faith,* p. 82.

[13]See Neal Gabler, *Life the Movie: How Entertainment Conquered Reality* (New York: Knopf, 1998), reviewed by Nicholas Lemann, "Lost in Post-Reality," *Atlantic Monthly,* January 1999, pp. 97-101.

[14]Beaudoin, *Virtual Faith,* pp. 157-58.

[15]Michael Casey, *A Thirst for God: Spiritual Desire in Bernard of Clairvaux's Sermons on the Song of Songs* (Kalamazoo, Mich.: Cistercian, 1988), pp. 63-64.

[16]Ibid., p. 72.

[17]For example, see Bernard of Clairvaux, "Sermons on the Song of Solomon," in *The Love of God and Spiritual Friendship,* abridged, edited and introduced by James M. Houston (Portland, Ore.: Multnomah, 1983), especially pp. 169-75.

[18]Homiletician Anna Carter Florence's exegesis of the Song of Songs offers the intriguing thesis that these texts may have been intended for the religious instruction of young people in the Hebrew community. See "Elihu: Job's Unexpected Prophet," "To Dwell in the Gardens," "Wise in the World" and "Bread on the Water," unpublished sermons on the Song of Songs, presented at the Princeton Forum on Youth Ministry, St. Simon's Island, Ga. (January 11-14, 1999), audiotape from Media Services, Princeton Theological Seminary, Princeton, N.J.

[19]Bernard of Clairvaux, *The Love of God and Spiritual Friendship,* pp. 169-75.

[20]See Catherine of Siena, *The Prayers of Catherine of Siena,* trans. Suzanne Noffke, O.P. (New York: Paulist Press, 1983), pp. 112-13. Cited in Robin Maas, *Crucified Love* (Nashville: Abingdon, 1989), p. 58.

[21]See Teresa of Ávila, *The Way of Perfection,* trans. E. Allison Peers, from the critical edition of P. Silverio de Santa Teresa, C.D. (New York: Image, 1964), especially chap. 6.

[22]I owe this observation to an untitled presentation by Susan Neder, Simpsonwood Retreat Center, Atlanta, Ga. (March 6, 1999).

[23]This exercise is adapted from Stephen Brookfield and Stephen Preskill's *Discussion as a Way of Teaching* (San Francisco: Jossey-Bass, 1999), p. 72.

Chapter 11: The Eschatological Significance of Summer Camp

[1]These results are part of the findings of the National Study of Youth and Religion. For the extended report, see Christian Smith with Melinda Denton, *Soul Searching: The Religious and Spiritual Lives of American Teenagers* (New York: Oxford University Press, 2005), p. 54.

[2]About half of American teenagers (49 percent) believe in life after death. Nine out of ten (91 percent) black Protestant teenagers, and 88 percent of conservative Protestant teenagers, believe in a judgment day when God will reward some and punish others. Only 63 percent of mainline Protestant young people believe this—and mainline Protestant teenagers were the least able to articulate what they believed and why. Understandably, Jewish youth ranked the lowest, with only 25 percent believing in a final judgment (Smith, *Soul Searching*, pp. 41-43; on the inarticulacy of mainline Protestant youth regarding their faith, see pp. 131-32).

[3]Martin Robinson, *Sacred Places, Pilgrim Paths: An Anthology of Pilgrimage* (London: Marshall Pickering, 1997), pp. 1-2.

[4]Mark Ralls, "Reclaiming Heaven: What Can We Say About the Afterlife?" *The Christian Century,* December 14, 2004.

[5]Jürgen Moltmann, *Theology of Hope* (San Francisco: Harper & Row, 1967), p. 16.

[6]Smith, *Soul Searching,* p. 157.

[7]These characteristics are part of a theological disposition of teenagers that Smith describes as "moralistic therapeutic deism." Smith concludes that "most religious communities' central problem is not teen rebellion but teenagers' benign 'whateverism'" (ibid., p. 266).

[8]Margaret Miles, "The Recovery of Asceticism," *Commonweal,* January 28, 1991, p. 41.

[9]This exercise is adapted from Stephen Brookfield's *Becoming a Critically Reflective Teacher* (San Francisco: Jossey-Bass, 1995), p. 78.

Chapter 12: What Are We Doing in These Mountains?

[1]This exercise is adapted from Stephen Brookfield and Stephen Preskill's *Discussion as a Way of Teaching* (San Francisco: Jossey-Bass, 1999), pp. 70-71.

Chapter 13: The Mission Trip as Global Tourism

[1]Zygmunt Bauman, *Globalization: The Human Consequences* (New York: Columbia University Press, 1998), p. 77.

[2]Ibid., p. 77.

[3]Ibid., p. 83.

[4]Karl Barth, "The Community for the World," in *Theological Foundations for Ministry,* ed. Ray Anderson (Edinburgh: T & T Clark, 1979), pp. 499-532.

[5]Ibid., p. 503.

[6]Ibid., p. 504.

[7]Ibid., p. 507.

[8]Ibid., p. 511.

[9]This exercise is adapted from Stephen Brookfield's *The Skillful Teacher* (San Francisco: Jossey-Bass, 1990), pp. 32-33.

Chapter 14: Doubt and Confirmation

[1]This exercise is adapted from Stephen Brookfield's *The Skillful Teacher* (San Francisco: Jossey-Bass, 1990), pp. 119-21.

Chapter 15: Ascension Deficit Disorder

[1]See J. R. R. Tolkien, *Tolkien on Fairy-Stories,* ed. Verlyn Flieger and Douglas A. Anderson, expanded ed. (London: HarperCollins, 2008).

[2]Bettelheim maintained that fairy tales help us overcome the "existential predicament" that unites us as a species—i.e., formless, nameless anxieties about death, abandonment and meaninglessness—by giving those fears concrete form, allowing children to master them symbolically before they have to confront them personally. See Bruno Bettelheim, *The Uses of Enchantment* (New York: Vintage, 1989). Other developmental theorists have developed similar theses; Martin Lubetsky notes that telling fairy tales "is one way to elicit a child's inner thoughts and frustrations, reduce anxiety, and gain mastery over developmental tasks" ("The Magic of Fairy Tales: Psychodynamic and Developmental Perspectives," in *Child Psychiatry and Human Development* [June 1989]: 19, 245). Bettelheim's scholarly reputation has been called into question since his suicide in 1990, though most critics agree that *The Uses of Enchantment* remains a useful example of psychoanalytic insight. Still, as Australian educator James Parson points out, parents should be judicious about taking Bettelheim's verdict on fairy tales to heart: "Presumably, Bettelheim himself was told such tales as a child. It did not stop him from suffering acute depression all his life or from committing suicide" ("Fairy Tales and the Existential Predicament" <http://parentingmethods.suite101.com/article.cfm/fairy_tales_and_the_existential_predicament>).

[3]Joseph Pearce, "The Catholicism of *The Lord of the Rings,*" in *Celebrating Middle-Earth: The Lord of the Rings as a Defense of Western Civilization,* ed. John G. West (Seattle: Inkling Books, 2002), p. 88; J. R. R. Tolkien, *The Letters of J.R.R.*

Tolkien, ed. Humphrey Carpenter (Boston: Houghton Mifflin, 2000), p. 147.

[4]Frederick Buechner, *Telling the Truth: The Gospel as Tragedy, Comedy, and Fairy Tale* (San Francisco: HarperOne, 1977).

[5]I am retaining the term "kingdom of God" for historic and literary reasons, though I admit it can invite problems in a gender-sensitive culture. The gender-neutral phrase "reign of God" could be substituted for the "kingdom of God" throughout this essay.

[6]This is in spite of a renaissance of academic interest in the subject, starting in the 1960s with Jürgen Moltmann's *Theology of Hope* and continuing today.

[7]I am borrowing this phrase, with permission, from youth pastor and cartoonist Cuyler Black; see <www.inheritthemirth.com>.

[8]Ann Morisy, *Bothered and Bewildered: Enacting Hope in Troubled Times* (New York: Continuum, 2009). I read Morisy's book after delivering this lecture, but the parallels are striking.

[9]See the excellent British Christian spirituality site *Re:jesus* <www.rejesus.co.uk/spirituality/celtic_spirituality/index.html>.

[10]See Morisy, *Bothered and Bewildered,* p. 21.

[11]2004 "Beliefs and Values Survey," cited by Albert Winseman, "Eternal Destinations: Americans Believe in Heaven, Hell," Gallup Commentary (May 25, 2004) <www.gallup.com/poll/11770/eternal-destinations-americans-believe-heaven-hell.aspx>.

[12]Results from an ABC News poll, reported by Dalia Sussman, "Poll: Elbow Room No Problem in Heaven," ABC News (December 20, 2005) <http://abcnews.go.com/US/Beliefs/story?id=1422658>.

[13]Christian Smith with Patricia Snelling, *Souls in Transition: The Religious and Spiritual Lives of Emerging Adulthood* (New York: Oxford University Press, 2009), p. 154.

[14]Don Peck, "How a New Jobless Era Will Transform America," *The Atlantic* (March 2010), p. 9 <www.theatlantic.com/magazine/print/2010/03/how-a-new-jobless-era-will-transform-america/7919/>.

[15]Ibid., p. 5.

[16]Cited in ibid.

[17]Christian Smith with Melinda Denton, *Soul Searching: The Religious and Spiritual Lives of American Teenagers* (New York: Oxford University Press, 2005), p. 263.

[18]Byron R. Johnson, "Religion and Delinquency: A Systematic Review of the Literature," presentation for the Coordinating Council for Juvenile Justice and Delinquency Prevention, Washington, D.C. (December 5, 2008).

[19]Kate Zernike, "Generation OMG," *New York Times,* Week in Review, March 7, 2009; also see Glen Elder, *Children of the Great Depression,* anniv. ed. (Boulder, Colo.: Westview, 1998).

[20]Morisy, *Bothered and Bewildered*, p. 13.

[21]Smith, *Souls in Transition*, p. 67.

[22]See Robert Wuthnow, *After the Baby Boomers: How Twenty- and Thirty-Some-things Are Shaping the Future of American Religion* (Princeton, N.J.: Princeton University Press, 2007).

[23]Rhonda van Dyke Colby, unpublished D.Min. thesis (Wesley Theological Seminary, 2000).

[24]Peter L. Steinke, cited in Morisy, *Bothered and Bewildered*, p. 75.

[25]William Meek, "Generalized Anxiety Disorder Prevalence Rates Based on Age," About.com Guide <http://gad.about.com/od/prevalencerates/a/prevage.htm> (accessed July 6, 2010). Information cited from the *Diagnostic and Statistical Manual of Mental Disorders* (Washington, D.C.: American Psychiatric Association, 2000); also D. H. Barlow, ed., *Clinical Handbook of Psychological Disorders*, 3rd ed. (New York: Guilford Press, 2001).

[26]Jonathan Reed, "Lost Generation" <www.youtube.com/watch?v=42E2fAWM6rA> (accessed July 5, 2010).

[27]Morisy, *Bothered and Bewildered*, p. 18.

[28]Studs Terkel, *Hope Dies Last* (New York: The New Press, 2003).

[29]Jürgen Moltmann, *In the End—The Beginning: The Life of Hope* (Minneapolis: Fortress, 2004), p. 27.

[30]Ibid., p. 28.

[31]Morisy refers to a similar phenomenon in her J-curve analysis, in which decline must be anticipated and prepared for as an antecedent to growth (*Bothered and Bewildered*, pp. 41, 60).

[32]Jacques Ellul, *Hope in Time of Abandonment,* trans. C. Edward Hopkins (New York: Seabury, 1973), p. 89.

[33]John Wesley, *The Heart of John Wesley's Journal*, ed. P. L. Parker and A. Birrell (New York: Fleming H. Revell, n.d.), pp. 35-36.

[34]These questions were posed in the book I coauthored with Ron Foster, *The God-bearing Life: The Art of Soul-Tending for Youth Ministry,* rev. ed. (Nashville: Upper Room, 2009), p. 17.

[35]Pope Benedict XIV, quoted in Morisy, *Bothered and Bewildered,* p. 18.

[36]Wikipedia describes Improv Everywhere as a "comedic performance group" based in New York City; the Improv Everywhere website (http://improvevery where.com) describes the group as a long-form improvisation troupe whose mission is to "cause scenes of chaos and joy in public places." Created in August of 2001 by Charlie Todd, Improv Everywhere has executed over one hundred "missions" involving tens of thousands of "undercover agents," usually random citizens pulled together for the sake of executing a short stunt. They have been featured on numerous media outlets and recently completed a public service stunt

for the New York Public Library based on *Ghostbusters*.

[37]Thanks to the Reverend Stephen Cady, who sent me the link. All Improv Everywhere "missions" are captured on YouTube (www.youtube.com/user/ImprovEverywhere).

[38]This exercise is taken from Stephen Brookfield and Stephen Preskill's *Discussion as a Way of Teaching* (San Francisco: Jossey-Bass, 1999), p. 83.

Postscript: Reflecting on Method

[1]See "Normativity and Context in Practical Theology," in *Practical Theology: International Perspectives,* ed. Friedrich Schweitzer and Johannes van der Ven (Berlin: Peter Lang, 1999).

[2]Bernstein explains the point of his project, a point which clearly has significance for practical theology: "The guiding principle of this study is that the investigation of the nature, status, and significance of praxis and action has become the dominant concern of the most influential philosophic movements that have emerged since Hegel. The essential aim of this study is to understand what each of these philosophic movements has been telling us about action, how it is to be characterized, what issues must be confronted in coming to grips with action, and what is the significance of action in the attempt to understand what man is" (Richard J. Bernstein, *Praxis and Action* [Philadelphia: University of Pennsylvania Press, 1971], p. xiii).

[3]Bernstein points to ultimacy in Hegel: "When Hegel speaks of Geist in this manner, he is thinking of Geist as God who does not abandon the world to chance and accident but guides it by Providence." Bernstein continues, "Hegel is claiming that if we take a world historical perspective, we will see that there is an inner logos to the seemingly chaotic multiplicity of events. This logos has a teleological form. There is a narrative or 'story' to be discovered in history—this is the epic of the devious ways in which Geist is realizing itself, moving from freedom and self-determination as an abstract idea to its concrete embodiment in human institutions" (ibid., p. 18).

[4]See Richard R. Osmer, *Practical Theology: An Introduction* (Grand Rapids: Eerdmans, 2008).

[5]Especially through her conversations with James Loder.

[6]Craig Dykstra and Dorothy Bass, "A Theological Understanding of Christian Practices," in *Practicing Theology,* ed. Miroslav Volf and Dorothy C. Bass (Grand Rapids: Eerdmans, 2002), p. 18.

[7]"The practices of the Christian community provide the human framework for faith, not its substance. At the same time, Jesus Christ, who knows better than to trust our sense of direction in trying to reach him, indwells these human actions and comes to us through them—and consequently, comes to the world through us. In the church, the Spirit moves and breathes through communities that imi-

tate Christ in these practices, supporting us as we wobble toward God" (Kenda Creasy Dean, *Practicing Passion: Youth and the Quest for a Passionate Church* [Grand Rapids: Eerdmans, 2004], p. 151).

[8]Ibid., p. 58.

[9]Ibid., p. 22.

[10]Ibid., p. 63.

[11]Ibid., p. 174.

[12]Ibid.

[13]"The church viewed the practices of faith as the Holy Spirit's chosen vehicle for conforming human passions to God's passion in order to construct a 'new creation' around the core of divine love, and to redirect human desire toward the One whose love we truly seek" (ibid., p. 58).

[14]Bernstein asserts, "Alienation is clearly, for Marx, a social category—a category for understanding 'political economy,' not an ontological category rooted in the nature of man" (*Praxis and Action*, p. 48).

[15]Bernstein explains Marx's view: "When man exists in a social situation where the objects that he produces and the 'system' in which these are exchanged is such that his products gain a mastery over him and dehumanize him, then this form of objectification is alienation" (ibid., p. 46).

[16]Ibid., p. 307.

[17]Ibid.

[18]Ibid.

[19]David White, *Practicing Discernment with Youth: A Transformative Youth Ministry Approach* (Cleveland: Pilgrim Press, 2005), p. 15.

[20]As I mentioned in the introduction to this article, just because these thinkers draw primarily from one form of action does not mean that they are not appropriating others as well. Here we see White's interaction with a neo-Aristotelian perspective: "To gain a sense of place, congregations need to engage their young people in practices that resemble the discernment practiced by Christian communities throughout history, engaging the gifts and problems of their context through experience, reflection, discussion, and prayer, bringing their lives more fully into partnership with God's work" (ibid., p. 6). Because White locates human/divine interaction in history, his understanding of discernment is radically different from, say, Ignatius. *Discernment* itself is a tricky word; as it can mean putting episodes, contexts and experiences into discrete categories of human (the world, etc.) and divine, it is critical to state up front where the divine actually works. White isn't discerning within practices; he is using practices to discern God's work in history. In some ways, practices do not have a telos of their own for White because all of human history is the telos of human/divine interaction.

[21]Ibid., p. 21 (italics mine).

[22]"These theological ideas and biblical clues help us to focus on often forgotten dimensions of youth ministry. Youth are not merely to be exploited by marketers, ignored or diminished by theorists, demonized by police, or patronized by adults with a status quo in view. Embraced by congregations seeking God's reign, the energies of youth can become something different than in the domesticated contexts of adolescence in which they are restrained, placated, distracted, or channeled for a productive adulthood" (ibid., p. 30).

[23]Ibid., p. 58.

[24]"In addition, youth ministry as it has evolved over these decades lacks significant critique of the shift in the social roles of young people in the second half of the twentieth century and into the twenty-first century, in which youth are increasingly ghettoized as passive consumers rather than treated as agents of faith influencing the common good" (ibid., p. viii).

[25]Ibid., p. 33.

[26]Ibid., p. vii.

[27]Bernstein, *Praxis and Action*, p. 213.

[28]Bernstein explains this perspective further: "Man from this perspective is seen as an active inquirer, and Peirce's theory of inquiry stands as one of the great attempts to show how the classic dichotomies between thought and action, or theory and praxis, can be united in a theory of a community of inquirers committed to continuous, rational, self-critical activity" (ibid., p. 199).

[29]Ibid., p. 190.

[30]See Chap Clark and Kara Powell, *Deep Justice in a Broken World* (Grand Rapids: Zondervan, 2007).

[31]Chap Clark, "Youth Ministry as Practical Theology," *Journal of Youth Ministry* 7, no. 1 (2008).

[32]Ibid., p. 14 (italics mine). I contend that this statement is a kind of transference. Clark believes from his pragmatist perspective that practical theology is about behavior, but he has failed to read even his own sources. Anderson's project seeks to place practical theology in the revelation of God, somewhere very different from behavior or conduct.

[33]Ibid.

[34]"The way to maintain the integrity of a practical theology model or method is to ensure that the Bible is the final definitive and authoritative source of truth, and all other data sets help to contextualize, understand, and align that truth in the service of God's kingdom" (ibid., p. 17).

[35]Clark really wants a process of inquiry to get to the right action, believing the right action can do much. Some pragmatists may feel his biblical obsession breaks down inquiry, which is anathema for a pragmatist. I can therefore understand

how some may be uncomfortable with Clark as a pragmatist, but in other ways it seems to fit. In other words, I am not saying that Clark is a good pragmatist in the eyes of other pragmatists, only that he is a pragmatist.

[36]Ibid., p. 15.

[37]Ibid., p. 29.

[38]"[A] communal process of reflection and discernment . . . can go a long way in dif-fusing the limiting impact of our theological and cultural blinders" (ibid., p. 19).

[39]This is the way Clark's use of Christopraxis in "Youth Ministry and Practical Theology" seems to be a misappropriation of Anderson's very point. Anderson constructs this theory to avoid rigid biblicalism. Anderson is working from a much more Kierkegaardian existentialism than Clark can see. Clark mistakes Anderson's focus on the community of cohumanity to be the same as the com-munity of inquiry.

[40]"Kierkegaard lucidly saw that his investigations led to a single terrifying conclu-sion: life is a form of despair from which there is no escape. . . . The thrust of Kierkegaard's dialectic is to show us the absolute absurdity of Faith and Christi-anity. This is the most absurd of all human thoughts" (Bernstein, *Praxis and Ac-tion*, p. 161).

[41]"Kierkegaard is not telling us to stand before our existential possibilities and cou-rageously and authentically choose what we are to become. He is not telling us that we are free to choose the aesthetic life, the ethical life, or even the religious life. On the contrary, Kierkegaard seeks to show us that all choice, decisiveness, and action leads to despair" (ibid., p. 117).

[42]"Ironically, Kierkegaard's point of view does not lead to a celebration of acting inwardly, but rather to the utter despair that overcomes one when he realizes the impossibility of this situation. There is no escape from this despair except a 'mir-acle'—the miracle of faith, but faith itself is only given to those who are saved by God's grace" (ibid., p. 118).

[43]The remainder of this section has been written by Blair D. Bertrand, which is why the third-person style of the above sections continues here.

[44]See James Loder's *Logic of the Spirit* (San Francisco: Jossey-Bass, 1998).

[45]Andrew Root, *Revisiting Relational Youth Ministry* (Downers Grove, Ill.: Inter-Varsity Press, 2007), p. 107.

[46]Ibid.

[47]This exercise is adapted from Stephen Brookfield's *The Skillful Teacher* (San Fran-cisco: Jossey-Bass, 1990), pp. 129-30.